① perhaps and my remarks wl ?
against strategic ambiguity

JIMMY CARTER, HUMAN RIGHTS, AND THE NATIONAL AGENDA

NUMBER TWENTY
Presidential Rhetoric Series

(3a) follow up project.
resistance to Am
effort of HR
hegemony

Jimmy Carter,
Human Rights,
and the National Agenda

Mary E. Stuckey

Texas A&M University Press
College Station

Frontispiece: Jimmy Carter addressing graduates
of the University of Notre Dame, May 23, 1977

This paper meets the requirements
of ANSI/NISO Z39.48-1992
(Permanence of Paper).
Binding materials have been chosen for durability.

Library of Congress Cataloging-in-Publication Data

Stuckey, Mary E.
    Jimmy Carter, human rights, and the national agenda / Mary E. Stuckey.
— 1st ed.
        p. cm. — (Presidential rhetoric series ; no. 20)
    Includes bibliographical references and index.
    ISBN-13: 978-1-60344-074-5 (cloth : alk. paper)
    ISBN-10: 1-60344-074-7 (cloth : alk. paper)
    1. Carter, Jimmy, 1924–   2. Human rights—Political aspects—
United States.   3. United States—Politics and government—1977–1981.
4. Rhetoric—Political aspects—United States—History—20th century.
5. Communication in politics—United States—History—20th century.
I. Title.   II. Series.
E872.S83   2008
973.926—dc22
2008012828

For Linda McCarty,
Jennifer Beese, and Beth Gylys:
The best friends ever

Peace is the work of many hands. It's the struggle for justice in many dark corners. It is striving to solve problems long stalemated and bitterly disputed. It's having the courage to rise above old failures and to act upon new hope. As we raise the shield against war, let us also hear the stricken voice of the homeless refugee, the cry of the hungry child, the weeping prayer of the political prisoner. We are one with the family of all people, and the concerns of the human family are many.

Jimmy Carter,
"Radio Address to the Nation on Foreign Policy,"
October 19, 1980, *Public Papers,*
2338–39

Contents

(handwritten annotations:)

but not the only articulation of "hr" (more than HR = globalization)

← very little on (Ch 2) — agenda, framing, priming — Carter

Chapter 3 — L as strategy — ┐ 38 — some ideological critique

Chapter 4 — "permanence term" — 73

Chapter 5 — good transition to Neolib / neocon — 78-9

Some ambiguity — Carter's ethos vs. American (42)
↓
41
47
56

multiple senses of ethos — I'm ambivalent on

Acknowledgments

As always, my debts far exceed my capacity to express my gratitude to all those who helped with this book and with so much else.

Writing is always hard, and sometimes it is harder than others. This book was written during one of the harder times, and I am all the more grateful to those who never lost faith in me or in my work. Their words of encouragement, often offered without knowing how badly I needed to hear them, meant more than I can say. My gratitude is thus all the more profound. In no particular order, Sarina Russotto, Victoria Sanchez, John Sanchez, Ira Strauber, Laura DeMarco, Damon Mosely, Chuck Carswell, Eric Willis, David Cheshier, Jeff Bennett, Isaac West, Davin Grindstaff, Jeff Baker, Holley Wilkin, Kay Beck, Tim Merritt, Kathy Fuller-Seeley, Alissa Perren, Carol Winkler, Mary Ann Romski, Wilbur Rich, Karen Hoffman, Chuck Morris, David Zarefsky, David Henry, Kathryn Olsen, Jerry Hale, Marty Medhurst, Tom Goodnight, Jason Edward Black, Jason Edwards, Rasha Ramzy, Joe Valenzano, and of course my family, deserve special thanks. You all mean a great deal to me. I am especially grateful to the special young people whose lives I have been privileged to share: Amanda, Robert, Philip, Dakota, and Brave Heart. You bring joy to my life, all of you. Linda McCarty, Jennifer Beese, and Beth Gylys are the best friends anyone could ever hope to have, and they have gone above and beyond this last year. Thank you.

I am grateful to Jeff Cohen, who took the time to educate me about non-attitudes, and to Jeff Bennett, who read much of the manuscript. Thanks again to Jeff and also to Isaac West for their help on ideographs. Bob Ivie's comments made the work much better. I had the help of two fabulous research assistants, Joshua Ritter and Kris Curry. They worked hard and cheerfully, and I am proud of them both. I look forward to reading their own work in print.

An early version of this project was presented at the 2006 annual meeting of the American Political Science Association. Parts of various chapters were presented at the 2008 meeting of the Southern States Communication Association. Part of chapter 4 was published in 2007 as an essay in *Presidential Studies Quarterly* (37, 646–66), coauthored by Joshua Ritter, "George Bush, <Human Rights>, and American Democracy." I'm grateful for the advice and encouragement I received through these venues, and I am especially indebted to Josh, whose work on neoliberalism made the work on ideographs much better than it could have been without him; he generously allowed me to use that work here.

This project was supported by two summer research grants from the Georgia State University Department of Communication. I am grateful to all of my colleagues in the department, and especially to my friend and chair, David Cheshier, who is still at least seven of the ten smartest people I know, and who is hereby forgiven for his secret, evil plan to prevent me from ever getting time to finish this book.

The archivists and staff at the Carter Library are smart, knowledgeable, and very helpful. Special thanks to Bob Bohanan, who never fails to be smart and encouraging—and a darn good luncheon companion as well.

I am immensely grateful to the editors and staff at Texas A&M, who made sure that there would be a book to finish. They are consummate professionals. Martin J. Medhurst, founding editor of this series is, of course, peerless. Mary Lenn Dixon is a great editor and a terrific friend. Thom Lemmons and Scott Barker deftly shepherded the manuscript through production. I also received much good advice from Denise Bostdorff and Colleen Shogan, who read this manuscript and offered valuable feedback at an early stage.

My students inspire me and make me proud. I think that I have a terrific job, and I am grateful to all those who help make it so.

Jimmy Carter, Human Rights, and the National Agenda

The Carter Administration and Human Rights in Context

As president, Jimmy Carter was famous, if not notorious, as a poor communicator.[1] Legions of authors, articles, and texts detail the various insufficiencies, absences, and problems with Carter's rhetoric, and with Carter as a rhetor. Many of these criticisms deal directly with Carter's lack of ability to communicate on matters of policy—one of the chief charges laid against him was his unwillingness and/or incapacity to motivate the electorate on matters of political and policy import. That being the case (and surely so many scholars cannot be wrong), the Carter presidency contains at least one puzzle that has never been addressed in the literature on his administration: If Carter was so poor a communicator, how did he get human rights on the national agenda? Moreover, having gotten his signature issue on that agenda, in a world where presidential rhetoric is purportedly ineffective, how did such a poor a communicator do so in such a way that it is still there more than a quarter of a century after he left office?

The answer involves expanding our understanding of presidential persuasion: all of the elements of Carter's communication on human rights that engendered problems for the formation of a coherent and consistent policy— the term's vagueness, the difficulties of applying it, its uneasy relationship with national security interests, the divergence between Democratic and Republican understandings of the term—allowed "human rights" to become a useful rubric for presidents who followed Carter, thus enabling its utility over time and ensuring it a place on the national agenda. That is, the kind of targeted, focused rhetoric we have long believed to be essential to effective presidential communication may in some cases work against rather than for an issue's longevity on the national agenda. What communication scholars think of as strategic ambiguity may be wielded, intentionally or not, in the service of a president's political and policy agenda.

To make this argument, I begin by discussing the key elements of how human rights got on the national agenda. I argue that the explanation for the creation and longevity of human rights as a national agenda item lies in the interaction of several distinct components: first, human rights did not originate with Carter, but was present in the *public mood* and, importantly, in the Congress. Second, the *fact of presidential communication* contributed to the national and international attention to the issue. Third, *the communication of this particular president* and members of his administration mattered as well. Fourth, *the nature of the communication itself* was a significant factor. Finally, the Carter administration furthered the *development of the human rights bureaucracy*, which contributed to the longevity of the issue. The project concludes with a discussion of how this case leads to the development of a model of presidential influence, one that relies less on focus and achievement and more on the virtues of an ambitious incompleteness.

Human Rights in the Carter Administration

Jimmy Carter took office in the wake of several national crises. The nation had sharply divided over the Vietnam War, which had ended in humiliation during the Ford Administration. It was still reeling from the shock of the Watergate revelations and from the continuing allegations of governmental misconduct that emerged as a result of the Church Committee hearings. Americans in the mid- to late-1970s were disenchanted with politics and suspicious of politicians. Into this political context came an outsider presidential candidate, a born-again Baptist who seemed to care more about morals than political expediency, who took human rights seriously, and who lacked any formal ties to the governing establishment in Washington. These conditions, which made it possible for Carter to be elected, also made it harder for him to govern once in office. In order to better understand the Carter Administration, a brief discussion of his political context, his rhetorical legacy, and the role human rights played in his administration is in order.

The Political Context of the Carter Administration
Carter's administration is widely considered to be one that held more promise than performance. Some of the reasons for this are structural and some are connected to Carter himself. Structurally, Carter lacked a real mandate;

he had neither experience nor contacts in Washington; he was not a tradi-tional Democrat and thus had political disagreements with Democrats in Congress; Congress itself had become more fragmented; and finally, gover-nance in general was increasingly difficult. Compounding these problems, which would have challenged even the most politically adept of politicians, was Carter's own attitude, which tended to be disdainful of politics and made him reluctant to use the tools at his disposal. Nonetheless, there was a consensus on the importance of human rights, and progress on that issue, at least initially, was possible.

Carter's problems, however, began with the campaign. He ran for office on a platform that had more to do with values than specific policy proposals,[2] which made it hard for him to claim a mandate once in office. One exception to this, however, was human rights. His position on human rights, which only came to the fore late in the campaign, was vague, but at least went by a clear and recognizable label. Campaign material, for instance, listed the Carter-Mondale position on foreign policy as "To stop treating our allies as if they were our adversaries. To make it clear that detente is a two-way street. To promote human rights abroad and to deal affirmatively with the social and economic problems of the developing world. To make our total commitment to the security of Israel as a Jewish state absolutely clear."[3] The only actual policy stance here was a commitment to Israel; other than that, the foundations on which his policies would be based may have been clear, but the policies themselves were less so. This allowed members of varying constituencies to infer support for their preferred policies, a time-honored strategic use of ambiguity common in campaign rhetoric. Still, it meant that once in office and responsible for crafting actual policy, Carter would inevi-tably lose some support among those whose preferences were not actually supported.

In addition, his was an "outsider" candidacy, and the nation's frustration with Washington was key to his electoral success.[4] Lacking ties to the national governing structure may have enabled Carter's candidacy, but it did not make it easy for him to lead the government once he made it to Washington. He had neither close friends not experienced advisors there—and after eight years of Republican presidents following a largely discredited Johnson Ad-ministration, the pool of experienced Democrats upon whom he could call was small. In any case, he chose not to summon many such people to serve in his administration, and his "Georgia Mafia" quickly became notorious for their inexperienced mistakes.[5]

Importantly, however, Carter did not run a negative campaign against government, but a positive one, stressing the ability of the American people to fix "the mess in Washington."[6] For him, government could still be considered part of the solution to the nation's problems—it was only later outsider campaigns, especially Reagan's, that began to define government as the problem. This meant that once in office he was able to argue that governmental resources could be appropriately marshaled in the service of his political preferences, and he was not shy about using them to advance the cause of international human rights. As we will see, this would turn out to be both an advantage, he could claim real progress on human rights, and a disadvantage, he was accused of doing the wrong things as well as criticized for not doing enough.

But doing anything at all presented something of a problem for Carter. His views differed from those of many traditional Democrats. This made his election possible, but also made governance more difficult.[7] Congressional Democrats did not recognize either Carter or members of his team as one of their own, and they quickly grew frustrated with his insistence on doing things his way rather than the way they were more accustomed to.[8] At the very least, it made cooperation between the Congress and the executive branch difficult.

The complicated relationship between Congress and the Carter Administration was further exacerbated by Carter's lack of support among the American people. Initially, Carter had broad support, but because it was tied to voters' reaction to Watergate, Vietnam, and Ford's pardon of Nixon, it was also shallow.[9] Thus, Carter could not count on a reserve of public approval when he may have needed it most.

These phenomena indicate structural issues that were becoming more and more apparent, and which together amounted to a nation that was becoming increasingly difficult to govern. Not only were interest groups gaining political strength, but the nation was also increasingly fragmented. The increased role money began to play in national elections, the rise of single-issue politics, and the fracturing of the political parties as inclusiveness and identity politics changed the nature and practice of representation all contributed to a fractious polity that was less organized and harder to manage. As Carter's chief of staff, Hamilton Jordan, put it, "We considerably underestimated the degree of fragmentation. We hoped that despite all of these differences, now that the Democrats finally had the White House and finally had a President, we were going to get more help and loyalty from these people and institutions than in fact we did. We were aware that it was there. We were not aware how extreme the fragmentation was. Either hopefully, wishfully, or naively, we thought that these people would fall in line with the President on some of these issues."[10] There was a widespread breakdown of consensus at the elite level, and a broader awareness at the mass level.[11] Ironically, these influences facilitated Carter's "outsider" candidacy, but made it harder to govern, especially as he lacked the "insider" experience required for navigating these increasingly complicated waters. As Carter aide Landon Butler put it, "We also had no unifying Democratic consensus, no program, no set of principles on which a majority of Democrats agreed. I often said, and I think some other people agreed, that the middle ground was not the high ground during the Carter years. The political high ground was on the extremes of right and left. The middle ground simply was not the position of strength during these years. So as we addressed this myriad of issues, we had to have an *ad hoc* approach to every issue. If we dealt with the natural gas problem, we put together one coalition; if we dealt with the Panama Canal, we'd put together an entirely different coalition. Our rhetoric would be aimed in different directions. We would wind up with a hodge podge, *ad hoc* approach to our initiatives."[12]

This need to build and rebuild a governing coalition meant that Carter's aides had to begin from scratch on every issue—good will would be at a premium. But the inexperience of Carter's team meant that they were not especially adept at either generating that good will or capitalizing upon what little they had.

Building coalitions was increasingly difficult, as the party system, never strong in the United States, was further weakened. In Carter's understanding, the Democratic Party was less able to offer rewards and engage in discipline of recalcitrant members than were interest groups.[13] So it seemed that Carter was enmeshed in a situation where he needed more and more resources and had access to fewer and fewer of them. Such a situation would require close attention to the politics of governance.

But Carter was entirely unwilling to provide such attention. He was notoriously intolerant of political processes and unwilling to engage in the activities and actions that help to grease the legislative wheels.[14] He tended to act as if his was the only reasonable and appropriate approach to policy, an attitude that those with more experience in Washington found both disrespectful and frustrating.

Nonetheless, and given these problems, somewhat surprisingly, Carter did make progress on some issues, and most specifically, on human rights. At least partially, this was due to the fact that human rights was one subject upon which everyone seemed to be able to agree—at least initially. Human rights had both the moral grounding and sufficient vagueness to offer real hope that it could serve a unifying function for the Democrats in particular and possibly for the nation in general. The ambiguity inherent in human rights provided something of a rhetorical resource for the president, even if he failed to realize it and to consciously exploit it as such.

Prior to Carter's election, the Democratic-controlled Congress was increasingly aggravated by what appeared to be a total absence of morality in the conduct of U.S. foreign policy. Vietnam, Watergate, and the revelations of various clandestine activities authorized by the CIA fed the impression that principle had become irrelevant to American actions abroad.[15] As Carter's national security advisor, Zbiginiew Brzezinski, put it, "Jimmy Carter took office sensing clearly a pressing need to reinvigorate the moral content of American foreign policy. After an almost unending series of revelations about the abuse of governmental power at home and abroad, the American people were dissatisfied with their government. In international affairs, there seemed to be a moral vacuum. The Carter Administration resolved to make a break with the recent past, to bring the conduct of foreign affairs into line with the nation's political values and ideals, and to revitalize an American image which had been tarnished by the Vietnam experience."[16] Carter built on this disaffection by promising not change but renewal—he would return the nation to its core values—and human rights was the most obvious way to do this.

This move was facilitated by the fact that Congress was developing an emerging consensus on the importance of human rights.[17] In the early 1970s, in cooperation with various and growing numbers of Non-Governmental Organizations (NGOs),[18] Members of Congress were advocating various methods of tying human rights to security assistance and other forms of foreign aid. By the time Carter was elected, thanks largely to these efforts of NGOs and Congress, human rights had added visibility, an increased role in important foreign aid decision making, and a growing bureaucratic presence.[19]

This congressional interest was both an advantage and a disadvantage for the Carter Administration. It was an obvious advantage in that there was a coalition already interested and active in the area of human rights. Significantly, it was a bipartisan coalition, which increased the chances of legislative victory on human rights issues.[20] But it is important to remember that this coalition was organized around a narrow vision of human rights—in fact, it was pretty much limited to agreeing on aid sanctions as a function of human rights abuses.

Furthermore, members of the bipartisan congressional coalition on human rights had very different reasons for advocating human rights sanctions.[21] Democrats thought it would be a way of improving human rights around the world, and of positively exerting American power on human rights—thus contributing to a resurgence of American moral authority, so badly needed in the mid- to late-1970s. Conservatives, however, signed on less because of their belief in foreign aid as an appropriate policy instrument for advocating human rights, and more because of a generalized hostility to foreign aid in general. Any limits on foreign aid, for any reason, would be approved by these members. So even the appearance of support for Carter in general and human rights in particular was more appearance than reality, and Carter's political situation was a difficult one indeed. It was a situation only the finest of communicators could have dealt with effectively. And whatever else one could say about the nation's thirty-ninth president, he was not the finest of communicators.

Carter's Rhetorical Reputation

Certainly, one of the most often cited reasons for the Carter Administration's political failures has to do with the president's lack of rhetorical skill.[22] Not only was he generally considered a poor orator, but critics have charged that "he never adequately articulated an overarching purpose and direction for his administration."[23] He placed human rights at the center of his administration, but that was not really tied to consistent policy or to a clear vision for the country. Given the political context of the times, Carter badly needed unifying themes and consistent application of those themes. The consensus is that he provided neither.

He tended to preach—he "addressed both sectarian and secular issues with religious-political rhetoric."[24] This allowed him to avoid specifics during the campaign, but meant that he risked his coalition every time he tried to make specific policy. In addition, this tendency toward didactic rhetoric led some to consider him self-righteous, and to resent his assumption that he was more moral than anyone else, his motives more pure, his means more efficacious, and his ends more valuable.[25] He tended to talk at, rather than to, the American public, and was, in general, unable to educate and persuade the public.[26]

At least in part, this inability was connected to unwillingness. Carter was markedly and persistently reluctant "to be rhetorical or inspirational."[27] His aide Jack Watson said, "Men and women will differ on this point, and God knows there is much ground for difference, but I'm among those who believe that one of the elements we need in our leaders is passion and a capacity for inspiring, an ability to use the rhetorical phrase and a call to duty.

You don't want to overuse it because its force will evaporate. But President Carter was almost always loath to do it. That particular characteristic affects other aspects of his presidency as well, such as his relationship with the Cabinet."[28] In the view of this aide, Carter declined to use the resources connected to the bully pulpit. In this regard, of course, he especially suffered in comparison to Ronald Reagan.[29] Carter's considerable political success was clearly grounded in elements that had little to do with impassioned public persuasion.

He was reluctant to use the full arsenal of rhetorical resources because he seemed to think that they were ineffective and unnecessary: "Carter's team assumed that public opinion on foreign policy was malleable and lacked structure. Thus, no effort was made to determine whether the contradictions pollsters found on the surface were actually held together by an underlying structure. Therefore, the Carter White House had neither an accurate gauge of public attitudes nor an understanding of those attitudes sufficient to build support for its policies."[30] It seems at least possible that Carter failed to persuade on many issues because, in his view, the public was not persuadable.[31] And he may well have been right, at least on many of the issues.[32] Clearly, to the extent that he attempted to argue for limits—on resources, on American power, on anything at all, while perhaps necessary, he was not endearing himself to either the American public or to the governing establishment.[33] As Carter himself put it, the open discussion of limits was "painfully prescient and politically unpopular."[34] This tendency also provided a pessimistic edge to Carter's communication, which, especially given his political context, proved to be particularly unwelcome.

Carter had both strengths and skills as a political leader; my point here is not that he was entirely inept, but that he was suspicious of and reluctant to use public persuasion, which he scorned as "merely" political, and distrusted as irrational and often misleading. He could be persuasive, and he could both stir and woo crowds. But as his presidency evolved, he increasingly chose not to do either of these things, and when he did, he tended to appear contrived.

As a case in point, his communication on human rights, initially a source of unification, became increasingly problematic. Not only were there problems of definition, but Carter's willingness to argue on the one hand that the United States was the world leader on human rights and to admit on the other hand that we were also guilty of human rights abuses upset those both on the Left and Right, albeit for different reasons.[35] Thus, "it became something of a commonplace, observable on both ends of the political spectrum, to accuse the administration of hypocrisy."[36] No matter what he actually did on human rights, it was seen in some quarters as too little, in others as too much, and in still others as simply wrong.

Les Altenberg and Robert Cathcart consider human rights to have been a "slogan," and state that Carter is "remembered only as a nice man who meant well but who lacked the capacity to be an effective president."[37] They argue human rights failed "as a social symbol,"[38] and conclude that, "rhetorically, Carter was quite successful in linking his administration with the human rights slogan. He was much less successful at convincing most of America's allies that human rights as a policy could sustain the Western Alliance in the bitter struggle with the Soviet Union."[39] And this may have been the crux of the matter—a human rights emphasis offered a way to transcend the Cold War, but it was not one that a majority in Congress or among the mass public could believe, especially as the Soviets invaded Afghanistan and the Iranians took Americans hostage.

Certainly, Carter could have been a better communicator, a fact that was clearly acknowledged by his own team. Zbigniew Brzezinski, for example, told the president as early as 1977 that:

> You need to express a more coherent vision of what we aim to accomplish, of what our priorities are, and of how you define the present historical era within U.S. foreign policy has to be shaped. You need to convey to the public your awareness of the complexity of the problems that we confront; disappointment and setbacks are normal in international affairs and accomplishments tend to be the exception. We are setting in motion a process, and the public must be made to understand that the President and his associates understand that the problems we face will be with us for a long time to come, and there will be no easy solutions, and that the effort to build a more cooperative world framework will be tedious, painful, and frequently disappointing.[40]

The staff understood better than the president the need for consistent, clear, and frequent public communication, but they were unable to change the chief executive's communicative behavior.

Carter's weaknesses as a rhetor were apparent, and it is true that Carter was not successful in getting Americans to consider human rights America's top foreign policy goal; but it is equally true that human rights had a higher place on the national agenda during and following his presidency than prior to it.[41] There is also evidence that his view of human rights was being absorbed and repeated in the media.[42] At least some Americans were happy to see the nation act in a way that was identifiable as "moral"; but morality is all too often associated with weakness, and presidents who are perceived as weak are vulnerable presidents. This proved true in Carter's case. But even after he left office, human rights remained an issue that his successor could not ignore. With all his problems as a communicator, Carter had put human rights on the national agenda permanently.

Carter's Human Rights Legacy

There is no doubt that Carter's legacy is centered on human rights. Because he has dedicated so much of his postpresidential career to human rights, that legacy has been made increasingly obvious and makes the issues all the more important, but his influence on the issue was the basis for his presidential legacy as well as for his postpresidential career. As president, Carter not only worked hard to get human rights on the national agenda, but there is good evidence that its presence there was due largely to his efforts.[43]

Carter helped put "human rights" on the national agenda, but interestingly and importantly, he did little to help us derive a coherent and widely shared definition of "human rights." For the purposes of this study, whenever I analyze rhetoric on human rights, I used every speech by the president that contained the phrase "human rights." For Carter, this generally referred to international rather than domestic issues, for which the phrase "civil rights" was usually used. But Carter also argued that advocating human rights abroad required attention to civil rights at home. And while he began his administration with the broadest possible definition of human rights, in practice, the term most often referred to political and civil rights. Defining human rights became a thorny issue, and definitions varied over time, but in general, he seemed to consider "human rights" to be related to governmental respect for and protection of an individual's person, beliefs, and spiritual practices.

For Carter, human rights was both a moral and a practical policy. Rather than completely abandoning the realism of the Nixon/Kissinger years, he argued that he could combine idealism and realism. He said, "I was familiar with the widely accepted arguments that we had to choose between idealism and realism, or between morality and power. To me, the demonstration of American idealism was a practical and realistic approach to foreign affairs, and moral principles were the best foundation for the exertion of power and influence."[44] He thought that by acting morally, the United States could increase its influence in the world—equally important given the Cold War context, he argued that American influence would be at risk if the nation failed to act in accordance with its moral principles.

Carter made the connection between morality and power central to both foreign and domestic policy,[45] but it was most apparent in foreign affairs: "from the first day of his presidency, Jimmy Carter set out to fundamentally alter the direction of American foreign policy."[46] While the idea that whatever the U.S. government does is moral has been a clear strand of American foreign policy since the nation's inception, and this reiteration of the myth of American exceptionalism thus resonated both at the time and in later administrations, Carter argued less that governmental actions were by definition moral and more that these actions had to be brought into line with widely shared views of morality. This, of course, created both problems and opportunities for the administration, as politics, especially international relations, involves both trade-offs and compromises and an overly simplistic view of morality will always collide with political reality.

Carter recognized this danger even as he dealt poorly with it. He emphasized the view that the United States was one among a community of nations, a stance that focused on what we would come to think of as interdependence.[47] Other presidents have been more inclined to focus on American dominance. Carter's communitarian vision was one that worried many observers of American politics, for it seemed to imply that the United States would take a less aggressive stance vis-à-vis the Soviet Union, and that Carter was more willing to criticize allies than enemies. Ronald Reagan would be quick to exploit both these fears throughout the 1980 campaign.

In addition to expressing a communal vision of international relations, Carter stressed the notion that the United States was not merely an exemplar—although for him, it surely was that. But he also argued that the United States had a more active role to play in the protection and advancement of human rights around the world. He argued that government could be an active agent for doing good in the world. This has been one strand of American exceptionalism since the Founding, but it took on added importance during the Carter years, and thus provided a rhetorical resource for later presidents.

Carter provided other resources as well: "in making human rights a key element of all discussions and considerations of American foreign policy, Carter succeeded in shifting the discourse on American foreign policy away from the dominant concerns of the Cold War and containment."[48] He objected to the singular focus on the Soviet Union, and hoped to move beyond that to a more value-based as well as a multilateral stance on foreign policy.[49] This stance clearly fits with arguments about the world's increasing interdependence, and has echoes in later presidents, especially Bill Clinton.

Many scholars have positive appraisals of his foreign policy,[50] but many others have less favorable analyses.[51] Most of the charges have to deal with inconsistency and "a public perception of weakness."[52] In general, the consensus is that Carter failed to understand and to adequately deal with the complexities of American security interests,[53] and that he failed to reconcile or otherwise deal with the conflicting stances of foreign policy represented by Carter's secretary of state, Cyrus Vance, and his national security advisor, Zbigniew Brzezinski.[54] Others object to his use of human rights to serve domestic political ends.[55]

Despite the human rights talk, there is some question about how different Carter's actions were from those of previous administrations. That is, the argument has been made that whatever the justifications offered for U.S. foreign policy actions, those actions remained substantially the same.[56] These critics claim that the United States seems to act in its own interest, and whether it justifies those actions with reference to human rights or in some other way seems to them insignificant.[57]

These criticisms notwithstanding, it is undeniably true that Carter's presidential image has been somewhat rehabilitated.[58] At least in part, this has to do as much with the performance of his successors and with his actions as an ex-president as much as it does with the perspective that historical distance provides.[59] It is also true that with the end of the Cold War, and as the structures of world politics have moved toward increased interdependence, Carter's views seem to resonate more and more. Indeed, Press Secretary Jody Powell may well have been correct when he said, "I think President Carter and the Carter administration will end up being most positively remembered for exactly those things that cost him the most politically."[60] Surely human rights would be one of those things.[61]

Human rights has consensus-building potential, but because of its vagueness and seeming inability to contend with security interests, alone it cannot create a new paradigm for American foreign policy.[62] Nonetheless, because his successors also used human rights to justify their policies, by the end of the Reagan Administration there was a sense that morality needed to play a continuing role in America's conduct of its foreign affairs.[63] That sense has never gone away, and a return to the blatant realpolitik of the Nixon/Kissinger years seems, even at this moment, dominated as it is by the pressures and demands of the global war on terror, to be all but unthinkable. This is due, in some part at least, to the efforts of Jimmy Carter.

As Carter aide David Aaron noted, "There are two kinds of failures. There are the failures in the sense that human rights might prevail and that didn't happen in this generation, and people died and were in jail and so forth. . . . The question is really whether we made it worse or better. I would argue we made it better."[64] From this historical moment, that seems to be a reasonable judgment—certainly, the Nobel Prize Committee thought so, awarding Carter the laureate in 2002.

At least in part, Carter has been credited with establishing "a climate of global concern that encouraged improvements in human-rights conditions as well as exhibited the gross violations."[65] That climate remains, after more than a quarter of a century. How exactly that happened is the subject of this book.

Human Rights and the National Agenda

This study relies on two important assumptions: (1) human rights has been a significant issue on the national agenda, and (2) Jimmy Carter had something to do with getting and keeping it there. Thus, part I of this book deals with these claims. Chapter 1, "Human Rights as a Public Concern," contains a brief history of human rights, with specific attention to the American context as Carter sought and occupied the presidency. I argue that human rights was an issue whose time had come and was thus already a minor item on the national agenda.

But having some resonance, as human rights did in the mid-1970s, is not the same as having national prominence, which human rights gained during the Carter years. Chapter 2, "Human Rights and the National Agenda," looks less at how human rights was defined and understood by key constituencies and more at how it was reflected and refracted through the lens of public opinion and the mass media. This chapter deals with public opinion on, and media coverage of, human rights and seeks to demonstrate the effectiveness of Carter's administration in getting it on the national agenda.

Once having made the case for presidential influence over the national agenda, I turn in part II to the specifics of Carter's rhetoric and political choices. Chapter 3, "The Ethos of Human Rights in Carter Administration Rhetoric," demonstrates how Carter tied his particular ethos and that of political party and nation to the idea of human rights. I argue that by making this connection so consistently, Carter virtually guaranteed the prominence of human rights on the national agenda.

But getting it there and keeping it there are different things, and human rights is still a matter of public concern because it has continuing usefulness to Carter's successors. Chapter 4, "<Human Rights> as an Ideograph," discusses how ideographs influence our political life and makes the case for <human rights> as an ideograph. Ideographs are culturally bound summary phrases that capture important ideological associations. They are high-order abstractions that function to unify a diverse audience around a vaguely shared set of meanings. As an ideograph, the single term <human rights> provided various presidents with a singular warrant for very different sorts of political actions. In order to make this argument, I depart from a strict focus on Carter, and delve into the use of <human rights> in administrations since Carter, specifically discussing the administrations of Ronald Reagan, Bill Clinton, and George W. Bush.[66]

The idea that presidential rhetoric matters is absolutely central to this book. But no one argues that rhetoric is the only thing that matters. Presidential rhetoric is institutionally produced and managed, and it resonates (or not) within the executive branch as an institution. Issues are more likely to have longevity if they have some institutional support. Consequently, chapter 5, "Implementing Human Rights," deals with the bureaucratization of human rights. It has less to do with specific policy actions on Carter's part than on the development of routinized procedures and institutions that meant human rights would continue to have a place in national policy making even after Carter left office.

Thus, I argue that the national agenda is a complicated entity, composed of personal, rhetorical, and institutional factors. The book concludes, therefore, with a discussion of what this case can tell us about presidents, the national agenda, and the study of political communication in general.

This work is related to the line of scholarship dedicated to "strategic ambiguity," or the notion that clear and focused communication may not be the only way to achieve persuasive goals. It relies implicitly on the idea of polysemy, or the multiple meanings inherent in a text, in order to better understand how audiences may react to and wield texts.[67] Importantly, polysemy may be exploited without intent—that is, in at least some cases, the multiple meanings of a text or texts are qualities of the text itself, and may have consequences that elude, defy, or are even irrelevant to a speakers' intent.

It is clear that Jimmy Carter intended to get human rights on the national agenda. It is not clear that many of the elements that helped him accomplish this goal—the lack of clarity about his definition of human rights, the inconsistencies in managing the policy, the availability of multiple meanings allowing for multiple policy outcomes under different administrations— were the products of intentional behavior on Carter's part. In fact, it is much easier to believe that these things were not strategic at all. Nonetheless, their presence points to what may be a viable presidential strategy.

The evidence presented here indicates that a president who wants to get an issue or set of issues on the national agenda, who wants to begin or further a national conversation on those issues, will have to have an issue that has at least some public resonance, or that can be tied to strong ideological beliefs or current events such that it can be given that resonance. He will have to communicate about that issue in ways that flag its importance to the administration in a variety of contexts, across a variety of issues, and over a long period of time. Members of his administration will have to similarly communicate. And there must be administrative mechanisms developed to ensure the longevity of the issue over time. Presidents who want a matter of concern placed on the national agenda, and kept there after they have left office, may do well to rely upon an open, ambiguous, and complicated strategy rather than a clear, tightly focused one. To rely on the metaphor so many of us use in our classes, the effects of a shotgun strategy may outlast those of a rifle. The rest of this book is dedicated to an examination of how such a strategy might work.

PART I

*Presidential Influence
over the National Agenda*

CHAPTER 1

Human Rights as a Public Concern

No political policy can arise out of thin air, and no policy can pass or succeed without at least a minimum of support at both the elite and mass levels. Human rights is no exception.[1] Thus, in order to begin to understand human rights as a national agenda item, this chapter provides a history of human rights with special attention to the United States, especially as Carter campaigned for, won, and occupied the presidency. I begin with a brief history of the idea of human rights, including material relevant to the American context and then devote my attention to the immediate political context in which human rights became an important national issue. This analysis makes it clear that without Jimmy Carter, human rights would not have received the level of national interest it attained under his leadership.

Human Rights in the American Context

While it is possible to trace concern for the human rights of some segments of populations back to the Code of Hammurabi, which included rights for women, slaves, and children,[2] or to the Stoics of Greece and ancient Rome, the idea of human rights as universal and inalienable is of much more recent vintage.[3] As Arthur Schlesinger Jr. noted, "Human rights—roughly the idea that all individuals everywhere are entitled to life, liberty, and the pursuit of happiness on this earth—is a relatively modern proposition. Political orators like to trace this idea to religious sources, especially to the so-called Judeo-Christian tradition. In fact the great religious ages were notable for their indifference to human rights in the contemporary sense—not only for their acquiescence in poverty, inequality and oppression, but for their addiction to slavery, torture, wartime atrocities and genocide."[4] Human rights have never been universally sanctioned nor consistently protected, even in theory. Regardless of the actual practices of established religions and governments, however, there is evidence that concern for human rights dates back further than the modern period, although such concern was sporadic and easily undermined.[5] Thus, Schlesinger is probably correct in asserting that in the West at least, "humanitarianism—the notion that natural rights have immediate, concrete, and universal application—is a product of the last four centuries,"[6] and that most human rights advances were made by political, rather than religious leaders.[7] So it is to political events that we now turn.

Human Rights in the West

Undoubtedly, one crucial moment in the history of Western conceptions of human rights came with the signing of the Magna Carta in 1215.[8] The Magna Carta established the principle that even the king was bound by a nation's laws, and while later monarchs established different interpretations and practices concerning that principle as the Divine Right of Kings met the notion of limited power, from the Magna Carta forward, all British monarchs were, to at least some extent, constrained by the idea that no one individual was above the law.[9] Making the monarch subject to legal restrictions was an important first step in the recognition and establishment of human rights.

For the West, the first modern expression of human rights[10] in political theory comes with the contract theorists, such as Rousseau, Hobbes, Locke, and Hume, who actually discussed "natural" rather than "human rights."[11] Importantly, for each of these theorists, the notion of natural rights was severely limited: Hobbes recognized only the right to life; in Locke that was extended to property, a move that would be consequential for American notions of liberty as they came into contact with slavery.[12] Both Hobbes and Locke grounded their idea of "natural" rights in a state of nature, which they conceptualized as communal life prior to the development of state institutions. For Hobbes, life in the state of nature was "solitary, poor, nasty, brutish and short,"[13] and he argued that the only security humans enjoyed came from state protections—the state was thus understood as the sole legitimate wielder of force. Locke's view, while milder than Hobbes's, also understood the state as an artificial construct, created to protect life and property.

Importantly, for these theorists and thus for the notion of human rights as it developed in the West, natural rights existed prior to the state, and the state's primary function was the protection of these rights. Should the state fail in its obligation to protect natural rights, its legitimacy was lost, and life reverted back to the state of nature. This was possible because for these theorists, rights were an inevitable and inalienable product of the human condition—rights, at least in some attenuated form, were given by God to all humans, and no one could be morally or lawfully deprived of those rights. Equally important, these rights were clearly and inextricably connected to the concept of duties—individuals owed something to the state and consequently received protections from it.[14] This is the first modern conception in the West of what would come to be called human rights.

This is crucial, because these philosophers, most notably Locke, located human rights in a religious—specifically Christian—conception of humanity. God made human life, and God gave humans rights. Since all governments were answerable to God—even those monarchs who ruled by divine right—governments were logically charged with protecting that which was given by God. No government could, therefore, violate natural rights and retain its legitimacy. Locke's reasoning was critical to the philosophical underpinning of the American Revolution.[15]

Because of the reliance the Founders placed on Locke and other European theorists, in the American context "human rights" has its origin in the documents that promulgated and justified the American Revolution, deriving from the notion of government as a result of a compact between the governed and the government. For those colonists advocating revolution, the British government had violated its part of the agreement, and revolution was therefore warranted on human rights grounds: "All men," announced the Declaration of Independence, "are created equal. They are endowed by their Creator with certain inalienable rights, among these are life, liberty, and the pursuit of happiness."[16] Both the American Revolution and the French Revolution which followed soon after were justified in terms of some conception of universal natural rights, and both the American Declaration of Independence and the French Declaration of the Rights of Man and Citizen acknowledge that these rights belong to all persons, regardless of class, status, or race.[17]

Even given the universal nature of these rights as they were articulated in the documents justifying revolution, natural rights were not understood as the same as "equal rights," but were bounded by both the formal and informal structures of class, gender, power, and privilege. As with the case of the Magna Carta, broad enunciations of principle met and collided with political practice.[18] As the American nation developed, the idea of universal rights was broadly accepted, at least in the abstract, and provided powerful warrants for political arguments concerning how war ought to be entered into and practiced,[19] whether slavery was legitimate,[20] and whether citizens could be tried by military tribunals.[21] As historian Lynn Hunt noted, "Rights questions . . . revealed a tendency to cascade,"[22] implicitly endorsing religious rights, women's rights, even as early as the late 1700s. Because human rights tend to be defended on the grounds of universal principles, once some form of human rights is accepted, it becomes increasingly difficult to stop the expansion of those rights.

Yet in the American context, the notion of natural rights was constrained by its Lockean roots. Charles W. Mills, for instance, argues that unequal and oppressive racial relations are implicit within the social contract upon which American notions of natural rights are based, and that the notion of equal rights is thus a sham.[23] The racial contract, for Mills, norms and racializes both spaces and individuals, and by definition contradicts the very principles that it is supposed to justify.

Mills makes a convincing argument that American democracy was implicitly and importantly racial in origin and character. Yet it is also true (as Mills acknowledges) that the American racial contract has also evolved over time, although some things remain constant. One important constant is the degree to which the centrality of property has mediated the stress on liberty. To a large extent, for instance, and due largely to the efforts of African American rhetors, by the end of the Civil War equality, liberty, and property were the essential constitutive values of the American republic.[24] This has tended to mean an emphasis on civil and political rights, and a stress on procedural rights, such as voting, rather than a focus on economic or cultural rights. Thus, for much of our national history in the United States, the emphasis has been on political, not social or economic equality.[25] Even labor unions, fighting for economic rights, have been most successful when it comes to issues such as regulating child labor and general work conditions, rights that can be easily understood as political or civil rather than economic.

Ironically, it seems that human rights advances have often come in the aftermath of war.[26] It is no coincidence that Woodrow Wilson was one of the first advocates of human rights,[27] nor that the first important international organization aimed at the protection of human rights, the League of Nations, was founded after World War I, in 1919. It is important to note, however, that the League was dedicated to the protection of the rights of minority groups, not to the protection of individual human rights.[28] This worked against racial minorities outside of Europe in particular.[29] Still, the League did commit its members to certain human rights principles, including humane working conditions, the elimination of trafficking in women and children, the reduction of disease, and fair treatment of colonized peoples.[30] Human rights were gaining a foothold in the West.

World War II was a watershed for human rights. Franklin Roosevelt enunciated a clear claim that human rights were at the foundation of the allied war effort when in 1941 he offered a defense of the "four essential human freedoms," which included the freedom of speech and expression, religious freedom, "freedom from want," and "freedom from fear." The speech included the claim that "Freedom means the supremacy of human rights everywhere."[31] By claiming that the war was fought in defense of those freedoms, it became ideologically imperative to protect them once the war was over and the Cold War began.

Certainly, the aftermath of World War II was critical for international conceptions of human rights, for it was in the 1940s that the term "human rights" gained international currency[32] and the first international courts were established.[33] Indeed, following World War II, the important context for human rights was international.[34] Because of the Holocaust, and remembering the promise of "never again" that provided rhetorical impetus to the founding of the United Nations, the General Assembly passed the Universal Declaration of Human Rights in 1948.[35] The Declaration constitutes the first important international effort to constrain the behavior of states toward their citizens,[36] and the first to explicitly include women.[37] Eleanor Roosevelt, who helped draft the Declaration, famously referred to it as the "international Magna Carta,"[38] and certainly, it had much to do with legitimating American human rights activism in the period following the war.[39]

The Declaration contains provisions for both political and economic rights, and thus could not garner enough support to have the force of a treaty. In particular, it fell victim to Cold War politics, as communist nations supported economic and cultural rights, and capitalistic nations such as the United States were only comfortable supporting political and civil rights, which were not supported by the communist bloc nations.[40] Consequently, and after nearly two decades of discussion and debate, in 1966 the U.N. General Assembly also passed the International Covenant on Civil and Political Rights and the International Covenant on Economic, Social, and Cultural Rights, both of which have been in force since 1976. These three documents together form what is often known as the International Bill of Rights.[41]

The International Covenant on Civil and Political Rights (ICCPR) is monitored by an eighteen-member Human Rights Committee, which meets periodically to review reports submitted by member states regarding their human rights practices. The United States ratified the ICCPR in the early 1990s, but expressed a variety of reservations, disallowing, for instance, the right of private action, and still maintaining the death penalty, despite the optional protocol banning it. Thus, even though the United States has long maintained the importance of civil and political rights, its national relationship with the U.N. document most concerned with them is complicated at best.[42]

The same cannot be said for the International Covenant on Economic, Social, and Cultural Rights, which was signed by President Jimmy Carter in 1977, but has never been ratified by the Senate. These rights remain much more controversial in the American context and receive significantly less support from the government than do political and civil rights.

The fact of the three documents reveals the lack of consensus concerning which rights are most entitled to international protection, and by whom. There are also important issues of enforcement. The original Universal Declaration of Human Rights is not legally enforceable, although the other two covenants are, but international law has always had difficulties with this, and many nations, including the United States, are ambivalent at best when it comes to obeying the dictates of the international community or exposing themselves to what they understand as the vagaries of international tribunals. Non-Western nations also take exception to what they consider the cultural biases implicit throughout these documents.[43]

Many of these issues percolated between the 1940s, when they were first proposed, and the mid-1960s, when they were enacted, and the late 1970s when they went into effect. During these years, as for the rest of human history, progress on human rights was slow, uneven, and often endangered by the geopolitical context,[44] in which African nations emerged from colonialism, but proxy wars were fought between the global superpowers, and human rights seemed to make clear gains in some areas, while suffering in others. In the United States, presidents supported the ideals of human rights, but also forged alliances with some of the worst abusers in the name of fighting the greater evil in the form of the Soviet Union.

The 1960s were a crucial decade for American understandings of human rights, as for so many other things as well. At the same time that the Vietnam War cast doubt on American morality in international affairs, the civil rights movement did the same for American government's treatment of its own citizens at home. Still, because of the constraints posed by the philosophical understanding of rights as it involved in the United States, the movement developed considerably more support for procedural rights such as voting, than for policies aimed at correcting economic and social equality, such as affirmative action and busing.

The fact of the Cold War has been important for American articulations of human rights, and much of American foreign policy was seen (at least by Americans and their allies) as an effort to more fully articulate and establish human rights internationally. This, of course, was cast into serious doubt by American actions in Southeast Asia during the prosecution of the Vietnam War.[45] That war, and the *realpolitik* policies of Nixon and Kissinger, had a good deal to do with the development in the United States of a national feeling that a more moral politics was called for. These debates were in process and were much in the minds of the international community as Jimmy Carter ran for, won, and occupied the presidency. In order to understand that context, a more detailed discussion of these debates is necessary.

Theories and Controversies Concerning Human Rights

As this discussion has made clear, there is no easy way to discuss human rights, for there are varying definitions of the term, and varying contexts in which it arises.[46] For the purposes of this study, there are two main justifications for human rights: those that rely on religious or moral foundations, and those that depend on a rational or procedural justification. In addition, there are a variety of categories of rights, and not everyone agrees that all categories are equally legitimate or important. In order to fully understand the issue of human rights as it arose during the Carter years, a brief discussion of these controversies is needed.

Justifying Human Rights

While some theorists have attempted to defend human rights based on biology[47] or even self-interest,[48] the most common justifications of rights are either moral-religious, such as those of Locke and the authors of the U.S. Constitution, and legal-procedural, such as those who defend some conception of rights as necessary for civil society or as a contractual means of protecting individual rights.[49] Both the moral-religious and the legal-procedural share a basic agreement on the principle that human rights are shared by all people, regardless of national origin, class, race, sexuality, or gender. Importantly, however, only those arguments resting on moral-religious grounds appeal to a transcendent principle; the grounds for legal-procedural arguments are less broadly applicable.

This is especially important because one of the major criticisms of international human rights policies is that they are grounded in, and continue to support, forms of Western cultural imperialism. Given that most of the philosophers of human rights as religious in origin have been Western, and that the notion of natural rights relies on Western religion and Christian conceptions of God, human rights as understood in the West can easily be seen as contributing to cultural imperialism. In addition, if the theory of human or natural rights is grounded in Western religion, then those who do not believe in a Western (Christian) God have no reason to support human rights; such rights may become little more than, as Jeremy Bentham famously declared, "rhetorical nonsense—nonsense upon stilts."[50] For Bentham, it is manifestly absurd to argue either that all men (which he explicitly argued included "all human creatures of both sexes,"[51]) are born free or in are any way equal in rights.[52] In his view, it is equally absurd—but infinitely more dangerous—to argue that the end of government is the protection of these rights.

For Bentham, rights are legal constructions, and therefore cannot exist prior to government, but are instead products of political associations such as governments: "The origination of governments from a contract is pure fiction, or in other words, a falsehood."[53] Therefore security, property, liberty, and other such "rights" are dependent upon government. Believing otherwise is dangerous, he argues, because it leads to contempt for those governments that protect rights, and thus renders political life unstable. For Bentham, the belief in natural rights leads to a belief in unbounded rights, which are both contradictory (the right to property implies abridgment of liberty, for instance) and impossible to sustain. Governments will therefore be rendered less legitimate, and less able to protect rights.

But legal-procedural conceptions of human rights are not immune to criticism either. Theorists such as Richard Rorty, who argue that human rights are based on a somewhat sentimental view of human beings,[54] and scholars such as Alasdair MacIntyre, who reject the notion of human rights as mere fictions,[55] come perilously close to arguing for an invidious form of moral relativism, by which there are no standards except expedience to judge communal human behavior. This became a particular problem in the wake of the Holocaust, as it exposed the weaknesses of consequentialist doctrines such as Utilitarianism.[56]

While there is widespread consensus that there are at least some rights associated with the human condition, there is thus clearly no agreement on the origin of rights, and it matters a great deal if one argues that they are given by God or by government, for the justifications of both government itself and the policies governments pursue differ depending on one's view. If government exists to protect rights given by God, then that is the primary function of government—and it is no coincidence that the nations in which this theory has been most popular are also the ones that used it to justify their revolutions. If, on the other hand, rights are given by government, then respect for government rather than justification for revolution, becomes an important consequence.

Just as there are important disagreements concerning the origin of rights, there are also controversies concerning their definition and nature. These apparently philosophical controversies have direct impact on American politics—for the republic's foundational documents explicitly connect the legitimacy of government to the protection of rights and argue that those rights come from God. So the task of the American government—and of its president—is the protection of rights. But the Founders had what would now be considered a restrictive view of rights, and it is not clear that the extension of those rights is warranted either philosophically or politically—and that lack of clarity proved to be important to Carter's efforts to put human rights on the national agenda.

Which Rights are Human Rights?
Defining human rights has proved to be a thorny matter, even in the abstract. Rights are often split into various categories: essential versus inessential, for instance, or political versus economic.[57] One of the more common divisions is that proposed by Karel Vasek, who understands rights as "generational." For Vasek, first-generation rights are confined to civil and political rights; second generation rights are economic, social, and cultural (such as a right to subsistence), and third-generation rights are importantly transnational, such as the right to peace and to a clean environment. Only the first two generations of rights are protected by law in any nation, and, as has been noted, in the U.S. even second generation rights are quite controversial.[58]

Where human rights legislation has been adopted, it is generally aimed at protecting *security rights,* or those that protect the integrity of the person, such as protection from murder, rape, and torture; *liberty rights,* or those that protect one's right to believe and worship as one chooses; *political rights,* such as those that guarantee the right to participate in the political system; *process rights,* which provide protections such as access to a justice system; and *equality rights,* such as those that endorse equal citizenship. All of these categories of rights are not very controversial to Americans and are generally accepted as necessary. More controversial are the categories of *welfare rights,* which are also known as economic rights, and which guarantee protection from economic deprivation; and *group rights,* which provide protections for specific groups against ethnic genocide or other forms of discrimination.

If rights are understood as given by God, then those rights may well be understood as quite expansive. It is no great leap, for instance, from the right to life to the right to clean drinking water. If, however, rights are understood as generated by the state, transnational rights become more problematic. But it is not that simple—in the United States, for instance, rights are understood as coming out of the natural rights tradition; yet second-generation rights are problematic, and third-generation rights are rarely even considered. This is because in the United States, as we have seen, notions of property, filtered through the lens of capitalism, have led to restrictions on the national understanding of rights that do not pertain in nations with stronger communitarian traditions. So while definitions of what constitutes a "human right" are connected to the origin of those rights, the correlation is not perfect, and the ideological tradition of the specific nation has a good deal to do with its understanding of rights.

In the United States, especially since "human rights" only really entered the American vocabulary in the aftermath of World War II, those rights are most often connected with the values of democratic capitalism. John Kennedy, for example, referred to the Twenty-third Amendment, giving citizens of the nation's capital the right to vote, in terms of "human rights."[59] He also used "human rights" as in at least one discussion of American race relations.[60] But for Kennedy, as for most American presidents during the Cold War, "human rights" were primarily used as warrants for action in the international realm—human rights were what Americans had, and what those under Soviet domination lacked, and he connected human rights to "representative democracy," as well as to "self-determination" and to "non-intervention."[61] Definitions of human rights by political actors have never been free of political implications.

One of the thorniest of those implications has to do with the issue of who is supposed to protect human rights. In the Western tradition, the state exists to protect at least a minimalist version of human rights, and, in that tradition, when the state fails to protect these rights, it loses its legitimacy. But in that circumstance, there is a question of who is charged with overthrowing the state and under what conditions is it acceptable to promulgate revolution. In one version, the people themselves must rise up and "alter or abolish" the government in question; in other versions, other nations, acting alone or in concordance with United Nations mandates, must do so.

This is not a small question, for there are clear policy implications for the U.S. national government (and for other governments as well) embedded in it. How is "oppressive regime" defined, and who gets to decide? Is support for human rights limited to rhetorical and symbolic support for those living under oppressive regimes, or is more direct action called for? Moreover, when can one nation intrude on the sovereignty of another, and when are human rights abuses purely domestic matters, and thus outside the purview of international interference? None of these questions have easy or obvious answers, and all of them have posed problems for the American government and specifically for the Carter Administration. They would prove to be serious issues for how human rights developed as a lasting part of the American national agenda.

There are also difficult questions of monitoring human rights activities and abuses. A considerable amount of monitoring is done by nonpartisan international organizations such as Amnesty International, but there are questions about the political biases—or lack thereof—of some monitoring groups, and there are always arguments concerning the politics of accusing allies—or nonallies—of human rights abuses. In a world where U.S. global and strategic interests are often understood as colliding with human rights, it is not easy to decide which should trump the other—there are arguments that U.S. military power is dependent on its wise use of moral power, and that the support of repressive regimes undermines the national interest both strategically and ideologically, but there are also arguments that our moral force must follow our military force, and that the United States is a force for good in the world and must act to protect its interests so it can continue providing a beacon light of freedom. These arguments, difficult in the abstract, become infinitely more complicated as a matter of political practice.[62]

This situation is further complicated by the fact that human rights abuses are not confined to dictatorships. In 2004, for instance, Amnesty International found that only the nations of Iceland, Costa Rica, the Netherlands, Norway, and Denmark were not guilty of at least some significant human rights abuses. On the other hand, at least ninety nations have now set up human rights organizations of some sort, designed to monitor, promote, and protect human rights. Pushing human rights internationally is always a matter of negotiating gray areas rather than dealing in the stark differences of black and white.

There are also controversies concerning how best to protect human rights in other nations. Observers disagree, for instance, about whether the United States should loudly and publicly denounce human rights abuses whenever and wherever they are found, or whether it is better to deal with them privately. There are disagreements about whether incentives should be offered to those who improve their records on human rights or sanctions imposed on those who fail to do so. These are both difficult and important questions, especially in an international political environment where some of America's most important allies in the Cold War were also numbered among the world's worst abusers of human rights.[63]

Many of these controversies, now well established as the subject of long and sometimes difficult if not acrimonious debates, were still nascent during the Carter presidency, but they were present and created difficulties for him and members of his administration. For the purposes of this study, the important thing to remember about how human rights was understood in the United States prior to the mid-1970s is that they were generally equated with civil rights for African Americans, although were also connected to women's rights and the rights of other minority groups.[64] On the international front, human rights were also generally understood as procedural rights such as civil and political rights rather than as economic or cultural rights.

But however they were understood, the discussion about human rights was just beginning to accelerate and deepen as Carter came to the presidency. This meant that even though there was no widespread agreement on what "human rights" were, how human rights ought to be understood, who was in charge of protecting them, or how they ought to be protected, there was a increasing number of people—inside and outside of Washington—who felt that they had a stake in human rights and who wanted the national government to take some sort of action on the issue.

The Public Mood on Human Rights in the 1970s

A good bit of the research on presidential agenda building relies upon stated or unstated assumptions about the centrality of executive leadership (see chapter 2). Jeffrey Cohen, for instance, notes that presidents are required to lead, but they are constrained in their ability to do so by the need for public responsiveness: presidents cannot lead where others will not follow.[65] This, of course, puts presidents in a difficult position—they need to display both leadership and responsiveness, and these two goals are not always compatible. Occasionally, however, presidents are able to stake out issues that resonate with the public as their own. Such was the case with Jimmy Carter and human rights.

There is good evidence that even while Carter was still "Jimmy Who?" human rights was "in the air" breathed by the denizens of the nation's capital.[66] In the context of the crises caused by Vietnam, Watergate, and revelations about the clandestine activities of the CIA, there was a reaction against the perceived immorality of the Nixon/Kissinger style of diplomacy and a renewed interest in instantiating the national morality in national policy.

"In the past year," noted the Friends Committee on National Legislation in their 1976 newsletter,

> "human rights" has changed from a rather tedious subject of low visibility to one of the most relevant and controversial issues on Capital Hill. Over strenuous [Ford] Administration objections Congress has written human rights into foreign military and economic aid bills. It has cut off military aid to Chile and Uruguay. Congressional hearings have been held on human rights violations in some eighteen countries. And the State Department, prodded by Congress, has created a Coordinator for Human Rights and Humanitarian Affairs. But the Senate failed to ratify the 28-year-old Genocide Convention which could have broken the logjam and led the way to approval of a number of pending UN human rights covenants and conventions. Why this new interest in human rights? The Indochina war appears to have sensitized many members of Congress. . . . A growing public awareness of the widespread use of torture and repression by regimes aided by U.S. tax dollars, has also sparked strong concern for human rights.[67]

There was thus significant congressional attention and activity dedicated to the issue of human rights—attention that was not due to the efforts of Jimmy Carter or the members of his administration, but that indicated widespread interest in and concern over human rights among members of Congress prior to Carter's election.

That attention may well have originally derived from events of the early 1970s, such as the military coup in Chile (1973), the publication of *Gulag Archipelago* (1973), and the completion of the Helsinki Conference and the signing of what has come to be known as the Helsinki Accords (1975).[68] The concerted efforts of various NGOs were also instrumental in getting some attention given to human rights issues.[69] Led by House liberals Tom Harkin (D-IA) and Don Fraser (D-MN), Congress began to notice and convene hearings on human rights as early as 1973.[70] Reports soon followed, and these reports are now one of the most important elements of human rights activity on the part of the U.S. government. Legislation followed the reports, including action tying foreign and military aid to human rights performance.

The most important example of this legislation is the Jackson-Vinik amendment to the 1974 trade agreement, which is the first legislative effort to link U.S. economic policy to human rights activities in other nations.[71] That amendment, signed by President Gerald Ford in 1975, denied normal trade relations—most-favored nation status—to nations that denied its citizens the right of emigration. It was clearly aimed at Leonid Brezhnev's Soviet government and its policy concerning the emigration of Soviet Jews. The amendment did make an important public statement about one right considered to be a "human right," but it also allowed the president to grant yearly waivers. Such waivers were long granted to China, for instance, reflecting the tension between maintaining economic and political relationships and remaining firm on issues of human rights.

Still, even some action was important, and Congress was not alone in its increased attention to human rights. During the decade of the 1970s, new groups dedicated to human rights were formed, and existing groups saw their memberships increase.[72] Their tactics changed as well, shifting focus from grassroots mobilization to lobbying—the number of these groups active in Washington grew from a few to over fifty by the end of the decade.[73] As with the congressional hearings of the decade, these groups also began to publish reports, and the cumulative outcome increased public awareness of and interest in human rights. Importantly, members of the U.S. government and members of these interest groups began both communicating and collaborating on issues of concern to them both.[74] Such behavior put pressure on the White House to respond with definitive action on human rights.

There was also a good bit of public and scholarly attention to issues of human rights in the 1970s.[75] In the summer of 1974, for instance, the *Virginia Journal of International Law* did a symposium on "Human rights, the National Interest, and U.S. Foreign Policy: Some Preliminary Observations."[76] There were other symposia and colloquia dedicated to the idea, however amorphously articulated, that the United States should have a more moral direction, especially in its foreign policy, than had been provided under Johnson, Nixon, and, by extension, Ford. Major foundations, such as the Ford and Rockefeller Foundations, also began funding human rights activists and human rights activity.[77] And it is surely significant that Amnesty International, founded in 1961, both experienced immense growth throughout the 1970s and was awarded the Nobel Peace Prize in 1977.[78]

The resonance of human rights had both realistic and idealistic components: "President Carter's human rights initiative was a direct response to this crisis of faith in American values. The attraction of human rights was that they were precisely not American, despite having a great deal of commonality with traditional American values. With its foreign policy at the service of universal human rights, America could conceivably avoid the charge of cultural imperialism. Significantly, Carter did not reject the exceptionalist tradition but intended rather, by this means, to save it. A human rights policy would ensure consistency and dispel hypocrisy in foreign policy, thus realizing at last the unity of American power and virtue."[79] Human rights was thus seen as both practical in terms of supporting U.S. power abroad and idealistic, as returning the United States to its exceptionalist ethical roots. Even Jeanne Kirkpatrick has noted that "In retrospect, it seems nearly inevitable that human rights should have become a central issue in American Foreign Policy once the U.S. became really involved in the world. The rights of individuals, whose protection we have always viewed as the purpose of a government, has always been a central preoccupation of America in politics."[80] When voices as conservative as Kirkpatrick's claim an inevitability to human rights, it is clear that even "in retrospect," there is something to this policy that unites Americans.

Human rights had the further advantage of bolstering both Carter's overall image and his efforts to unify the Democratic Party and the nation as a whole.[81] As Hamilton Jordan wrote to the president in late 1977, "Of our numerous foreign policy initiatives, it is the only one that has a broad base of support among the American people and is not considered 'liberal.' With Panama and SALT II ahead of us, we need the broad based, non-ideological support for our foreign policy that human rights provides."[82] There was evidence that even those who did not approve of Carter still found something appealing in his talk on human rights.[83] Just as human rights had helped to unify the Democrats leading up to the 1976 election, the hope in the White House following that election was that human rights could help solidify Carter's position as the leader of an ideologically cohesive nation. As badly as Watergate and Vietnam had divided the country, a clear commitment to human rights had the potential to bridge the various fissures that the previous decade had widened—among members of opposing parties, ideologies, and generations.

This unification was seen as possible not least because "human rights" seemed to call on the best of the American past, but was vague enough that members of these conflicting groups could each pour their preferred meaning into the term. However unwittingly, Carter was aided by the polysemy inherent in "human rights," and gained politically by its ambiguity. In addition, "in making human rights a key element of all discussions and considerations of American foreign policy, Carter succeeded in shifting the discourse on American foreign policy away from the dominant concerns of the Cold War and containment."[84] Emphasis on human rights allowed Carter to move attention from foreign policy constraints and possibilities as articulated by Nixon and Kissinger and toward a view of national relationships that was more congenial to him and more expressive of his political preferences. Human rights worked to Carter's advantage in two distinct ways: it provided a potential basis of unity and it allowed Carter to distract attention from debates he did not want to encourage in favor of debates he did want to encourage. It is no wonder that he increasingly focused on them.

Jimmy Carter and Human Rights

Any southerner running for national office in the wake of the civil rights movement would have to stake out a clear position on issues of racial relations, and Jimmy Carter was no exception. While his early record on civil rights was somewhat ambiguous,[85] by the time he was elected governor, Carter's actions were clearly on the side of racial progress: "From the day he was inaugurated as governor on, his whole line was to embrace civil rights and put all that behind us."[86] As governor, he moved forward on issues of what would now be called racial reconciliation and pursued both substantive and symbolic policies that forged a multiracial coalition in support of his reelection as governor and candidacy for the presidency.[87]

As a presidential candidate, he continually stressed the themes of "competence and compassion."[88] Carter did not emphasize human rights until after the Democratic National Convention, and indeed, "The human rights issue emerged not in any Carter speech, but in the writings of the 1976 Democratic Platform."[89] As Senator Daniel Patrick Moynihan (D-NY) recalled, "We'll be against the dictators you don't like the most . . . if you'll be against the dictators we don't like the most."[90] With that, the Democrats were able to unite and create "the strongest platform commitment to human rights in our history."[91] Reacting, in large part, to the policies of the Nixon Administration, the Democratic Party led the way on human rights. Carter was not slow to follow.

Having won the nomination, Carter experienced a brief honeymoon of sorts with the media, and it was no real surprise when the afterglow began to fade, and criticism of the candidate stepped up, and his poll numbers fell a bit.[92] Human rights enabled him to regain some of that lost standing. Especially after Ford's gaffe regarding Soviet domination of Eastern Europe in the debate, Carter's stance on human rights allowed him to both claim the moral high ground and to criticize his opponent.[93]

Once elected, Carter maintained a visible position on human rights: "The President's single sentence in his inaugural address—'Because we are free we can never be indifferent to the fate of freedom elsewhere'—had led to press speculation, then queries, then to a sequence of presidential acts—e.g., the letter to Andrei Sakharov, the meeting with the Soviet dissident Vladimir Bukovsky, and partial statements such as those in the address at the United Nations on March 17—but still nothing that could be described as a policy."[94] From the earliest days of his administration, it was clear that Carter was committed to something called human rights, but it was considerably less clear what that commitment might actually mean for U.S. action in foreign policy.

Where anticommunism had long been the single most dominant justification for foreign policy, by 1977 it was clear that the Carter Administration was motivated more by human rights than by strict anticommunism.[95] Senator Henry M. (Scoop) Jackson (D-WA), two-time presidential candidate and cosponsor of the Jackson-Vinik amendment, for instance, noted that "In the area of the defense of human rights the new Administration has departed markedly from its predecessor. Those of us in Congress who have labored long and hard on behalf of the rights of men and women everywhere to those basic liberties set forth in the Universal Declaration of Human Rights are gratified by the new American emphasis on these matters."[96] Jackson was eager to welcome Carter's participation in the issue, but was equally eager to remind the president that there were people fighting for it long before Carter entered national politics. As historian Arthur Schlesinger Jr. noted, "By 1977 the world was well prepared for new human rights initiatives. Up to this point, Washington had lagged badly behind. But the new President, in a remarkable display of leadership, seized the standard of human rights and succeeded in presenting it to the world as if it had been American property all along. He was able to do this because the time was ripe and because the cause fulfilled the old American conviction of having a mission to the world."[97] It was that element of locating human rights in the best of the American ideological traditions that provided its unifying impetus—liberals and conservatives alike could point with pride to American traditions rather than to its failed policies in Vietnam.

Still, it was significant that the president joined the human rights conversation, and this president joined in most forcefully: "No president in American history," notes one author, "gave the promotion of human rights a higher priority in foreign policy than did Jimmy Carter."[98] Because of this attention, there was evidence that the Carter Administration's support for human rights touched an important—and preexisting—chord among the American people.[99] That chord, however, led to some problems for Carter, as expectations for domestic action were raised,[100] and increasingly, people demanded that he speak out on all human rights-related issues, at home and abroad.

Noted columnist William Raspberry, referring to the Wilmington 10 case, commented, "Because it is a state case, not a federal one, President Carter may be as powerless to do anything about the Wilmington 10 as he is in the case of, say, Russian dissidents. But it would be a most useful thing if he could bring himself to speak out on it. Human rights, after all, don't begin at the water's edge."[101] Such criticism, as we will see, became all too frequent. Carter's constituents were interested in human rights, happy to see the president speaking out on them, concerned with the foreign policy repercussions of such speech, and eager to hear him be more explicit about human rights abuses at home. Human rights created many opportunities for this president, but like most opportunities, there was a large cost associated with his espousal of the issue.[102] Those problems would come to haunt him the longer he stayed in office, but ironically, may well have been one of the reasons behind the longevity of the issue.

Conclusion

Human rights in the West are generally understood to stem from the religious and political traditions of the Enlightenment, and American conceptions of those rights are firmly rooted in the theories of Hobbes, Locke, and other contract theorists as refracted through the lens of the colonists hoping to justify and incite revolution against England. In the United States, then, human rights are most easily understood and defended as political and civil rights. Procedural rights, such as the right to vote, are those that gain the broadest base of support. That has been true through the long, and often painful, history of inclusion and exclusion in the nation.[103]

The national mood in the wake of Vietnam, Watergate, and the revelations of various instances of governmental malfeasance had led to a decline in trust, increase in cynicism, and growth of a certain nostalgia for simpler times, when the exercise of U.S. power had seemed both effective and moral. In that context, both public and congressional interest turned to human rights, and Jimmy Carter, the born-again Southern Baptist, was well positioned to capitalize on that interest. The nature of his campaign and his personal ethos contributed to his ability to take the issue and make it his own. But that would only matter if his communication could be said to have effectiveness as well.

CHAPTER 2

Human Rights
and the National Agenda

H uman rights have been a motivating force behind political
action for centuries, but there has been no clear universal or
even widely shared notion of what exactly is entailed in the
phrase "human rights." Even in the American context, the
phrase has meant very different things at different times. In
this chapter, I look less at theoretical or even elite definitions of human rights
and more at how the phrase resonates between the presidency, the media,
and the mass public. I make two important assumptions: that human rights
has been a significant issue on the national agenda, and that Jimmy Carter
had something to do with getting and keeping it there.

Human Rights as an Agenda Item

There are at least two ways to understand human rights as an item on the national agenda: as a function of public opinion, measured through polls, and
as function of media coverage, which for my purposes, is measured through
the opinions and comments of journalists. When we talk about polls on
human rights, it is important to note that these polls are relatively recent in
origin—and that in itself is interesting. When we talk about media coverage,
I am more interested in the sense among journalists that human rights was
a "real" topic than I am in measuring column inches dedicated to human
rights—if members of the media see it as an issue, it is an issue.

Polling Human Rights

There seems to be little doubt among pundits and scholars that although the contemporary push for human rights dates back to the U.N. Charter, Jimmy Carter's presidency coincided with an increase of interest in, and attention to, human rights by the media, politicians, and the general public.[1] Questions about human rights, for instance, did not appear on national surveys prior to 1978, and once there, responses remain quite stable, as the following table, which reports responses on the importance of human rights as a national goal, indicates. (Numbers indicate the percentage of respondents giving a particular answer.)

YEAR	VERY IMP.	SOMEWHAT	NOT	DON'T KNOW
1974	n/a	n/a	n/a	n/a
1978	39	40	14	7
1982	43	42	9	6
1986	42	45	9	4
1990	58	33	13	3
1994	39	47	10	4
1998	39	47	10	4

Source: The Gallup Organization, *Attitudes of the American People Related to Foreign Policy,* Submitted to the Chicago Council on Foreign Relations, December 1998, 8.

Other data show that in 1975 the public was largely concerned with the economy; and even as late as 1978 people were paying relatively little attention to foreign as opposed to domestic news. And while majorities of the public supported human rights in the abstract, support fell when it was connected to specific policies.[2] Together, these data indicate that there was diffuse support for the idea of human rights and increased attention to it in the 1970s, but that it was poorly connected to specific programs. Moreover, broad consensus did exist for some form of human rights, at least early in the Carter Administration, but that support proved to be shallow and shifted depending on how human rights was being defined.[3]

Because of this preference for issues broadly defined, there is a certain inertia about the public agenda, and the issues that appear on it are remarkably consistent over time.[4] Attitudes on human rights policy certainly show that level of consistency: a Gallup Organization poll reveals that in the twenty years between 1978 and 1998, only about 1 percent of respondents list human rights as one of the two or three biggest foreign policy problems.[5]

Yet support for human rights is high: in 1978, 79 percent of respondents called human rights very or somewhat important; and those numbers also remain remarkably consistent over time: in 1982 it was 85 percent, in 1986, 87 percent, in 1990, 91 percent, in 1994, 86 percent, and in 1998, 86 percent.[6] Events seems to have the capacity to elicit short-term effects—note the rise in 1990, immediately after the fall of the Berlin Wall, for instance—but those effects appear ephemeral. Absent such events, Americans may not think of human rights when listing important problems, but they respond to the phrase when prompted—as we have seen, human rights clearly connects to values that Americans find important but not necessarily to specific policies that are considered important.

There is a partisan dimension to these attitudes; Democrats are consistently more supportive of human rights than are Republicans.[7] This fact probably does have a policy dimension, as Republicans are also more likely to rely on notions of nongovernmental influence on human rights—relying on the free market, for instance, rather than seeking to put governmental muscle behind the enforcement of human rights.

Partisanship aside, the data on public opinion and human rights have not changed significantly since 1998. In 2006, a poll by the Chicago Council on Foreign Relations reported that "A very large majority believes promoting human rights is an important priority for U.S. foreign policy. A very strong majority feels that with the increased economic involvement that has come with globalization, the U.S. should be more concerned about human rights in other countries. Majorities feel that promoting human rights serves U.S. interests. Denying human rights is seen as leading to political instability, and a majority believes that using U.S. military forces to remove a government that is abusing human rights is justified. A majority also supports using foreign aid as a means of promoting human rights."[8] Thus, it is clear that human rights are effective as a warrant for political action. Americans do not so much consider them a free-standing issue as a motive and a justification for action on other issues. They seem to encourage consideration of human rights when formulating policy, but not to the exclusion of other policy interests. This is entirely consistent with how Carter treated human rights.

It is interesting that majorities of Americans display attitudes that are so consistent with Carter's claims for human rights during his term in office. Whether these attitudes developed in the White House or Congress and filtered down to the public, or whether they were present among members of the public and filtered up is less important (for the moment) than the fact that these attitudes are shared by elites and the public. For it is that shared sense of the issue and its place in national politics that determines its place on the national agenda.

According to that same report, "an overwhelming majority says that promoting human rights should be an important priority of U.S. foreign policy." When asked in a February 2005 Gallup poll how important "promoting and defending human rights in other countries" is as a U.S. foreign policy goal, 86 percent said it was important (52 percent said "very important" 34 percent said "somewhat important"). Only 10 percent said "not too important" and 2 percent said "not important at all." Numerous other polls on the topic in recent years have found similar results. Yet, "when ranked against other objectives . . . human rights falls below several other concerns. In Gallup's End-of-Year Poll 2004, only 4 percent of respondents selected "improving/maintaining human rights" as the most important priority for leaders of the world, while 29 percent chose "the war on terrorism" and 13 percent selected "restoring trust and honesty in government, in business and in international institutions."[9] These data tell us that the public responds to the idea of human rights when prompted but does not usually consider them an important problem when individuals are asked to generate their own lists of important problems. This is precisely the sort of situation in which presidential framing and agenda setting are most likely to have the greatest effects. The attitudes are "out there," as potential warrants for presidential action; all that is needed is a nationally prominent rhetor ready to make the case. That is precisely what Americans got when Jimmy Carter was elected to the presidency, and both public opinion and media coverage reflect that fact.

As we have seen, the U.S. public is sporadic at best in its attention to human rights, but once it gets on the agenda, the effects can be widely felt. One author noted, "The human rights stand of President Jimmy Carter and public opposition to U.S. support for repressive Third World governments added to public concern for human rights. When the issue has been raised, there is little public opposition to defending, in principle, international human rights: Americans oppose the murder or arbitrary imprisonment of political dissenters in all countries, and torture is opposed without reservation. Nevertheless, throughout U.S. history the defense of human rights has been a strikingly unimportant issue for the American public."[10] That is, Americans will rally to a call for human rights, but absent such a call, are likely to place their concern on other, more personally pressing matters. And it is the media who tell the public what issues merit their concern.

Covering Human Rights

What attention does get paid to human rights is generally credited to the presidency of Jimmy Carter. Numerous pundits and authors clearly connect Carter to the upsurge in interest in human rights. Catherine Cassara, for instance, tells us that "foreign correspondents active during the period report that the Carter policy fundamentally altered how the U.S. press covered Latin America."[11] Anthony Lewis credited him with "raising a standard. He is giving not just Americans but people in the West generally a sense that their values are being asserted again, after years of silence in the face of tyranny and brutality."[12] *Newsweek* noted, "In the last half year, human rights have suddenly become a major theme in world diplomacy,"[13] while the *New Republic* said that Carter had "made the world more aware of human rights."[14] And there was enormous coverage granted to individual cases, such as those of Sakharov, Ginzburg, and Scharansky.[15] Even today, human rights abuses continue to get intense, if sporadic, coverage.

Observers also noted that Carter's emphasis on human rights was not without risk: The *ABC Evening News* said in March of 1977 that "It is possible that the most important development anywhere in the world at present is President Carter's personal crusade for human rights. No president or other world leader has ever tried such a risky venture before. It could end up a calamity for U.S. influence as offended governments withdraw cooperation, as some South American countries and Mr. Brezhnev threaten to do. It could, if it catches on, change the human tone of the world vastly for the better. It's far too early to guess which way things will go. But one thing we may not have suspected is clear: Among people there is a hungry market for his stand. . . . It feels rather good to be on the side of the angels again, the way Jefferson prescribed, 200 years ago."[16] Note that ABC here is both crediting Carter with the increased prominence human rights issues have attained and assuming the frame he offered for the issue. Carter worked hard to use U.S. political history in general, and the Founders in particular, as he argued that a commitment to human rights was consistent with and even required by the American national ethos. When the media pick up not only the issue but also the way in which presidents frame the issue, and treat both as if they were inevitable, that amounts to a pretty good case for presidential influence over the media agenda.

And that influence was clearly intentional. At least one reason for the prominence accorded human rights during the Carter Administration was the willingness of members of that administration to encourage and facilitate media coverage of human rights. Prior to the Carter Administration, even interested members of the media were constrained in their efforts to cover human rights because of lack of access to information,[17] and changes in coverage that made human rights more visible were directly traceable to Carter Administration policies: "The Carter human rights initiatives changed the lax attitudes towards human rights violations. Suddenly there were embassy sources willing to talk and official U.S. government reports of rights abuses became available. U.S. diplomats were ready to provide official sources and facts, 'giving reporters legitimate pegs to write at length on the subject.' As additional assistance to correspondents, the Carter administration's concern with human rights legitimized rights monitoring groups, such as Amnesty International and America's Watch, as news sources."[18] Carter Administration policies were thus part of the agenda-building process; they helped lead to agenda setting, and thus to public opinion on the matter of human rights. Without administration support, the media would have had a more difficult time finding ways to cover the constellation of issues that are "human rights." With that support, sources became more available, and topics that were previously ignored became more acceptable to editors and to readers as well.

Even criticism of the president's human rights policy helped keep the issue alive in the public mind. And his human rights policies were quite heavily criticized throughout the Carter presidency. He was, for example, charged with fostering "the widening gap between the promise and the reality,"[19] of human rights, for endangering Soviet dissidents,[20] for failing to follow the policy consistently,[21] and for failing to maintain the original high level of attention given to human rights concerns.[22] There were also charges that the emphasis on human rights led to an incoherent and sometimes contradictory foreign policy.[23] Many of these criticisms were not without foundation, but for the moment the point is that coverage of human rights, both positive and negative, increased during the Carter years, as a direct result of intentional Carter Administration policies.

Looking at polling data and media coverage, it is possible to conclude that while human rights are poorly understood by the U.S. public and salience is low, when prompted, Americans support human rights, and human rights became a major issue for the media both at home and abroad during the Carter Administration. Both the U.S. public and media began to accept human rights as a legitimate area of concern, and while human rights will probably never be a leading issue on the national agenda, it has retained the status it gained during the Carter years. The available evidence indicates that "Presidents can influence the public's policy agenda,"[24] and that in the case of human rights, Jimmy Carter did so. That argument is only plausible, however, if it can be shown that presidential rhetoric has an effect on public opinion and the national agenda.

Does Presidential Communication Matter?

Pundits, journalists, and presidents all act as if they believe that presidential communication can and does influence both the media agenda and public opinion. But scholars are not necessarily so sure. Presidential scholars in both political science and communication are engaged in a vigorous debate (which, sadly, is not always interdisciplinary), over the question of whether presidential rhetoric matters.[25] Some authors argue that presidents talk more and more, but mostly, it is to hear themselves talk. They believe that this constant chatter has both debased the office of the presidency and the quality of public discourse in the United States.[26] Others argue that presidents speak to specific purposes and that these purposes are more or less met, depending upon, among other things, the quality of the communication.[27] This debate is complicated by issues of definition (what does it mean that rhetoric "matters"?) and measurement (how do we know if it matters?).

Issues of Definition

Issues of definition are central to the question of whether presidential communication matters, because they go to the heart of the issue: what does it mean to "matter," and how will we know? It is hard to define effectiveness in presidential communication, but there are numerous scholars who have endeavored to do so. Generally, they find that indeed, there is evidence, that under at least some circumstances, presidential speech does seem to have an impact both on the media and on the general public.

Jeffrey Cohen, for instance, has found that the more attention the president gives to an issue in his State of the Union Address, the more concerned the public becomes with that issue.[28] This is true whether or not presidents rely on substantive arguments to support their case. He concludes that "Presidents can influence the public's policy agenda."[29] Importantly, as Cohen points out elsewhere, while the president is the only nationally elected official, it does not follow that he must influence national opinion.[30] Presidents build coalitions around specific issues and for specific purposes. They can afford to be—indeed, they have every incentive to be—strategic in how they approach the challenges of trying to create, lead, or manage public opinion.[31] Indeed, there is likely a reciprocal relationship at work: presidents attempt to be responsive to public opinion while at the same time helping to set the public agenda.[32]

It is helpful at this point to distinguish between agenda setting, priming, and framing, for it is likely that presidents will have different abilities in each of these categories. *Agenda setting* is the ability—usually associated with the media or powerful political actors such as the president—to influence issue salience among the mass public. That is, the more coverage an issue receives, the more likely it is that the mass public will find that issue significant.[33] *Framing* is the process of identifying an event with its cause: it is the heart of problem identification.[34] As Robert Entman put it, "The social world is . . . a kaleidoscope of potential realities, any of which can be readily evoked by altering the way in which observations are framed and categorized."[35] When an issue is framed, it is also defined—one pattern is chosen from the kaleidoscope of possibilities. Finally, *priming* influences the judgments the audience makes about the issue and its cause.[36] To define a problem is also to render a judgment about it, and the ability to influence the judgments the public makes about events, issues, and people can translate into enormous political power. Of all these elements, agenda setting is the most often studied and probably the most clearly understood.

Agenda Setting

The most common definition of agenda setting is that it involves telling people what to think about, rather than what to think. That is, agenda setting is the process by which issues move from being invisible or irrelevant as matters of public concern to becoming problems that are worthy of public and governmental attention. There is evidence dating back to the early 1970s that the media play an important role in agenda setting.[37] By 1996, there had been over 300 studies substantiating this finding.[38] It seems indisputable that the amount of news coverage given to an issue matches the public's identification of the nation's most important problem.[39] That is, unsurprisingly, the more often members of the public hear and read about an issue, the more likely they are to consider that issue important. Agenda setting does not necessarily influence how people think about a given issue—attitudes are, as we shall see, considerably more complicated than that—but it does influence the public's perception of which issues are most deserving of governmental time, attention, and resources.

Some scholars separate agenda building from agenda setting. Agenda building is the process whereby media stories are created. Gladys and Kurt

Lang, for instance, have proposed a four-step model of agenda building, in which first, a topic is covered by the media; second, a common frame for the topic is developed; third, the topic is linked to secondary symbols, thus rendering it recognizable to a mass audience; and finally, officials and their spokespersons comment on the topic, giving the media something to cover. In this formulation, both the media and public officials are key players in the process, and no topic will make it onto the national agenda without the participation of both.[40] Presidents are both initiators of and reactive to the media agenda.[41] That is, agenda building is one step back from agenda setting—it is the process by which political actors get their issues noticed by the media and thus by the public.

If political actors think that an issue will resonate with the public, a belief that may be fostered by extensive media coverage of the issue, they may try to position themselves vis-à-vis that issue, thus perpetuating and extending the coverage of it. Or, political actors with an interest in an issue area may try to create coverage of it and thus influence public opinion and public policy in the direction they prefer. Paying attention to public attitudes is not necessarily "pandering": politicians may be attentive to the public in order to better craft their appeals rather than to decide which appeals to craft.[42] The relevance to Carter's actions on human rights is clear.

Clearly, a topic does not need to originate with the media; just as clearly, a president can have an impact on what stories the media decide are newsworthy, although it is unclear how much of an impact he can have.[43] Presidents seem to have more influence when an issue is the subject of a major speech or when the issue is one to which the president devotes considerable time and energy. Ronald Reagan, for instance, helped make the Nicaraguan Contras very well known throughout the 1980s, even though he consistently failed to get the policies he wanted accepted by the people or passed by Congress. It is thus important to note that success at agenda building or agenda setting is not a guarantee that the media or the public will agree with a president's position—that is not the claim I am making here. I *am* arguing that the more attention a president gives an issue, the more likely that issue is to receive coverage, and that this was the case with Jimmy Carter and human rights.

Importantly for the issue of human rights, the president's ability to affect the national agenda seems strongest in foreign policy.[44] This is, of course, consistent with how we understand presidential power in general, as his greater unilateral power, more extensive informational networks, and broader bureaucratic resources generally enhance his power in foreign policy vis-à-vis other national institutions. This means that when a president declares a foreign policy issue to be of primary importance, there is likely to be an increase in media coverage and in public attention to that issue. For this reason, advocates of various causes work very hard to get presidential attention and time, even presidential endorsements, for their issues.

Presidential power over the tone and content of the national agenda is also enhanced whenever there is a lack of controversy among elites. When there is such consensus, as there was, for instance, in the case of human rights during the Carter years, the frame proposed by the White House is likely to be very influential in determining how the media will frame a story, through the process of what Robert Entman calls "cascading activation."[45] Entman argues that frames move from an administration to the media and thus to the public when four variables work together: the frame must be packaged in a way amenable to the media; the president must be seen as a credible source with effectiveness over the policy area in question; the communication strategy (word choice, distribution, timing) must be effective; and finally, the substance of the issue or event must be understood as having cultural congruence—it must have relevance and resonate. All of these elements pertained concerning human rights in the 1970s.

So the agenda-setting literature tells us that when a president has an issue that can be clearly connected to the mass public, is seen as credible on that issue, and clearly and consistently communicates on it in a way that is friendly to the media's organizational needs, the president is likely to have an effect on the media agenda, and through the media, on the national agenda. This was the case with human rights during the Carter Administration. But getting an issue on the agenda is only part of the battle. Another important element is getting the media—and the mass public—to see the issue as the president sees it—to get them to accept his frame.

Framing

Framing, notes Robert Entman, involves two key elements, selection and salience: "To frame is to select some aspects of a perceived reality and make them more salient in a communication text, in such a way as to promote a particular problem definition, causal interpretation, moral valuation, and/or treatment recommendation for the item described."[46] That is, different frames take the same set of facts and foreground different elements, rendering different interpretations of the same event and encouraging different preferred judgments about it, and different courses of action regarding it. The bully pulpit is an important source of frames for both the mass public and the media.[47]

There is good evidence that presidents avail themselves of the opportunities offered by their institutional position. As far as presidential rhetoric goes, there is, Donna Hoffman and Alison Howard note, "remarkable consistency in the policy areas that are given high priority (foreign policy/defense policy, economic policy, governmental affairs, and social welfare policy) and low priority (labor issues, agriculture, resources, and civil rights/civil liberties) over time."[48] Presidents generally speak as presidents—they do not tend to vary much in the overarching nature of the issues they present as important. But this does not mean that they do not have different emphases within these areas—one president may turn toward Europe while focusing on foreign policy, another toward Africa or China. And it is these smaller realms of emphasis that, at any given time, will comprise the national agenda.

It seems likely that the most potent presidential influence over public opinion would lie in his ability to frame issues. As Cohen points out, "The president plays a critical role in shaping the systemic agenda by affecting problem identification and issue prioritization in the mass public."[49] In other words, presidents have at least some ability to set the national agenda, as we have seen, and to frame issues—what Cohen calls "problem identification." Frames "set the boundaries of public policy debates."[50] The research on frames focuses almost exclusively on media frames—but those frames come from somewhere. And while many of them derive from organizational and institutional norms and practices,[51] political elites play a role in frame definition. In fact, a good bit of political debate revolves around the competition between elites over frames,[52] and we know that elites are more able to establish a given frame among members of the public when they are united on the frame—the more competition there is among elites, the less likely it is that a single frame will dominate[53]: "When citizens are exposed to complete rather than an edited version of political debate, they do not succumb to ambivalence or fall into confusion. On the contrary, even though as part of the process of debate they are exposed to an argument at odds with their general orientation, they tend to "go home," to pick out the side of the issue that fits with their deeper-lying principles. This suggests that political argument, when it takes its full form . . . may facilitate rather than distort consistency in political reasoning, and it may facilitate political reasoning."[54] When there is political debate, the public is well able to understand the terms of the arguments and to decide among competing frames in ways that are consistent with its political beliefs. In this competition the president is singularly advantaged.[55]

Of course, it is but a short step from identifying a problem to proscribing its solution. "Frames," according to James Druckman, "work by altering belief importance."[56] That is, each possible frame of an event delineates different aspects of that event as important. Frames are thus significant rhetorical devices as well as cognitive structures.[57] It is possible to see the same military action as either a war to liberate oppressed people or a trade of blood for oil. It may be either or both; but each frame carries within it judgments about past action and proscriptions for future endeavor. Entman notes that frames function by drawing attention to some elements of a problem but also draw attention away from other elements: "Most frames are defined by what they omit as well as by what they include, and the omissions of potential problem definitions, explanations, evaluations, and recommendations may be as critical as the inclusions in guiding the audience."[58] To frame an issue is to implicitly argue not only for understanding that issue, but also for the appropriate means used to address it.

This is why one of the key factors in understanding framing effects is the credibility of the source. It is possible, for instance, that citizens delegate to elites the responsibility for deciding which of many possible frames is the most appropriate for any given issue.[59] Once a frame is accepted, everything else follows from that. But is seems implausible that either the media or the public uncritically accept a frame without considering its source: there are reputable political actors—most presidents, most of the time; mainstream media outlets; other well-known public figures—and less reputable ones—presidents who have lost their credibility such as Lyndon Johnson and Richard Nixon; many tabloid media outlets; and political actors who are seen as "extreme," or somehow tainted, such as David Duke.

No political actor's ability to frame is without limits. They are constrained by "the public mood, the partisan composition and organization of interests of the representative's constituency, the historical lines of conflict surrounding an issue, and the level of institutionalization of the issue."[60] No one discusses political issues, and thus no one can frame, in a vacuum. In some ways, all political rhetoric is framing rhetoric, and all political arguments are arguments over frames. In making arguments political actors are limited by their understanding of the audience (the public), the history of the issue, and the level of flexibility they have (or lack) regarding the possible means of addressing the issue.

Political actors seeking to establish a preferred frame need to pay close attention to the mood of the relevant public as well as other structural issues,[61] for "real-world phenomena influence the public far more than does the president in every policy area."[62] Frames are not imposed unilaterally upon the public but are created and sustained by political actors and the media in an unequal collaboration with that public.[63] And they are integral to political discourse by providing a common vocabulary through which issues and events may be understood and debated.[64] That vocabulary may revolve around metaphors, which function to frame issues, such as Lyndon Johnson's choice of the war metaphor to frame his policies on poverty.[65] It may involve analogy, such as the use of Pearl Harbor as a device for understanding the events of 9/11 or Vietnam as a tool for understanding the Iraq war. Some frames are more enduring and vibrant than others. The Cold War frame, for example, seems to have considerable power, and presidents and the media have returned to it time and again when seeking explanations and justifications for governmental actions.[66]

Research—either qualitative or quantitative—can be useful in locating frames within a text. Textual evidence, however, will not give us evidence as to how any given audience or set of audiences will receive any political message, but can only inform us regarding the speaker's preferred frame. It seems at least plausible that there is no one mass audience that receives a frame as given and accepts it without processing it first—and sometimes in idiosyncratic ways that are difficult to predict.[67]

If this is true, it would explain a good deal about what appear to be the vagaries of public opinion, which we know to be affected by frames,[68] at least when that public is aware of and influenced by a particular political message.[69] That is, frames are influential, but not necessarily determinative of how the public constructs political meaning. But for the purposes of this study, we do not need to show that the president's influence is all-encompassing for it to be important. And it does seem clear that presidents, in collaboration with the media, can influence which issues the public considers important; they can also influence the terms through which the public comes to understand those issues and can also affect the values used to make judgments about those issues.

Priming

From framing it is a short step to priming: the solution to a problem is inherent in its definition, and every frame brings with it assumptions that reflect values—and those values underlie political judgments.[70] In fact, frames activate values, and it is more than possible that "the clash of political arguments increases the chances that [citizens] will anchor their specific preferences in underlying principles."[71] Whereas framing is about the narrative through which an event, process, or person can be understood, priming is about the evaluative criteria brought to bear when making judgments about that event, process, or person.[72] That is, while frames are more likely to be accepted by the media and the mass public when there is elite consensus, lack of such consensus activates the values that underlie frames, and political disagreement among elites heightens the opportunities for nonelites to make accurate judgments based on their own political values. Think, for instance, about of the difficulties facing those who challenged the president immediately after the invasion of Iraq. The consensus among elites sharply reduced coverage of dissent, and made those engaged in such dissent appear unpatriotic at best. Several years later, there was no elite consensus, and the range of opinions about the war proliferated both within the media and among the mass public.[73] The more the public is exposed to a range of opinion, the more they will respond to issues in ways that are authorized by their own values and beliefs.

But political actors can also influence the way those values and beliefs are activated. We know, for example, that by rhetorically setting the standard by which they will be judged, presidents can have a "substantial effect" on their own approval ratings.[74] By placing so much attention on the global war on terror, for instance, George W. Bush appears to have significantly affected public perceptions of his administration, for better and for worse. Approval ratings seem to tap into deep-seated predispositions among the public rather than merely reflecting day-to-day events and as such are an important, if problematic, measure of the president's relationship with the public.[75] Absent dramatic events, approval ratings remains stable; if a president can help determine the standard by which he is judged, then that standard may prove quite durable.

Because frames are intimately connected to the values that underlie them, they are more stable than not. There is evidence that once a frame is established and institutionalized, it is difficult to dislodge it.[76] As with the data presented on human rights, it seems that in all issue areas, once people have decided what to think about (agenda building and setting) and how to think about them (framing), their opinions can be expected to be stable over time. Thus, once an issue gets on the national agenda, it can be difficult to remove it completely, although its salience can be expected to fluctuate over time.

Most media scholars believe that the media have three important impacts: agenda setting, by which the media influence what issues, events, and people the public find important; framing, by which they influence the narratives through which events, actors, and issues are understood; and priming, through which the influence the judgments citizens make about political actors, events, and issues.[77] At least this is true when individuals are aware of and influenced by political messages,[78] which leads us to the issue of measuring the impact presidents have on these complicated processes.

Measuring the Effects of Presidential Communication

When scholars argue that presidential rhetoric "matters" (or fails to matter), it can be difficult to know precisely what that means. At least since the 1980s, scholars have focused on the "rhetorical presidency," or the idea that the institution has changed to accommodate an increased need for the president to engage with the citizenry.[79] Much of this research has centered on the demands and potential of "going public," the tendency of the president to attempt to influence Congress by communicating directly with the people.[80] The theory is that presidents think they can achieve certain ends through public speech, and so they speak increasingly often.[81] But there are still issues about how to understand and measure the efficacy of that speech.[82]

For some, claiming efficacy means being able to demonstrate that the president had an impact on public opinion measured through polls. Brandon Rottinghaus, for instance, declared in his doctoral thesis that presidents "are only modestly able to successfully lead public opinion with their rhetoric."[83] Instead of leading public opinion, Rottinghaus argues, presidents choose rhetoric that is congruent with that opinion, preferring to be led rather than to lead.[84] This finding is consistent with much of the literature on the presidency and public opinion, which generally argues that presidents are constrained by public opinion even as they try to lead it.[85]

No one has taken a starker view of this question than George C. Edwards III. Edwards has argued, in numerous venues over a long period of time, that presidential rhetoric does not really matter at all, and that if presidential speech can be said to have any effect, on either Congress or on the public, it is decidedly minimal. For Edwards, "going public" is generally best understood as a waste of valuable presidential time.[86] He argues that even the most able presidential speakers are still unable to penetrate the mass public and have proven historically incapable of either affecting their own approval ratings or mobilizing the public around their preferred agendas.

Other scholars agree with Edwards that presidential communication may not affect public opinion, but argue that it may have other uses. It is even possible that the president is not actually trying to influence public opinion directly, but speaks in order to send signals to other elites—in this case the public is background or prop rather than audience.[87] Presidents may speak to solidify support among key constituencies rather than to change public opinion, and in the process, they inform other elites of their agenda and priorities.[88] In this model, it at least makes sense for presidents to continue talking, but it implies that scholars have been wrong about the nature of the audience. The mass public is not the target of presidential persuasion, and its response to presidential speech is incidental at best to the policy process.

Part of the problem in measuring the impact of presidential communication is that for a political message to have an effect, there must be an audience that is both attentive to that message and open to its influence. There is considerable debate concerning both of these assumptions.[89] Many scholars argue that presidential communication, like much public discourse, faces increasing barriers in gaining public attention: there is more competition, more apathy, higher partisanship, and more disengagement from politics than ever before among members of the mass public.[90]

As Edwards exemplifies, the evidence increasingly indicates that presidents have difficulty changing public opinion and are only barely able to increase issue salience among members of the mass public.[91] But some scholars consider this an artifact of the general incompetence of the public rather than the fault of the president or other elites.

Phillip Converse, for instance, is probably the most famous exponent of the view that the mass public is inattentive, unaware and, frankly, not very smart when it comes to politics.[92] Converse argues that, at best, the U.S. mass public has opinions that are ambivalent, inconsistent, and only very loosely related to one another—in keeping with a long line of research in political science,[93] he argues that those opinions lack "constraint."[94] He notes the persistence of "nonattitudes," and argues that because the public is so poorly informed, he doubts their ability to identify elites who agree with their predispositions and are thus but minimally qualified to judge issues or leaders.[95]

Not all researches agree with Converse's rather stark view of the public. John Zaller argues that members of the mass public are more properly understood as "ambivalent," and concludes that democracy is really about debates among elites.[96] Because the public lacks "real" attitudes, according to Zaller, public opinion is unstable and is susceptible not only to manipulation by elites, but to the ways in which questions measuring public opinion are framed and ordered.[97] Elites are able to play on the inherent contradictions in the public mind. "'Political leaders,' Zaller writes, 'are seldom the passive instruments of majority opinion. Nor, as it seems to me, do they often attempt openly to challenge public opinion. But they do regularly attempt to play on the contradictory ideas that are always present in people's minds, elevating the salience of some and harnessing them to new initiatives while downplaying or ignoring other ideas—all of which is just another way of talking about framing."[98] That is to say, the public has opinions, but they may not form into policy preferences without guidance, which most often occurs in the form of framing.

And so we are back to the issue of presidential communication as framing. Both presidents and the media can frame issues, and much of political communication may be understood as competition among and between frames.[99] Presidents, who speak with a single, consistent voice, have more potential influence over frames—and thus also over the national agenda—than do other political actors. Of course, presidents have made varying use of the bully pulpit and have had uneven success at wielding it to their purposes. But for the moment, it seems reasonable to conclude that presidents can, at least under some circumstances, use the media to affect the national agenda.

That effect does not have to be understood as dramatic and immediate change, even when the efficacy of presidential rhetoric is measured by short-term public opinion polls taken immediately after a single speech. The assumption is that change must be both instantaneous and significant or it does not happen at all. It is equally likely that small changes may occur over time, and an audience may be led incrementally to very different positions than those initially held. Education and persuasion are both effects that may well be seen only in the long term.[100]

It is even possible that the effect does not have to be understood as change at all. When public opinion is measured, especially in efforts to locate the precise nature of presidential influence over it, there is a tendency to focus on opinion change. But influence can be felt as reinforcement as well. There is evidence that presidents may not be able to take an inert public and create opinion on an issue that coincides with their preferred policy position. But that may not be the best way to understand the relationship between the public and presidential rhetoric, and it certainly is not the best way to understand the role Jimmy Carter played in getting human rights on the national agenda, where the public was by no means inert or uninterested in human rights prior to his time in office.

It seems reasonable to conclude that under some circumstances, presidents can exert at least some influence over the national agenda, congressional activities, and public opinion. The breadth and longevity of that influence may be in question for the common incidence of presidential speech—clearly, a president cannot hope to exert influence over a topic that is ineptly articulated, inadequately publicized, or insufficiently resonant. But it is plausible that in some instances, presidential speech can have a determinative effect on the public agenda. That is clearly the case with Jimmy Carter and human rights.

Conclusion: Carter's Influence on Human Rights and the National Agenda

Certainly, under Carter, there was more attention paid to issues of human rights—internationally, nationally, and even locally—than there had been under previous administrations[101]: "Media attention did receive a dramatic boost during Carter's early years in office . . . and while this coverage declined after peaking in 1977, it did not return to its earlier low levels after Carter left the White House."[102] If a president can influence the media agenda (agenda building) and the media can influence the public agenda (agenda setting), then it should be possible to connect the pieces of this complex puzzle and then to argue that the actions of the president and his administration can effect public opinion, but that these effects are not likely to be consistent across time or issue domains, and are not likely to be revealed in studies that focus on a single speech and look for immediate changes in public opinion.

Now that there is evidence of both the historical context for human rights as an item on the national agenda and for the president's ability to facilitate agenda items, we can turn to the specifics of the case of Jimmy Carter and the influence of his public communication on the salience of human rights as an agenda item. I turn first to his use of ethos as a communicative strategy, then to the nature of human rights as a persuasive term in its own right, and then to the importance of Carter's implementation of human rights policy.

PART II

*Jimmy Carter
and Human Rights*

Chapter 3

The Ethos of Human Rights in Carter Administration Rhetoric

Much of the power of human rights rhetoric stems from the timing and the fact of presidential speech on the subject. But there is still the issue of whether *any* president's speech would have had the same effect, or if *this particular* president was a deciding factor in getting human rights on the national agenda. Of course, we cannot really determine the merits of a counterfactual case, but it is worth thinking carefully about the factual case we do have. We cannot go back and redo history with a different president, but we can analyze the actual example history provides.

All presidents have the institution in common, even though the contours of that institution develop and change over time. Institutionally, the individual characteristics of presidents matter less than their function as presidents.[1] To the extent, for instance, that all presidents will engage in a specific action as a product of the presidential role, their individual preferences and idiosyncrasies matter very little. Much of what any president does comes under the heading of this sort of routine, even bureaucratized, behavior.

But a presidency is generally notable less for this routine behavior and more for those areas in which individual presidents made choices that reflected their own individual preferences and the demands of their electoral and governing coalitions. I argue that for Jimmy Carter, human rights was one such choice. Carter, who came to the presidency with a specific set of imperatives and a specific public image, was positioned to put human rights on the national agenda in a way that no other national politician could have matched. In so doing, he turned the relatively new term "human rights" into an ideograph. Ideographs, or words and phrases we are socialized to valorize, are culturally bound summary phrases that capture important ideological associations. They are high-order abstractions that function as attempts to unify a diverse audience around a vaguely shared set of meanings. They serve to garner support for specific policy positions (civil unions) through association with long-held foundational beliefs and values (equality). Ideographs function as God-terms[2] in authorizing action and justifying policy. We know a good bit about how ideographs function but relatively little about how they become established. I contend that by connecting "human rights" to the American ethos, Carter created it as an ideograph.

Human Rights in Context

One of the consistent problems of policy making in a democracy is that it is rooted in abstract ideals that are claimed as timeless and universal, yet actual policy is always located in particular, specific, and material political conditions. These issues are clear and are clearly problematic in the rhetoric produced by the president and his administration on the subject of human rights.

For Carter, human rights were both a natural extension of the national ethos and also a product of a particular national and international political context. His human rights policy was central to his administration and to his definition of national identity: "The very heart of our identity as a nation," he said, "is our firm commitment to human rights. We stand for human rights because we believe that government has as a purpose to promote the well-being of its citizens. This is true in our domestic policy; it's also true in our foreign policy."[3] So for Carter, human rights was a natural extension of everything that unified Americans—history, ideology, and political practice. This enabled the birth of human rights as an ideograph. The political utility of having a single theme that could unite the nation was clear—and given the political times, was clearly necessary.

National Context

For Carter, the crucial national political context involved very recent history: the Cold War, Vietnam, Watergate, and the revelations concerning CIA activities as revealed by the Church Committee.[4] These events were, for Carter, both cause and effect of American moral failures and for the divisions that rent the nation. He (correctly) understood the 1976 election as a revolt against the existing structural arrangements and political practices of Washington[5]: "Carter understood the national mood perfectly, and he attacked Washington in a positive way, emphasizing not so much what was wrong in the nation's capitol as the power of the American people to set things right and appealing not to their cynicism but to their idealism."[6] In appealing to American idealism, Carter enacted the sort of behavior he also promised—behavior based in principle and morality. As Jon H. Patton has it, Carter returned "transcendence" to our national politics, providing an ethical grounding for policy—a grounding that many felt had been entirely absent under the Nixon Administration.[7] Carter claimed that such behavior would allow Americans to be united and proud of their government again.

On Vietnam, for instance, he said, "The Vietnamese war produced a profound moral crisis, sapping worldwide faith in our own policy and our system of life, a crisis of confidence made even more grave by the covert pessimism of some of our leaders."[8] Human rights allowed the United States to recapture both its own meaning and the approval of the world, both of which, for Carter, had been lost due to the excesses of previous administrations. Upon returning from a European tour in the spring of 1977, for instance, he said, "We've been successful in the recent summit meeting, I think, and also in my visit throughout England and Switzerland, in reestablishing a clear-cut concept of what our Nation is, what it stands for. And the outpouring of affection and approbation that was demonstrated on this recent trip was not, I don't think, for me a personal thing but just an appreciation of our European allies that the devastating times for Watergate and Vietnam and CIA revelations and Cambodia, and so forth, are over, and that the United States once again is a clean, admirable, strong, competent entity."[9] He understood his task as a purification of sorts: as the restoration of U.S. prestige, which could only be accomplished through a return to the values and practices that had made America "clean, admirable, strong, [and] competent." Human rights thus had a restorative, rather than a generative effect. Carter could argue he was not asking for anything new, just a reestablishment of long-held beliefs and practices, which would in turn lead to a reestablishment of national pride and international prestige.

This worked domestically as well as internationally. For Carter, human rights, which he understood as deeply rooted in national values, served a specific political as well as a necessary moral function, restoring Americans' faith in themselves and in their government, and he was deeply committed to that restoration.[10] In his inaugural, for instance, he said, "Let our recent mistakes bring a recent commitment to the basic principles of our Nation, for we know that if we despise our own government, we have no future."[11] The renaissance promised by human rights began at home. Indeed, the national commitment to human rights was Carter's solution to the problems caused by the combination of Vietnam, Watergate, and other unsavory revelations. As a result of these events, he argued, "Our country had lost its spirit."[12] But recommitting to the ideals that had been lost through the politics of pure self-interest could restore that spirit. He said, "We've come through a long period of turmoil and doubt, but we've once again found our moral course, and with a new spirit, we are striving to express our best instincts to the rest of the world."[13] That moral courage would restore our certainty, and that certainty would restore respect.

As the person most able to articulate national values, Carter's values and those of the nation were presumed to be aligned. He could not only speak to but also for the nation. As president, he also represented the nation, and his values became, presumptively, ours as well.[14] But he stopped short of claiming the president could dictate national values or national policy, even in the area of his greatest institutional strength: foreign policy. He said, "In our foreign policy, the separation of people from government has been in the past a source of weakness and error. In a democratic system like ours, foreign policy decisions must be able to stand the test of public examination and public debate."[15] Human rights promised a reunion of morality and pragmatism, and of the people and the government from which they felt increasingly estranged.

He also argued, "The healthy self-criticism and the free debate which are essential in a democracy should never be confused with weakness or despair or lack of purpose."[16] Instead of assuming unilateral definitional power, Carter argued that this power was checked by the American people—only definitions that had the demonstrable support of the people were viable. For Carter, human rights was one such definition.

On human rights he consistently argued that he had the support of the nation behind him. He said, "As far as the human rights effort is concerned, this is a position that is compatible with the character of the American people. It is one that is almost overwhelmingly supported by the American people."[17] That support provided the basis for the policy, legitimated it, and established Carter as its spokesperson: "And I knew then and I know now that our country always has to be the well-recognized leader and bulwark in protecting basic human dignity, basic human liberty, basic self-respect, known by the words, 'human rights.' And they will be protected as long as I'm in Washington and you give me your support."[18] Carter argued that his political success was inextricably connected to the success of his human rights policy, and that success was understood by him as measured by the support of the American people.[19]

The political utility of this argument is clear, for it places those who opposed Carter on human rights in a triply untenable position: they were morally wrong, they were opposing the entire national history and ideology, and they were standing in opposition to prevailing public opinion as well. In all of these ways, Carter used human rights to argue for a dominant position in the national context. But the political and strategic benefits did not stop at the water's edge. Human rights worked for him when it came to the international context as well.

International Context
Because his own previous political experience included no real foreign policy work, Carter needed to bolster his international credentials. Human rights offered one way for him to do that. He argued, in keeping with most post–World War II presidents, that the world had become increasingly interdependent and that the United States had an important leadership role, both for moral and for self-interested reasons.[20]

In talking about the moral reasons for U.S. leadership within the international political context, Carter said, "As you know, 204 years ago today America declared its independence with a truth that still sets people free throughout a troubled world, that all people are endowed with rights that cannot be bought or sold, rights that no power on Earth can justly deny."[21] Here, he relied on universals and offered the often-used idea of America as an exemplar of freedom. For Carter, human rights was a natural outgrowth of that ideological tradition. As human rights helped restore national confidence in U.S. political leadership, Carter expected it to work in a similar way among U.S. allies on the world stage.

But stressing the moral value of human rights led to charges that he was overly moralistic, perhaps weak, probably naive. To counter those charges, he was careful to argue that, given the prevailing international context, human rights had practical value as well as moral impetus. Discussing practical reasons for U.S. leadership on human rights, Carter said, "The world is still divided by ideological disputes, dominated by regional conflicts, and threatened by danger that we will not resolve the differences of race and wealth without violence or without drawing into combat the major military powers. We can no longer separate the traditional issues of war and peace from the new global questions of justice, equity, and human rights. It is a new world, but America should not fear it. It is a new world, and we should help to shape it. It is a new world that calls for a new American foreign policy— a policy based on constant decency in its values and on optimism in our historical vision."[22] The world had changed, he argued, the imperatives of foreign affairs were now different, and the nation's policy needed to reflect those differences and changes. In addition to its moral value, the protection of human rights would lead to a more peaceful, and thus a more stable, world.[23]

Indeed, he argued, "And as Americans we cannot overlook the way that our fate is bound to that of other nations. This interdependence stretches from the health of our economy through war and peace, to the security of our own energy supplies. It's a new world in which we cannot afford to be narrow in our vision, limited in our foresight, or selfish in our purpose."[24] For Carter, the crucial fact of the international context was global interdependence. Stressing human rights would help the United States successfully navigate this interdependent world in ways that previous policy paradigms would not.

He argued that at least in part, human rights put the United States in the forefront of an inevitable and important international movement: "The passion for freedom," he said in his inaugural, "is on the rise. Tapping this new spirit, there can be no nobler nor more ambitious task for America to undertake on this day of a new beginning than to help shape a just a peaceful world that is truly humane."[25] For Carter, a more just world was a more humane world, a more humane world was a more peaceful one, and a more peaceful world was a more stable one. Stressing human rights was thus the right thing to do, both morally and practically.

These arguments were facilitated by the fact that in making such pronouncements about the international context, Carter tended to speak in universals. "Our country," he said, "espouses human rights which is a hunger that exists among people in every nation, no matter where they might live."[26] Appealing to the national sense of mission, Carter connected human rights to national tradition, rendering the United States both exemplar and activist. That tradition was based on unquestioned acceptance of universals, and all humans, in Carter's rhetoric, lived on common ground: "What are the goals of a person or a denomination or a country? They are all remarkably the same: a desire for peace, a need for humility, for examining one's faults and turning away from them; a commitment to human rights in the broadest sense of the word, based on a moral society concerned with the alleviation of suffering because of deprivation or hatred or hunger or physical affliction; and a willingness, even an eagerness, to share one's ideals, one's faith with others, to translate love in a person to justice."[27] Because all humans wanted the same things, common ground could be found among and between even the most diverse nations, and a just, humane, peaceful and stable world would naturally result.

So for Carter, human rights was a morally necessary and politically useful set of policies that responded to the political exigencies of both national and international contexts. The policies connected to his advocacy of human rights allowed Americans to unite at home and to reclaim America's stature internationally following Vietnam. Importantly, he advanced these policies in a particular way, through a collection of arguments based on ethos, or the public character of the speaker, that would have significant consequences for human rights policies throughout the Carter Administration and beyond, as it is this connection to the national ethos that helped establish human rights as an ideograph.

The Ethos of Human Rights

Ethos was particularly useful for Carter, as he was able to wield it both for his policies and against the preferences of his opponents. Through his use of ethos, he defined human rights in opposition to his critics, "the politics of selfishness,"[28] the Republican Party, our own national past, and other nations, especially the Soviet Union and Iran.

It is a truism, present since Aristotle, that communication is more likely to persuade when its source is perceived as credible.[29] And on human rights, Jimmy Carter quickly rendered himself a credible source. While he did not focus on human rights during the 1976 presidential primary campaign, at the convention the efficacy of the issue for uniting a fractious Democratic Party became clear.[30] As an issue, human rights also resonated with the argument Carter had made since the beginning of his campaign: that new, more moral leadership, "government as good as the American people," was required.

Furthermore, Carter had run a campaign based on values and personal characteristics [31] and continued this emphasis after the election.[32] As one biographer noted of Carter, "In him, consummate personal ambition was linked to a compelling sense of public purpose; though spiritually content and eminently successful in nearly everything he did, Carter was not complacent but driven."[33] His drive was directed less toward personal aggrandizement and more focused on doing what he considered good in the world. This focus was particularly clear in foreign policy.[34] As Carter himself said, "I had adopted, I'll use the word pious again, I think an attitude of piety that aggravated some people, but also was the root of my political success in 1976. People wanted someone who wasn't going to tell another lie, who was not going to mislead the public and who was going to try to reestablish, in my judgment, ethics and morality in international affairs. That's what I tried to carry out."[35] Human rights thus fit in with Carter's image as both a candidate and as a president and became his signature issue.[36]

His communication was clear on this point. Beginning with his inaugural, where he declared that "our commitment to human rights must be absolute,"[37] Carter was unequivocal about the need to emphasize human rights as a foundational principle in U.S. foreign policy. Indeed, "Carter offered four principles to guide U.S. foreign policy: 1) open, honest, decent and compassionate policies consistent with the character of the American people. 2) U.S. policies that treat others with the respect and dignity that Americans demand for themselves. 3) U.S. policies that build a peaceful and just world. 4) using the Presidency to restore the moral authority of the U.S., to support humanitarian policies, and to reject policies that strengthen dictators, create refugees, prolong suffering, postpone racial justice."[38] Human rights were central to all four of these principles.

Carter did not simply base human rights on his own personal ethos, although he certainly did that. He also argued that human rights was a natural extension of his entire administration, of the nature of the Democratic Party, the nation and, indeed, the world. In so doing, he identified all of these separate entities with one another, using each to bolster his claims about all. Human rights, as Carter's signature issue, thus became difficult to separate from the Democratic Party, the national identity, or even world history. As an issue, human rights thus achieved a level of unprecedented national prominence and began life as an ideograph. To see how this process played out, it is necessary to examine each element in turn.

Personal Ethos

Carter's own personal ethos was closely connected to his stance on human rights. Even though he came to human rights rather late in his political career—and even rather late in his first presidential campaign—he nonetheless had the proper credentials to make human rights his own, and was thus able both to help maintain human rights as a national agenda item and to use it effectively as a rhetorical weapon against his opponents. As one of his top aides put it, "Carter's personal philosophy was the point of departure for the foreign policy priorities of the new administration. He came to the Presidency with a determination to make U.S. foreign policy more humane and moral. In part because of his religious feelings, in part because it was useful in the campaign, he went on record not only in rejecting the 'Lone Ranger' style of the preceding Administration but in criticizing it for an excessive preoccupation with practicing balance-of-power politics. I know that he genuinely believed that as President he could shape a more decent world."[39] Human rights were thus both a natural extension of Carter's own personality and an important source of rhetorical power for him.

He established his own credentials on human rights as a man of God, with a specific personal history, who recognized the accomplishments of, and associated with, others who were dedicated to the cause of human rights, all of which, especially as president, enabled him to function as the appropriate and authoritative spokesman for the issue.[40]

Carter used his personal history and also his regional identity to make claims about ethos connected to human rights.[41] As he told an Alabama audience in 1980, "As the first man from the Deep South in 140 years to be President of this Nation, I say that these people in white sheets do not understand our region and what it's been through, they do not understand what our country stands for, they do not understand that the South and all of America must move forward. Our past is a rich source of inspiration. We've had lessons that we've learned with a great deal of pain. But the past is not a place to live."[42] By both lauding the South and distancing himself from the more despicable aspects of its history, he could play both on regional pride and his own regional identity to make claims that would be less acceptable to southern audiences had they come from someone from outside that region.[43] The South here served the same role that the nation's checkered history would in other contexts. It allowed him to admit to mistakes and to argue that such admissions made reconciliation and progress possible.

After he left office, Carter presented the most detailed and compelling statement of the association between his regional identity and his commitment to human rights: "To me, the political and social transformation of the Southland was a powerful demonstration of how moral principles should and could be applied effectively to the legal structure of our society. The same lesson has been learned many times in our dealings with other nations."[44] Ignoring the importance of federal legislation and, at times, federal troops in the development of civil rights, the changes in the South since the civil rights movement exemplified for Carter the political possibilities of moral suasion.

Naturally, faith played an important role in Carter's ethos. Certainly, his reputation as a religious man did a great deal to further his ethos on human rights.[45] For Carter, human rights had both political roots in the foundational documents of the American republic, but also religious roots, authorized by God. He was not shy about discussing his religion—and its connection to advocating human rights—in public: "My own religious convictions are deep and personal. I seek divine guidance when I make a difficult decision as President and also am supported, of course, by a common purpose which binds Christians together in a belief in the human dignity of mankind and in the search for worldwide peace—recognizing, of course, that those who don't share my faith quite often have the same desires and hopes."[46] Enacting the tolerance he saw as rooted in human rights—recognizing that those who did not share his religion could still share his values—strengthened his ethos and his argument. Similarly, he claimed to "worship daily," and argued that religion represented a "stabilizing factor in my life."[47] Yet he was also clear that "I have never detected nor experienced any conflict between God's will and my political duty."[48] For Carter, enacting human rights in national policy was the best example of the confluence between his duty and God's will.[49]

Because of that confluence, he took a position as spokesman for the human rights cause: "The best way to enhance human rights around the world is not to go to war and to kill people; it's to keep constantly before the leaders and the people of this world the possibility of freedom, of liberty, of democratic processes, of equality of opportunity."[50] Carter put himself in the position of one well versed in the options of how to concretize human rights and to know what approach was best. In a meeting with European broadcast journalists, for instance, he said, "My own best approach has been to treat the countries' violations in a negotiating way so that I can talk to a president of a country or to the leader of a country and say this is a very serious problem between us, we don't want to put public pressure on you which would make it embarrassing for you to release political prisoners, for instance."[51] In such ways, he relied upon the president's traditional dominance in matters of foreign policy to underline his personal claim to expertise on the specifics of how a human rights policy ought to be properly conducted.

Interestingly, this was something of a double bind for Carter. His willingness to work behind the scenes sometimes made it appear that he was not taking action on human rights or that he was willing to compromise on human rights in the name of protecting U.S. security interests. So on the one hand, he was lambasted for advocating human rights at all—and thus harming U.S.-Soviet relations for instance—while on the other hand, he

Kairos, etc

produdil

130

was criticized for not doing enough on human rights. Knowing when to go public and when to remain private while still advocating for an active human rights policy was a rhetorical morass of difficult choices, the complexity of which he never quite explained to anyone's satisfaction.

He did try, however. He argued that his job was "to try and analyze the most difficult questions that face our Nation and not to be timid or reticent about seeking solutions for them, recognizing that some of them are historic in nature, some of them have very difficult aspects that almost defy solution, but that they're all important to our country."[52] Human rights was one such issue. For Carter, the point was to work on a problem and to improve the situation, not to give up because the problem defied solution.

Moreover, his role was to facilitate national debates, even difficult ones or those where his preferences did not always win: "I think it's better to get it on the table, have an open debate, let the people be involved in it, let the Congress start learning about it, let the private sector of our country become involved in the debate, the universities, the economists, the business leaders, the labor leaders."[53] While this complicated the policy process, Carter strengthened his ethos on human rights by enacting a form of the democratic openness he rhetorically espoused.

He did this more directly as well. Upon being interrupted by demonstrators while speaking before the World Jewish Council, for instance, he said, "One of the basic human rights that we cherish in our country is the right to speak, and I have no objection to it."[54] He was willing to allow others the right to speak, even if at his own expense. Such examples functioned to tacitly support his claims to personal belief in the importance of human rights.

He bolstered his public connection with human rights in other ways as well. For example, he established himself as able to recognize the achievements of others. Giving a speech at Notre Dame's 1977 commencement ceremonies, for instance, he noted that, "In his 25 years as president of Notre Dame, Father Hesburgh has spoken more consistently and more effectively in the support of the rights of human beings than any other person I know." He also lauded the works of the three men chosen to receive honorary degrees from Notre Dame that year, saying, "In their fight for human freedoms in Rhodesia, Brazil, and South Korea, these three religious leaders typify all that is best in our countries and in our church."[55] Similarly, he praised the members of the World Jewish Congress for their efforts to "promote human rights in a universal way,"[56] and noted that "I know what the NAACP stands for, and I also know what the NAACP organization in the last 80 years has meant to this Nation and has meant to my life as an American."[57] Of course, all speakers use such tactics to establish identification with their audiences, but the forms of such identification are not without consequence. By claiming to be able to recognize the efforts and accomplishments of others, he bolstered his own individual and institutional authority. Implicitly, of course, that also undermined the authority of his critics, who were individually and institutionally disadvantaged in comparison. These effects were strengthened by his claims to deep personal and political commitment to human rights.

He reiterated over and over that "It's an undeviating commitment that I intend to maintain until the last day I'm in office. And through various means, either public statements or through private negotiations, through sales policies, we are trying to implement a renewed awareness of the need for human rights in our dealing with all countries."[58] He had argued consistently that his leadership was important; because of his personal ethos, his history, and his role as president, all of these claims were more plausible than would otherwise have been the case.[59]

He also argued that the cause of human rights transcended his leadership, setting the stage for its continuance after his departure from office: "Some claim . . . that Jimmy Carter elevated human rights and democracy on the international agenda and that the agenda will change when I leave my office. They are wrong. Hemispheric support for human rights is a historic movement."[60] In this way, Carter connected his personal ethos to a wider movement, giving both added credibility.[61]

Throughout his administration, Carter tied his personal life, values, experiences, and political commitments to human rights. It became his signature issue because of the effort he made to claim human rights as his own. That effort extended from his personal ethos to that of his administration as a whole.

Administration Ethos

Carter placed a great deal of emphasis not only on his personal ethos and commitment to human rights, but also on that of his administration and its personnel.[62] Members of his administration proudly assumed the banner of human rights. Zbigniew Brzezinski, Carter's national security advisor, put it this way: "The Carter administration resolved to make a break with the recent past, to bring the conduct of foreign affairs into line with the nation's political values and ideals, and to revitalize an American image which had been tarnished by the Vietnam experience. . . . Both during the campaign and afterwards [Secretary of State Cyrus] Vance and I supported this policy.

While [Ambassador to the United Nations] Andy Young gave it a special Third World orientation, with emphasis on Africa."[63] While there were differences within the administration over the best way to define and implement a human rights policy, apparently the commitment to some form of such a policy was pervasive.

And there is no doubt Carter wanted it that way. During Human Rights Week, for instance, he declared that "a concern for human rights is woven through everything our Government does, both at home and abroad."[64] He contrasted this position with the politics of selfishness,[65] again maintaining the position that his administration was morally superior to its alternatives.

Carter was not alone in speaking on human rights, as many members of his administration were called upon to articulate, explain, and defend the president's new policy.[66] The most often discussed example of such rhetoric is undoubtedly Secretary of State Cyrus R. Vance's 1977 speech at the University of Georgia.[67] That speech was specifically designed to promote the administration's position on human rights.

Like Carter, Vance grounded that position in U.S. political tradition: "Our concern for human rights is based upon ancient values. It looks with hope to a world in which liberty is not just a great cause but the common condition. In the past it may have seemed sufficient to put our name to international documents that spoke loftily of human rights. That is not enough. We will go to work, alongside other people and other governments, to protect and enhance the dignity of the individual." He thus rooted human rights in the past while promising growth in the present and development in the future. This set up human rights as extending well beyond what most understood as the American tradition, which was centered on the political and civil rights of the individual, and emphasized a series of rights that resonated more deeply in other nations than in the United States. Following Carter, Vance specifically defined human rights as "the right to be free from governmental violation of the integrity of the person . . . the right to the fulfillment of such vital needs as food, shelter, health care, and education . . . the right to enjoy civil and political liberties . . ." and argued that "our policy is to promote all these rights." This was a very expansive version of human rights. By arguing for such an expansive definition of rights, and by claiming that U.S. policy was dedicated to their promotion, Carter was clearly attempting to lead where others—including some members of his own administration—were unwilling to follow. Indeed, the overly ambitious nature of Carter's definition of human rights ranked high among the criticisms of his policy.[68]

Some of those criticisms came from inside his own administration. Andrew

Young, for instance, garnered significant attention for his claim that the United States was also guilty of holding political prisoners, a statement that Carter characterized as "unfortunate" and noted that "I do not agree with it."[69] This created some level of dissonance, for he appeared to be contradicting a highly placed member of his own administration as well as the more expansive version of his own definition of human rights. The difficulties he experienced with finding definitions and policies that would enjoy widespread consensus may have worked against the establishment of a clear and consistent human rights policy, but those difficulties worked for keeping the issue alive as an agenda item, for the controversy helped keep the issue in the minds of the media and the public. Ambiguity, whether strategically exploited or not, is an important element in keeping a complex issue on the national agenda.

So, while some of the members of his administration argued that Carter's definition of human rights may have been unwieldy and overexpansive,[70] and others, like Andrew Young, believed that it was too restrictive and too narrowly applied,[71] the issue is not whether there was agreement on human rights but whether the Carter Administration was consistent about connecting some version of something called "human rights" to the goals and actions of the administration.[72] It is clear that the administration did make such connections.

Carter and his team shared a commitment to human rights, and he connected both his personal identity and that of his administration to human rights, and in so identifying them, buttressed the position of both regarding the issue. In addition, he connected the ethos of the Democratic Party to the issue and extended the potential reach of human rights as a politically unifying issue.

Partisan Ethos

In addition to locating human rights as a reflection of his personal and administrative ethos, Carter also connected it to the ethos of the Democratic Party. This connection served both principled and political ends. While the partisan advantage human rights gave to Carter was plain, and while he was quite willing to use that advantage in campaign contexts, Carter also often argued that his commitment to human rights was not partisan—it was a deeply moral position that must be articulated in a balanced fashion, not just against the communist demons of the Right or the authoritarian demons of the Left. This stance, however, did not prevent him from taking partisan advantage of the issue. Speaking at a fundraising dinner for the Democratic

National Committee, Carter noted, "As you well know, our nation has been deeply wounded in the last few years. The war in Vietnam—our withdrawal from that country caused our people to be embarrassed and brought the condemnation of most of the rest of the world on our Nation. We have been embarrassed by the Watergate revelations and by the CIA investigations. There was a sense of malaise and discouragement and a sense of distrust of our own Government, a sense of betrayal of the fine ideals on which our country was founded. I think it's accurate to say that a strong emphasis on human rights and every aspect of them has restored to our people a sense of pride again."[73] For Carter human rights would restore integrity to government practices and thus would also restore citizen trust in government. What the Republicans had ripped apart, Democrats would reunite.

He argued that these political accomplishments were not, for Carter, without risk, and were therefore all the more laudable. Speaking to a group of Chicago-area Democrats in 1978, he said, "And I'm proud to say that we've put our national prestige on the line for human rights in every corner of the world. Whether a country is behind the Iron Curtain or not, we will no longer be silent as a nation about oppression and injustice."[74] Americans, according to Carter, were willing to support their principles with whatever action was required. The Democrats had been equally bold on the domestic front: "Our concern with human rights which is the foundation of the Democratic Party, begins here at home. We've chipped away at decades of neglect, and we've tried to root out examples of blatant prejudice. We've placed minorities, qualified in every way, in many decisionmaking jobs in the Federal Government. We've whacked away subtle forms of discrimination. We've improved the enforcement of Federal equal opportunity laws. We've brought more minorities and more women into our judicial system than in all the rest of American history combined. And we're not through yet."[75]

Human rights were thus clearly connected to domestic policy, and he could claim progress both at home and abroad. Apparently ignoring significant chunks of U.S. history, he noted that the Democratic Party (unlike the Republicans) had "never betrayed those principles. And one of the things that I wanted to do when I came into the President's office, after Vietnam, after Watergate, after the CIA revelations, was to have some standard that I could raise to make Americans once again part of their country."[76] Again, human rights served a purifying and thus a restorative function. Moreover, he claimed that "We're a nation that believes in compassion, and we're a party that represents a compassionate attitude to those not quite so fortunate as we. We've been the party of civil rights; and we are the party of human rights, not only in our own country, but around the world."[77] The Democrats thus represented the best of the nation's practices and beliefs, which could be understood as his signature policy: human rights. In tying the Democrats to both human rights and to the national traditions and ideology, Carter was also well positioned to speak to human rights as a natural extension of the national ethos.

⭐ National Ethos

Carter consistently maintained the importance of human rights to the entire nation, connecting them to the foundational principles of the American republic: "In ancestry, religion, color, place of origin, and cultural background, we Americans are as diverse a nation as the world has ever seen. No common mystique of blood or soil unites us. What draws us together, perhaps more than anything else, is our belief in human freedom. We want the world to know that our Nation stands for more than financial prosperity."[78] Relying on the notion that the United States is less a place than an idea, Carter claimed that this idea was best understood as "human rights."

For Carter, U.S. policy should be grounded not in material interests, although he never denied their importance, but in timeless issues of ethics: "Our policy is based on an historical vision of America's role. Our policy is derived from a larger view of global change. Our policy is rooted in our moral values, which never change. Our policy is reinforced by our material wealth and by our military power. Our policy is designed to serve mankind."[79] For Carter, his policy was more consistent with both American history and American values than were the policies of his immediate predecessors, and his stance on human rights was a powerful warrant in support of that argument.

In fact, "To establish those values, two centuries ago a bold generation of Americans risked their property, their position, and life itself. We are their heirs, and they are sending us a message across the centuries. The words they made so vivid are now growing faintly indistinct, because they are not heard often enough. They are words like 'justice,' 'equality,' 'unity,' 'truth,' 'sacrifice,' 'liberty,' 'faith,' and 'love.' These words remind us that the duty of our generation of Americans is to renew our Nation's faith—not focused just against foreign threats but against the threats of selfishness, cynicism, and apathy."[80] Here, Carter again relied on the rhetoric of purification, arguing that by returning to an unabashed commitment to our fundamental values, the American republic could be morally, and thus politically, rejuvenated.

Consequently, his dedication to changing the direction of U.S. foreign policy away from the actions of his immediate predecessors was clear. He said, "For too many years, we've been willing to adopt the flawed and errone-ous principles and tactics of our adversaries, sometimes abandoning our own values for theirs. We've fought fire with fire, never thinking that fire is better quenched with water. This approach failed, with Vietnam the best example of its intellectual and moral poverty. But through failure we have now found our way back to our own principles and values, and we have regained our lost confidence."[81] Claiming as fact what remained as hope was overly optimistic, but given the nature of his political times and the fragility of his political coalition, the political utility (if not the political necessity) of claiming unity was obvious. Equally obvious was the centrality of human rights to the cre-ation and protection of that unity—and to Carter's own political future.

As Carter stated in a well-publicized and much discussed speech to B'nai B'rith in September 1976, "As long as I am president, the government of the United States will continue throughout the world to enhance human rights. . . . No force on earth can separate us from that commitment."[82] Here as elsewhere Carter committed U.S. military and moral might to the cause of international human rights.

He argued this commitment was both possible and realistic because U.S. military and political strength was intimately associated with its moral strength. Believing that "America is a religious nation,"[83] he said, "To me, as to most Americans, this country has always stood for something special in the world. We were the strongest country in the world, and we were the country most devoted to some higher idea—some striving for something beyond mere self-interest. To me, as to many people from my part of the country, there was nothing inconsistent in striving for peace and justice and freedom in the world, and maintaining a military defense structure that pro-tected our nation. In fact, not only was there nothing inconsistent—but I felt, and I feel today, that the two elements must go hand in hand."[84] For Carter, human rights was not inconsistent with protecting U.S. security in-terests. He argued that moral strength of purpose complemented military strength—that the former gave purpose to the latter.

Carter understood that many in his international audience might con-strue this policy as another means to assert American ideological dominance, and he consistently denied any such intent: "We must recognize that basing our own behavior on American values does not mean that we should insist on identical standards from every other country. We must realize that ours is not the only system of government that is acceptable to people; ours is not the only set of values by which men and women can live happily. I do not want to see us abandon the cynical manipulation of nations and peoples only to see a return to the excessive moralistic zeal of an earlier era—a moralism which often cloaked other motives and helped lead us into the tragedy of Vietnam."[85] Carter thus defined his human rights policy as a reaction against the "bad old days" of American moralism as equivalent to American imperialism, and as a more positive expression of American beliefs and values. It entailed respect for others, not a willingness to dominate them.

For Carter, the United States is "a strong nation. But we don't have to be a bully to show it. We want to be the kind of nation that arouses the understanding and the admiration and the friendship of smaller countries, those that are poor, those that are uncertain, those that are new, those whose citizens might be black or brown or yellow. We're trying to extend the influence of our Nation and its principles throughout the world in a good, decent way, to make Americans proud."[86] American influence would be felt through its example, not through its willingness to enforce that example through its military. So Carter tied his personal ethos and those of his administration and political party to that of the nation. Carter argued that unlike Republicans, who had tarnished the American image by neglecting American core values, Jimmy Carter and the Democrats would restore American power by emphasizing their commitment to those values.

For the United States to act as an exemplar, it had to remain faithful in action to the values it was so willing to espouse rhetorically. He said, "The best way to enhance freedom in other lands is to demonstrate here that our democratic system is worthy of emulation. To be true to ourselves, we must be true to others. We will not behave in foreign places so as to violate our rules and standards here at home, for we know that the trust which our Nation earns is essential to our strength."[87] Carter claimed that only by acting consistently with fundamental American principles at home and abroad, could the United States reclaim its role as moral exemplar for the world.

It was important for the United States to act as an exemplar, both for our own sakes and for others' as well: "There are brave men and brave women in many nations striving against great odds to taste the freedom which you and I take for granted. They look to America to hold high the lamp of freedom and liberty, and they must know that they are not alone."[88] For Carter, the United States had a responsibility to itself and to individuals and nations around the world to espouse human rights—it was the national mission as well as his personal mission, and as president, he could speak to both.

He said, "This is a troubled world; it's an unpredictable world; it's a complex world. It's almost impossible to understand. We cannot dominate others; that's not the American way. But we can provide them with a vision of the future and an assurance of their own security and a realization of the hopes and dreams of people who live under subjugation that provides some glimpse of how we can work together in the years ahead."[89] In Carter's public speech, human rights was not an automatic anodyne for all of the world's ills—that, he argued, would be naive. But if there was to be hope extended to this troubled world, the American espousal of human rights was necessary to that effort.

Furthermore, he was willing to acknowledge that the United States would take the lead not only in talking about human rights abuses in other nations, but in admitting and working on improving the situation at home. In his 1980 State of the Union Address, for example, he vowed, "We will never abandon our struggle for a just and a decent society here at home. That's the heart of America—and it's the source of our ability to inspire other people to defend their own rights abroad."[90] He agreed that some of the past practices used against internal demonstrators, for instance, were "inappropriate," and stated that he would "oppose" the use of such tactics in his own administration.[91] He also removed restrictions on overseas travel, and claimed, "We're going to open up our borders for a change so visitors can come to our country. . . . I want to see our country set a standard of morality."[92] In all of these examples, Carter argued that it was necessary to practice at home what he preached abroad.

Setting that standard also meant openness in government: "In the past we've had too much of top Government officials going off in a closed, locked room and evolving a foreign policy for our country and negotiating in secret and then letting the American people know about it when it's over. I want you to know about it ahead of time, and you can depend on what I tell you."[93] While this meant he had less unilateral control over policy, in the wake of the Nixon Administration's abuses, the political utility of this argument is clear, and Carter did not hesitate to exploit it, with such tactics becoming increasingly prevalent in election years.[94]

Having admitted that the United States was also guilty of some abuses did not, for Carter, lessen his ability to speak out on human rights. At an early press conference, for instance, he said, "I think it's entirely appropriate for our own country to take the leadership role and let the world say that the focal point for the preservation and protection of human rights is in the United States of America. I'm proud of this. And I intend to adhere to it with the deepest possible personal commitment, and I believe I speak accurately for the American people on this subject."[95] He also argued that, "I think it's something that our country ought to assume as a permanent, clear-cut commitment of our people. I think it's compatible with our constitutional stance, the framework of our societal structure. It's something that appeals to our own people. It restores a kind of beacon light of something that's clean and decent and proper as a rallying point for us in all the democracies of the world."[96] Even if its own practices were flawed, the United States, for Carter, still had an important role to play in the protection and extension of international human rights.

For Carter, the real task of government was to offer that "beacon light of something that's clean and decent and proper." Everything else government did was secondary. He tied that belief to his personal ethos, and to the ethoi of his administration, his political party, and his nation. But because he rested so much of his argumentation concerning human rights on universals, he was also able to argue that the nature of humanity itself required commitment to human rights.

International Ethos

For Carter, there was no doubt that the world shared a faith in certain universal truths, and that was a strong sense of commonality among what he called "the human family."[97] Speaking in response to a question about the Palestinians, he said, "But I think all human beings have the same basic yearnings for freedom, for human self-respect, for a home in which they can live, for a right to raise a family, to have education, health care, food."[98] All humans, for Carter, shared common ground. He argued that "Our work for human rights makes us part of an international tide, growing in force. We are strengthened," he insisted, "by being part of it."[99] Because all humans were linked, human rights were a natural extension of the basic political rights Americans enjoyed.

He told the United Nations in 1977 that, "The basic thrust of human affairs points toward a more universal demand for fundamental human rights. The United States has a historical birthright to be associated with that process."[100] He thus advocated action intended to control the arms race,[101] to ameliorate poverty and inequality, and to focus more stringently on human rights. "Our commitment is not just a political posture," he argued, and "I know perhaps as well as anyone that our own ideals in the area of human rights have not always been attained in the United States, but the American people have an abiding commitment to the full realization of these ideals. And we are determined, therefore, to deal with our deficiencies quickly and openly. We have nothing to conceal."[102] American ideals have had, as he argued elsewhere, political utility, but they were not, he claimed, reducible to politics. Because of our dedication to our values, we could be—indeed, must be—as open about our deficiencies as about our assets. In this, he was, of course, implicitly doing as all Cold War presidents have done: contrasting the virtues of the United States to the villainy of the Soviet Union.

Sometimes the comparison was direct: "Our country's a peace-loving nation, and a lot of nations around the world are trying to build governments based on the value of a human being, like ours, using us as a pattern. I don't know of a single other nation on Earth that's trying to structure their own government patterned after the Soviet Union."[103] Because of our commitment to our values, we served as an exemplar in ways others could not. He castigated the Soviet Union for "The abuse of human rights in their own country, in violation of the agreement which was reached at Helsinki," which "has earned them the condemnation of people everywhere who love freedom. By their actions they've demonstrated that the Soviet system cannot tolerate freely expressed ideas or notions of loyal opposition and the free movement of peoples."[104] Unlike the United States, the Soviet Union cynically manipulated values rather than acting upon them. He criticized them for accusing Anatoly Scharansky and Vladimir Slepak of espionage and argued that these actions damaged the Soviets in the eyes of the world community: "And I believe that even though they obviously have a right to make decisions within their own country, this works against the best interests of harmony and peace between the Soviet Union and other countries, because they look with concern upon the attitude of the Soviet Union towards its own citizens and they see in these actions the violation of an agreement, a solemn agreement, which the Soviet Union voluntarily signed."[105] According to Carter, such cynical manipulation undermined both their international reputation and the stability of the world. And, of course, as a result of the Soviet invasion of Afghanistan, he boycotted the 1980 Moscow Olympic Games.

Often accused of naiveté regarding the Soviet Union, Carter himself argued that he harbored no illusions regarding the Soviet Union. He said, "As we negotiate with the Soviet Union, we will be guided by a vision of a gentler, freer, and more bountiful world. But we will have no illusions about the nature of the world as it really is. The basis for complete mutual trust between us does not yet exist. Therefore, the agreements that we reach must be anchored on enlightened self-interest—what's best for us, what's best for the Soviet Union."[106] Carter argued here as elsewhere that his commitment to human rights was not naive, but amounted to smart as well as moral politics.

He argued that, "We must always combine realism with principle. Our actions must be faithful to the essential values to which our own society is dedicated, because our faith in those values is the source of our confidence that this relationship will evolve in a more constructive direction.[107] Here, he claimed that the realists like Nixon and Kissinger were the naive ones, thinking that politics based exclusively on power was in the nation's long term interest. Addressing the issue of naiveté directly, he argued, "There are those who say we ought not to do it. Some say it's naive for America to stand up for freedom and democracy in other lands. But they are wrong. But don't take my word on it. Ask those who are suffering under tyranny around the world about human rights. Ask them if America should stop fighting and speaking out for American principles, ask the American people. We'll go on defending human rights for our own country and for people throughout the world."[108] Carter argued that the best way to end tyranny was to call it by name, to add a moral force and support to those who suffered under it.

Carter also argued that his foreign policy regarding the Soviet Union also had practical benefits: "we are encouraging democracy, yes, but we are also strengthening our ability to compete effectively with the Soviet Union. Those who are most concerned about Soviet activism in the world should be the strongest supporters of our foreign aid programs designed to help the moderate transition from repressive tyranny to democratic development and to bolster the strength and independence of our friends."[109] For Carter, an America that acted in ways that were demonstrably consistent with its highest ideals would earn the approbation and trust of the rest of the world. That trust would have practical benefits in terms of trade and other economic relationships, allowing us to become more competitive with the Soviet Union, and thus further undermining the Soviet system.

Carter's stance vis-à-vis the Soviet Union did create some tension between the two nations, but the president seemed unwilling or uninterested in discussing those problems, claiming that, "I don't have any sense of fear or frustration or concern about our relationships with the Soviet Union," nor did he see his harsh rhetoric abut the Soviet Union as affecting "our defense or SALT negotiations."[110] Oddly, while he argued on the one hand that human rights was clearly connected to every aspect of the U.S.-Soviet relationship, on the other hand, he appeared to believe that he could criticize the Soviet Union on human rights while cooperating with it on arms reduction and that the tension caused by the former would not affect the latter.[111] He failed to see this willful blindness as naive.

The Soviet Union did not bear the brunt of Carter's criticism alone. Other communist nations were also compared unfavorably to the United States in terms of human rights. Carter refused to consider the restoration of diplomatic relations with Cuba, for instance, absent "demonstration . . . of their commitment to the human rights concept."[112] Iran was also cast as clear antitheses to American virtue, for while he criticized the Iranian government for its role in the taking and keeping of American hostages, calling it "an act of terrorism,"[113] at the same time he pledged both prudent and restrained responses, as "our Nation is fully committed to the enhancement of human rights, the protection of legal rights, and the enhancement of civil justice."[114] Again, American virtue was contrasted to foreign villainy, with human rights the point of comparison.

Carter's claim that his human rights policy was based on an international ethos was premised on his belief that "We live in an interdependent world,"[115] that the United States was connected to important elements in world, that the U.S. political and economic systems were compatible with international human rights. All of this was made possible because of his reliance on universals. For Carter, all "people want freedom, they want democracy, they want an opportunity in life."[116] So therefore, "We must understand that human rights and human dignity are indivisible. Wherever our fellow human beings are stripped of their humanity, defiled or tortured or victimized by repression or terrorism or racism or prejudice then all of us are victims."[117] These universals meant that the whole world could come together, despite political, social, and economic differences.

For Carter, international capitalism led to decreased international tension and increased international cooperation, and this in turn led to peace, which would support the protection of human rights around the world. Signing the Trade Agreement Act of 1979 into law, he said, "Expanded international trade brings strength and growth to economies throughout the world. It enhances understanding, it opens up thousands of unpublicized avenues of consultation and cooperation and the sharing of responsibility which quite often can help to alleviate political tensions and eliminated divisions that sometimes make international borders an obstacle rather than an avenue for cooperation. Peace and the expansion of human rights are natural by-products of this lessening of tension and this increase of an acknowledged and productive interdependence."[118] For Carter, therefore, the rhetoric of human rights, which stemmed naturally if not inevitably from his personal ethos and that of his administration, party, nation, and understanding of the world, had important practical consequences. Thus, it is to the intersection of human rights rhetoric and the material conditions of the political world that we now turn.

Human Rights in Rhetoric and Practice

Like most presidents, Carter advanced an unrealistically optimistic view of American ideals as they have played our historically. He claimed, for instance, that "Our society has always stood for political freedom. We have always fought for social justice, and we have always recognized the necessity for pluralism. Those values of ours have real meaning, not just in the past, 200 years ago, or 20 years ago, but now, in a world that is no longer dominated by colonial empires and that demands a more equitable distribution of political and economic power."[119] While these claims were, strictly speaking, so optimistic as to border on the false, they were also consistent with the celebratory nature of most presidential speech. But whereas many presidents, especially his immediate predecessors, had frequently been accused of offering rhetoric that celebrated American ideals while acting in ways that clearly controverted them, Carter argued that he attempted to align ideals with action. This led to criticism that he was too naive, too idealistic, even too good a person to be a good president,[120] criticisms he tried to counter with arguments concerning the practical benefits of human rights.

Idealism in Human Rights Policy

Carter argued consistently for human rights as the only acceptable policy based on moral principles. And indeed, his entire corpus of rhetoric on human rights is full of references to American ideals. He rarely if ever mentioned human rights without connecting them to some American or universal ideal. For Carter, "There is something clean about America. There is something decent about America. There's something idealistic about America. There's something unselfish about America. There's something strong about America. It's what makes people love our country. And I want to see those basic commitments restored. And in that restoration will come strength based on American people themselves (*sic*), where those commitments have never changed in spite of mistakes made in the past by some of our leaders."[121] For this president, the real strength of the United States lay in its grounding in and commitment to universal principles, principles that always motivated the American people, even as they were ignored by the government. For him, that strength underpinned and was the only morally acceptable justification for American economic, military, and political strength.

The idealism was not just for the United States, but extended to the rest of the world as well: "The American people are deeply committed to peace. But along with that, there has to be peace not just for Americans. We've used our strength and our influence, our national will, our political courage not only to avoid war for ourselves but to pursue fundamental human principles for ourselves, yes, but also for others."[122] Free ourselves, we had an obligation to advocate freedom everywhere. At peace ourselves, we had a duty to advocate peace. Of course, the shining example of those efforts was the Camp David peace agreement between Israel and Egypt.

American presidential rhetoric is, of course, supposed to appeal to both idealism and pragmatism. The Nixon Administration had been seen as too aggressively pragmatic; Carter needed to ensure that he was not understood as too meekly idealistic. In defending his idealism, Carter rejected the idea that it was inconsistent with practical politics. He said, for instance, "I was familiar with the widely accepted arguments that we had to choose between idealism and realism, or between morality and the exertion of power; but I rejected these claims. To me, the demonstration of American idealism was a practical and realistic approach to foreign affairs, and moral principles were the best foundation for the exertion of American power and influence."[123] Such statements were easily attacked as the hopeful delusions of an eager optimist, and while it was relatively easy to argue for in the abstract, it became much more difficult to argue for when ideals met the rocky ground of political practice, both in domestic and in foreign policy.

Pragmatism in Human Rights Policy

At least partially in response to the chorus of criticism that his human rights policy was naive, Carter also argued that grounding policy in human rights was also in the best interest of the nation—it was pragmatic policy, that clearly served American self-interest.[124] "Americans," Carter said, "must be mature enough to recognize that we need to be strong and we need to be accommodating at the same time. We need to protect our own interests vigorously while finding honorable ways to accommodate those new claimants to economic and political power which they have not had in the past."[125] By this, he meant that the best practice of foreign policy had both eyes open— and while one eye was fixed firmly on unchanging principle, the other was equally focused on the shifting terrain of self-interest.

While offering a more moral basis for the practice of U.S. foreign policy, Carter also argued that, "This does not mean that we can conduct our foreign policy by rigid moral maxims. We live in a world that is imperfect and which will always be imperfect—a world that is complex and confused and which will always be complex and confused. I understand fully the limits of moral suasion. We have no illusion that changes will come easily or soon. But I also think it is a mistake to undervalue the power of words and of the ideas those words embody."[126] Human rights rhetoric, for Carter, had value because it could change opinion, which could lead to a political climate where material change would be facilitated. But this process would be difficult and slow: "Our goal has not been to reach easy or transient agreements, but to find solutions that are meaningful, balanced, and lasting."[127] He admitted that the progress was "very slow, tedious."[128] But he argued that it was progress nonetheless: "It's a difficult and sensitive issue, because it's easy to say you're for human rights but it's difficult to force other nations over whom you have no control to honor the principles of human rights. We've made very good progress."[129] Thus, he argued that gradual progress was possible and that moral suasion, if properly practiced, would have practical benefits.

Carter also recognized that there was still a long way to go in terms of domestic human rights.[130] In his 1978 State of the Union Address, for instance, he balanced praise for national progress with calls for further action: "We've already passed laws to assure equal access to the voting booth and to restaurants and schools, to housing and laws to permit access to jobs. But job opportunity—the chance to earn a decent living—is also a basic human right, which we cannot and will not ignore. A major priority for our Nation is the final elimination of barriers that restrict the opportunities available to women and also to black people and Hispanics and other minorities. We've come a long way toward that goal. What we inherited from the past must not be permitted to shackle us in the future."[131] Carter both acknowledged the progress that had been made and the work that still needed to be done.

In this context, the case of the Wilmington 10 caused enormous difficulty for the Carter Administration, presenting as it did a potentially explosive example of human rights violations in the United States. The Wilmington 10 were a group of students, involved in protesting racial segregation in North Carolina. During the protests, violence broke out, a store was firebombed, and ten students were convicted of the crime, causing a national outcry and demands for presidential action.[132] Carter consistently argued that while he was "against unjust imprisonment," he "had no jurisdiction" in this case, and could not intervene.[133] It was one of the cases that raised troubling questions for the Carter Administration's human rights policy concerning the question of whether he was as committed to correcting violations at home as he was determined to denounce them abroad.[134]

There were other issues that offered apparent contradictions between Carter's avowed stance on human rights and the actual practices of the U.S. government. One potentially troubling one was abortion, which, in the wake of the 1973 *Roe v. Wade* decision, was in the earliest stages of gaining the national importance it would claim decades later. Abortion, which potentially at least, places two human rights positions—that of the unborn child and that of the mother—in competition, is a difficult one. Carter argued against federal funding for abortion, but also argued that the solution lay in eliminating the need for them: "I have to abide by the laws of the land as interpreted by the courts. Joe Califano, who's the new Secretary of HEW, feels the same way I do against abortions. I think he has done everything possible within the law to prevent Federal funds from being used to pay for abortions. . . . And I don't know what else I can do, except under the law itself and with the appointment of my own top administrators, to try to hold down the need for abortion. . . . The other thing that we will do is this: Under the new and revised welfare system, we'll do everything we can to provide a permanent, nationwide system of family planning, to make sure that as much as humanly possible to encourage that every child is a wanted child (*sic*)."[135] As with the case of the Wilmington 10, Carter's position on abortion unsettled some of his supporters on the Left while also drawing fire from the Right. The interstices thus opened allowed other prominent political actors (most notably Ronald Reagan) to disagree with Carter on policy specifics while also relying on human rights as a warrant for action.

Carter recognized that the centrality of human rights to his foreign policy—and indeed to his entire administration—would pose problems, and indeed there were complaints that the administration's policies rested on misunderstanding of other nation's practices and cultures and were further evidence of American paternalism.[136]

Not least of these problems was the belief, especially prevalent among Republicans, that human rights was "a weapon aimed primarily at allies," and was weakening our relationships with those allies.[137] Carter responded that there was consensus among our allies on the moral and political efficacy of protecting human rights,[138] but it is doubtful that critics were convinced.

Carter was well aware of the problems and criticisms occasioned by his policy, but he argued that its results were well worth the criticism: "And, of course, we've tried to raise the banner of human rights throughout the world.

But we've been sometimes criticized for this, because the very concept of human rights, which seems to us kind of a hazy but admirable concept, in some countries is like a razor. It slashes through the obfuscation and the confusion to the very bone of people's sensitivities and yearnings and aspirations, and has caused governments to change. It's caused attitudes to change. It's created differences, sometimes, between us and our potential adversaries or our friends, but I feel that our Nation ought to stand firmly for the protection of the individual human being and basic concepts of human rights as was espoused when our own Nation was founded."[139] For Carter, human rights was pragmatically defensible, but even were that not the case, it was a policy the nation could not avoid supporting and still remain true to itself, for its long term benefits were more important than the short term gains associated with selfish politics.

He also implicitly argued that there was an important difference between being idealistic and stupid, and that his policy was the former, not the latter: "We have no illusions that the process will be quick or that change will come easily. But we are confident that if we do not abandon the struggle, the cause of personal freedom and human dignity will be enhanced in all nations of the world."[140] Those long-term benefits outweighed the alternatives. He also argued that "Our own actions in the field of human rights must vary according to the effectiveness of one kind of action or another, but our judgments must be made according to a single standard, for oppression is reprehensible whether its victims are blacks in South Africa or American Indians in the Western Hemisphere or Jews in the Soviet Union or political dissidents in Chile or Czechoslovakia."[141] For Carter, the principles behind human rights were universal and unchanging, but the tactics required to align political action in a complex world with those principles had to be varied and flexible.

But Carter clearly argued that as an issue, human rights should not serve a particular agenda. After losing to Ronald Reagan in 1980, he went before the General Assembly of the Organization of American States and said, "The cause of human rights will be all the stronger if it remains at the service of humanity, rather than at the service of ideological or partisan ends, and if it condemns both terrorism and repression. In the phrase 'human rights,' the 'rights' are important; but the 'human' is *very* important."[142] For Carter, who was often accused of using human rights against our allies rather than our enemies,[143] the moral force of human rights was only sustainable if it was also politically neutral.

He also recognized that human rights diplomacy was slow, difficult, and sometimes success was achieved in the absence of publicity. He noted that human rights diplomacy could be both public and private and was reluctant to discuss "negotiations that go on between ourselves and other governments about release of prisoners in general or specifically."[144] This led to some problems, because any such successes were not helpful in defending his policy to an increasingly skeptical national audience.

There were other issues as well. He recognized, for instance, that no U.S. president could presume to control another nation's internal affairs. He said, "We can't change the structure of governments in foreign countries. We can't demand a complete compatibility in a system of government or even basic philosophies with our own, but we reserve the right to speak out freely and aggressively when we are concerned."[145] There were practical limits to what he could actually accomplish. He did not think, however, that this meant he had no role to play in influencing those governments: "But I think it's proper for us to either enhance or reduce our trade with a country depending upon its own policies that are important to us and to the world. I think it's important for us to decide when we should and should not sell weapons to other countries, when we should or should not invest in another country, when we should or should not encourage government programs, loans, and grants to apply to another nation. I don't look upon that as interference in the internal affairs of another country."[146] So Carter was primarily concerned with right moral action on the part of the U.S. government in managing its affairs, but the difficulties presented in limiting trade with human rights abusers when those abusers were economically or strategically important were difficult to reconcile.

Yet Carter remained committed to denouncing human rights abuses. He argued, for instance, that failure to speak out on human rights concerns would violate the very principles he attached to human rights: "America's concern for human rights does not reflect a desire to impose our particular political or social arrangements on any other country. It is, rather, an expression of the most deeply felt values of the American people. We want the world to know where we stand. We entertain no illusion that the concerns we express and the actions we take will bring rapid changes in the policies of other governments. But neither do we believe that world opinion is without effect. We will continue to express our beliefs—not only because we must remain true to ourselves but *also* because we are convinced that the building of a better world rests on each nation's clear expression of the values that have given meaning to its national life."[147] Even where our closest allies were concerned, our national obligation to denounce human rights abuses was paramount.

Despite the difficulties associated with instantiating human rights as national policy, Carter consistently claimed that even the imperfect efforts had important consequences. During the 1980 campaign, for instance, he said, "For the past four years, the United States has been at peace. We've strengthened the foundations of our security. We have pursued our national interests in a dangerous and often unstable world. And we've done so without recourse to violence and war. This is no accident. It's the result of a careful exercise of the enormous strength of America."[148] Carter claimed the primacy of human rights raised international awareness of human rights concerns, it brought about some real and important changes, and it brought the United States closer to achieving what he considered to be our national destiny.

Over and over, Carter argued, "I think there are very few leaders in the world now who don't realize that their attitude toward the basic question of human rights is a crucial element in our future relationships with them,"[149] and that, "I think it's accurate to say that almost the entire world leadership is now preoccupied with the question of human rights."[150] In more concrete terms, he stated, "We've had 25 to 30 nations who have made very substantial moves toward enhancing the quality of human rights in their nations. Almost every time they take such an action, they will inform me directly that, 'We have done this action, and we are very proud of it.' And we have complimented them on it, quite often quietly through diplomatic channels."[151] For Carter, these counted as very real successes in his campaign for human rights.

He also made more specific claims. He told German reporters that, "In many areas of the world the recommitment to human rights initiated by us and many others, I might say, has borne rich dividends. There's been a strong shift toward democratic principles in Latin America. In Indonesia there have been tens of thousands of people liberated from prison. I think we've reexamined in our own country some possible violations of basic human rights. I think other Western democracies have done the same. And I think raising the issue in a responsible, clear way has been a very constructive element throughout the world in ensuring human freedoms in which we believe so deeply."[152] He argued that there was success in South Africa and other nations,[153] that political prisoners had been freed as a result of his policy,[154] and, while he stopped short of claiming credit for the challenges to Soviet authority in Poland, he did argue that they were both part of an interconnected international movement.[155]

Certainly, one of the more prominent events in his human rights policy activity was the signing of the Panama Canal Treaty. He acknowledged that the treaty had been politically risky, even damaging, but also argued consistently that it had been both the right thing to do and that it would have instrumental as well as moral benefits for the nation. He said, "It made me proud, because it was the right thing to do, it was a decent thing to do. And it wasn't entirely an unselfish gesture, because I say flatly to you that the United States will reap rich dividends from this action in the years ahead."[156] Those benefits included "new respect in this hemisphere,"[157] and "improved relations with the Third World in general."[158] He concluded, "I have no doubt that history will show that it prevented violence, it treated a small nation fairly, and it provided for the security and continued use of a vital waterway joining the two oceans that spans our shores." In other words, doing "the right thing" was also doing the self-interested thing. Carter claimed to understand and accept the political consequences of his human rights policies, and remained certain that principle should and could triumph over political expediency. In all of these instances, despite the problems occasioned by the collision between the ideal and the practical, Carter claimed some very real successes in human rights policy, a subject we'll return to in later chapters.[159]

Conclusion

The Carter presidency provides some evidence that, at least in this case, the actions of the particular individual who was president were a decisive factor. While it is possible that given the nature of the national and international political climates, any chief executive might have jumped on human rights as an issue, but no other nationally prominent politician was as committed or as well-positioned to make human rights a national issue as was Jimmy Carter.

Carter tied human rights to his personal ethos, grounded in his religious and regional identity; he connected it to the overarching goals and ethos of his administration and to his political party. He made human rights an issue that stemmed logically, if not inevitably, from the widely shared sense of national identity and argued that given the nature of the contemporary world, human rights was inevitable there as well.

Now, if any action is actually inevitable, no arguments need to be made for it; often, the strongest arguments are most necessary when the action in question is most contingent. So I am not arguing that action on human rights was inevitable once Carter was elected. But I am arguing that in his election, in the actions and rhetoric of this particular president, human rights reached a level of national prominence as an agenda item that would otherwise have been highly unlikely.

But raising national and international interest in some amorphous thing called "human rights" is one thing. Getting widely shared agreement on what "human rights" is and how it ought to be implemented is something altogether different.

Chapter 4

<Human Rights> as an Ideograph

In the previous chapter, we saw how ideographs[1] are born—rhetors connect them as words or phrases to key values deeply embedded in the American mythos, and by associating them with other ideographs and the American ethos, develop new associations that suit contemporary times. But one speaker's use of a word or phrase in such a way does not necessarily make it an ideograph; ideographs have enormous staying power. So while it is possible to argue that Carter got human rights on the national agenda in the first place because of his astute use of the phrase and his ability to connect it to his own ethos, that of his party, his nation, and his global environment, the longevity of human rights is also due, at least in part, to its ability to function as an ideograph—an ability that was facilitated by Carter's use of the phrase.

While Carter used <human rights> with one set of associations, and with one kind of intent, those associations changed as later presidents added layers of meaning to <human rights>, and one of the reasons <human rights> is still with us as a powerful warrant for national action is because presidents continue to find it useful, even to justify and explain actions of which Carter himself would not approve.[2] That is to say that language can take on an ideological life of its own, and this is particularly the case with ideographs.

Ideographs and the Myths of American Democracy[3]

Ideographs are culturally bound summary phrases that capture important ideological associations. They are high-order abstractions that function as attempts to unify a diverse audience around a vaguely shared set of meanings. This vagueness allows for meaning to be adapted to fit time, circumstance, and rhetorical exigency, although they are not entirely flexible and do require the creation and maintenance of cultural consensus.[4]

Ideographs are not the only important element of our shared rhetorical culture. Metaphor and narrative, for instance, are also crucial in the creation and transmission of shared meaning. According to Celeste Condit and John Lucaites, "it is the ideograph that seems to be the most resistant to change. Whereas other components of the public vocabulary tend to disappear from view once their meaning calcifies, ideographs rarely disappear, even though their meanings and usages change. Accordingly, ideographs provide an element of the public vocabulary that is central to the definition of the life of the community, and which maintains a discursive constant that allows us to observe the social and political movement of the community across time."[5] That is, ideographs like <equality> or <freedom> remain and continue to resonate throughout our public culture, even though the meanings assigned to them vary considerably over time and across speakers.[6] Since the Carter Administration, <human rights> has functioned as an ideograph.

Ideographs are terms that are ordinarily found in common language but tend to resist change—<liberty>, or <equality> are two examples, although ideographs can be visually driven as well.[7] Ideographs possess a certain fluidity, but their use within a cultural vocabulary produces an ossification into the public imagery as an empty signifier that may be attached to various meanings in different rhetorical situations. This is how they function discursively and why they are so powerful—they possess a certain "givenness" that is also highly variable.

Because of the ordinariness and variability of ideographs, they are useful windows into the motives of rhetors. Michael McGee, for instance, calls ideographs "figure[s] of thought,"[8] which reveal how rhetors choose to frame any given debate. By examining the context and specific use of an ideograph, it is possible to reason backward to the motive of the speaker. James Jasinski notes that "Ideographs constitute a structure of 'public motives'; they are the terms we use to impart values, justify decisions, motivate behavior, and debate policy initiatives." The vocabulary of politics may be limited—there are only so many foundational values to draw upon—but rhetors can use this vocabulary for very different purposes.

Ideographs are thus tools of both consistency ("we have always been dedicated to the cause of freedom") and change ("therefore we must initiate this new action"). They can be used to promote reactionary, conservative, liberal, or progressive causes, depending upon the context and the goals of the speaker. Therefore, ideographs can tell us a great deal about the rhetorical culture at any given moment and about the myths animating that culture. The reasonableness of a given term's usage is an important standard by which the effective use of an ideograph can be measured. For example, that use can lead to policy change as well as serve as an important means of social control. McGee says, "Because they are rhetorical determinants, ideographs are not revolution friendly. They support political, social, and cultural stability by constituting the lines outside of which politicians rarely color."[9] Thus, ideographs are constrained by a certain level of narrative rationality—the stories they tell must be coherent, faithful to accepted values, and probable—that is, they should not defy commonly accepted standards of reasonableness.[10]

Ideographs must function in concert with other rhetorical terms, gaining their specific power at any one time through the wealth of associations created, which work both in a single moment and over time.[11] They are clearly connected to myth, because myths are the narratives that rely on these associations, and ideographs are the individual elements that have ideological power because of their ability to call upon and occasionally substitute for those myths. The frontier myth, for instance, which resonates through centuries of U.S. history, implicates specific ideographs, e.g., <progress> and <freedom>. Ideographs can be attached to a variety of myths. <Progress> and <freedom>, for example, are both components of the myth of American exceptionalism as well as of the frontier myth. The rhetorical and ideological power of both myth and ideographs result from the synergy created by their union—a synergy that can change over time and across circumstances. It is the notion of <progress>, for example, that allows us to understand space as a frontier.

It is important to note that audience reactions to ideographs are not "rigidly determined."[12] Instead, ideographs work to "exert social control by shaping political consciousness."[13] That is, the meanings of ideographs are negotiated, and audiences and speakers must share some sense of the meaning of an ideograph for it to function persuasively. Ideographs work best when they are unnoticed—when their use seems so natural and so inevitable that the response is not so much persuasion as recognition, an identification that is persuasion—audiences do not need to be convinced because they are already interpellated into the narrative itself. The meaning of the ideographic narrative is so "obvious" that it can pass unremarked.[14] It is important to remember, however, that this meaning is not static. It will change over time and across audiences. U.S. conservatives, for instance, have a complicated relationship with <progress>, and they react to it differently than do U.S. liberals.

Consequently, communities of meaning are created through the development of shared agreement on the meaning(s) of ideographs at any given point in time. Ideographs are always therefore culture-bound. As Condit and Lucaites note, "To participate in a rhetorical culture one must pay allegiance to its ideographs, employing them in ways that audiences can judge to be reasonable."[15] Ideographs do not create automatic reactions in audiences. They must resonate with how those audiences understand the political world and must seem to be deployed in a reasonable way to be recognizable and thus persuasive.

One reason ideographs are effective is because they cannot be empirically verified; there is an amorphous quality to them. That is, the degree of presence or absence of <liberty> or <equality> is always contestable and contested. The meaning of an ideograph at any given point in time is determined through such contestation. They are, according to McGee, floating signifiers,[16] and they are important because they are simultaneously so full and so empty of meaning. An ideograph is full of meaning because it operates over time and acquires a vast array of historical meanings and usages. Yet it is empty of meaning because at any given moment the action and attitude required by commitment to an ideograph is open to rhetorical negotiation. Every instance of concretizing an ideograph adds to the range of meanings associated with it. Ideographic meanings are thus always open *and* constantly constrained: "Rhetors who employ ideographs in public discourse seek to achieve the assent of a particular audience and thus are constrained to use such terms in ways that are more or less consistent with the rhetorical culture. They must, therefore, be sensitive to the moral tensions between the term's history of usages for the community being addressed and the range of plausible interpretations of its use in relationship to other culturally and situationally relevant ideographs."[17] As warrants for action, ideographs exist within the rhetorical culture historically and contemporaneously; they are both synchronic and diachronic. Audiences must agree that their understanding of <progress>, for instance, fits with the claims being advanced for it at any given moment by any given speaker.

It is not enough, however, simply to label a term an ideograph. The point is less to name and more to analyze, because ideographs can provide important windows into the myths that animate our shared rhetorical culture. Understanding <human rights> as an ideograph is not merely a matter of providing a label. Knowing that a word or term works as an ideograph is the first step in unpacking its ideological function in political speech. As Condit and Lucaites observe, "Public discourse cannot afford the attempt to function on the basis of single, absolute, or transcendental principles. No single principle can ever be enacted effectively into a government, for the successful operation of any government always depends on ordering manifold and competing experiences. Such ambiguity makes political language important, precisely because it allows for the possibility of a multiplicity of political meanings. Individuals and groups use public language to shape and negotiate the common interests of governance, a governance made meaningful through public language."[18] By understanding a term's ideographic function, then, embedded as it is within various societal myths, we are prompted to examine its ideological import as a warrant for political action.

‹Human Rights› as an Ideograph

Ideographs are ideologically loaded concepts whose appeal lies in their resonance with American political history and culture and their connection with American foundational myths; they are words and phrases we are socialized to valorize that are high-order abstractions representing a commitment to a particular, but ill-defined goal. Because of both their vagueness and their connection to American political ideology, ideographs function discursively in the rhetorical negotiation and renegotiation of differing political agendas within the mythological structure of political discourse itself.

As an ideologically freighted term, ‹human rights›, grounded in the theories of natural rights that were integral to the American Revolution,[19] has long had an important role as a justification for political preferences and governmental policy.[20] Franklin D. Roosevelt, searching for ways to legitimate World War II in a political context initially dominated by isolationists, relied upon appeals to a human rights tradition, citing the "Four Freedoms" as the cause and justification for military action.

Following the war, progress on ‹human rights› was slow, uneven, and often endangered by the geopolitical context in which African nations emerged from colonialism and proxy wars were fought between the global superpowers. In this context, ‹human rights› seemed to make clear gains in some areas while suffering in others.[21] In the United States, presidents supported the idea of ‹human rights›, but they were markedly uneven in policy, as that idea often collided with what was understood as U.S. security interests in the context of the Cold War. The contradictions between the ideals we espoused and the policies we practiced became increasingly apparent throughout the tumultuous decades of the 1960s and early 1970s.

Neoliberalism and Neoconservatism

One form of rights gained considerable support and power following these times of upheaval—a particular vision of economic rights—which largely began with the turn away from Keynesian economics towards a new international world order constituted by the Bretton Woods agreements along with the development of several other institutions like the United Nations, the World Bank, and the International Monetary Fund.[22] This turn to economic rights brought a reconfiguration of "rights" within a global economy so that <human rights> now included the right to consume within the context of unfettered access to the market—a type of consumer citizenship. Economic neoliberalism as well as a strong move in the direction of political neoconservatism facilitated this transition. In order to clarify this argument, some discussion of neoliberalism and its connection to neoconservatism is in order.

Neoliberalism revolves around "the primacy of economic growth; the importance of free trade to stimulate growth; the unrestricted free market; individual choice; the reduction of government regulation; and the advocacy of an evolutionary model of social development anchored in the Western experience and applicable to the entire world."[23] Largely rooted in the classical liberal ideals of British moral philosophers like Adam Smith, David Ricardo, and Herbert Spencer, but radically reinterpreting their theories, neoliberalism desires to "liberate" all markets (globally) by instituting laissez-faire capitalism across all borders and boundaries in order to create a single global market, which neoliberals consider to be a "self-evident" and "natural" order of the era.[24]

Adherents of neoliberalism argue that the "private" interests of the market will govern the "public" passions of the people [25] and bring democracy to the world—a triumph of markets over governments.[26] Neoliberal ideology—and its influence over how Americans understand <human rights>—first gained a foothold in the 1970s with Carter's deregulation of the economy. Reagan's administration, with the considerable aid of Margaret Thatcher, strengthened and extended the reach of neoliberalism, both as an ideology and as an economic practice.[27] Bill Clinton accepted much of the underlying premises of neoliberalism, thus increasing its hold on American ideology. George W. Bush has continued this neoliberal economic tradition of what Bradford Vivian terms "neoliberal epideictic," which is particularly popular for civic ceremonies.[28]

What these new economic interests mean for "rights," is a type of "closure of political discourse." John Gray writes, "In the United States, as it has been reshaped by the neo-conservative ascendancy, the authority of rights has been used to shield the workings of the free market from public scrutiny and political challenge. An ideology of rights has been used to confer legitimacy on a novel successor to American liberal capitalism."[29] Gray argues Reagan set the agenda for following presidencies by creating a culture that no longer distinguished among the free market, the interests of corporations, democracy, and the demands of human freedom. Thus, ideographically, <human rights> is now rhetorically linked to neoliberal ideology, and the "rights" associated with <freedom> and "democracy" also include the right to consume and the right to promote free market capitalism.

Rhetorically, it is particularly interesting that <human rights> is so closely linked to democracy *and* free markets since free market neoliberalism is significantly antidemocratic. Essentially, the private economic interests of the individual always outweigh any form of universal "democratic" concern, says David Harvey.[30] A type of market fundamentalism ensues in order to maintain neoliberal orthodoxy as consumerist orthopraxis, but "imperialist interventions" are frequently needed, which are typically justified as "military humanism" connoting the protection of freedom, democracy, and human rights.[31] "Rights," then, "cluster around two dominant logics of power—that of the territorial state and that of capital. . . . Rights are . . . derivative of and conditional upon citizenship."[32] "Rights" therefore, particularly <human rights> thusly constructed, remain empty until they are rhetorically linked directly to "democracy" and "free markets" while they are at the same time being antidemocratically enforced in order to maintain neoliberal free market capitalism under the auspices of humanitarianism and a defense of <human rights>. As we will see, this has been a characteristic of all presidential rhetoric on <human rights>, but it has become particularly dangerous under George W. Bush, who has linked neoliberalism with neoconservatism in a marked way.

Neoconservativism is precisely why "democracy" must be linked to "free markets"—why rights must be included within neoliberal discourse—because neoliberalism's reliance on competition and fierce individualism ultimately points the way towards social anarchy and nihilism, and neoconservatism offers the "moral" response to this chaos[33]: "Neoconservatism sustains the neoliberal drive towards the construction of asymmetric market freedoms, but makes the anti-democratic tendencies of neoliberalism explicit through a turn into authoritarian, hierarchical, and even militaristic means of manipulating law and order."[34] Essentially, neoconservatism is concerned primarily with the restoration of order over the chaos created by the neoliberal belief in the market's ability to replace society's role in ethical decisions—and the response is always a "moral" response that will allegedly unify "us" against the threat of the Other ("enemies") both within and without. Neoconservatives desire to restore a sense of moral purpose to society by a type of "social control through construction of a climate of consent around a coherent set of moral values."[35] Thus, the neoconservative move embraces neoliberalism while remaining in tension with it by reinscribing the limits of radically unfettered free market capitalism.

One set of moral values American presidents are particularly adept at wielding are those values connected to <human rights>: "The aim of human rights activism 'is not merely intervention to protect human rights but the creation of a moral community.'"[36] <Human rights> functions within neoconservative discourse as a powerful example of what must occur rhetorically in order for neoliberal ideology to remain effective: a set of "moral" values is rhetorically constructed around neoliberal ideology in an attempt to bring order to the chaos that is actually created by neoliberalism. These moral values, incidentally, also serve to justify any military interventions as "military humanism." <Human rights>, particularly in the United States, functions ideographically to promote and facilitate this neoconservative agenda. Indeed, <human rights> has become the ideograph *par excellence* of neoconservative discourse.

The Ambiguity of <Human Rights>

Although <human rights> has a rich history within the American context and functioned differently at various times across audiences, not everyone considers <human rights> an ideograph. Writing without the benefit of the historical perspective we enjoy, for instance, Les Altenberg and Robert Cathcart noted that during the Carter Administration there was no single major address on <human rights>, and they argue that as a social symbol <human rights> failed because it could not be used to do the same rhetorical work as <freedom> and <democracy>. They consider <human rights> too vague to have sufficient rhetorical power.[37]

I argue that the vagueness is the root of its rhetorical power, and that this power is demonstrated by the fact that presidents since Carter, specifically including Ronald Reagan, Bill Clinton, and George W. Bush, wielded that ambiguity as they used <human rights> to further ends very different from those espoused by the Carter Administration.[38] As John Kane notes, "The beauty of human rights was that they seemed simply moral, unideological, almost apolitical."[39] This is an apt description of the invisible nature of the work ideographs do. They go by unnoticed, providing warrants for action and connecting actions to deeply held beliefs and the narratives we have constructed around those beliefs. "Civil rights" were associated with specific policy actions within the domestic context of American politics, and as such, were a prominent source of political division among Americans. <Human rights>, on the other hand, was, at least initially, unattached to any specific policy, and was understood more as impacting foreign rather than domestic policy. It was, however, initially a source of political cohesion.

Carter, Reagan, Clinton, and Bush all connected <human rights> to "the myth, central to the exceptionalist tradition, of the essential unity and compatibility of American power and American virtue."[40] Kane argues that Carter relied heavily upon notions of American exceptionalism, and sought to salvage that myth, which had been damaged by the actions of the Johnson and Nixon administrations. Carter explicitly argued that through a policy grounded in <human rights>, American power would be put at the service of American moralism. For Carter, Kane notes, <human rights> would redeem America from its sins—a neoconservative response to the "enemy" within. His presidency was followed by that of Ronald Reagan, who chose to deny American sin and simply assert the superiority of American values. For Reagan, <human rights> was a weapon to wield against the Soviet Union and other communist states—a neoconservative response to the "enemy" without; it did not imply, as it did for Carter, American guilt, but American wealth and the right to consume. As Kane notes, where Carter used <human rights> to foster an idealized notion of global community, and understood <human rights> in the most expansive of ways, Reagan focused almost exclusively on <human rights> as a way of bludgeoning the Soviet Union.[41] As Carter emphasized American sin as a way of restoring national belief in the exceptionalist myth, Reagan chose to simply reassert that myth by relying on American machismo.[42]

Bill Clinton, relieved of the burdens of the Cold War, also lacked the warrants for action the Cold War provided. As head of the world's only remaining superpower, Clinton was faced with the challenge of asserting American moral superiority, but had no commonly accepted foil against which to do so. So Clinton tended to argue in terms of context—the world had changed, new challenges and new opportunities were on the horizon. Like the presidents who had gone before him, he also understood <human rights> as best protected through democratic capitalism. Like Reagan, he often talked about the importance of individualism, and like Carter, saw the world as interdependent and communal. He stressed the importance of process—for Clinton,

<human rights> was connected to proc   owed him
to gloss over some important questions   content of
these rights, and yet to stress the centra   ndividual-
ism under democratically elected govern   ated a little
from both Carter and Reagan, seeking   the "third
way" of governing.[43]

Finally, George W. Bush adopted the language of <human rights>, but as a wartime president, used it to justify actions that quite clearly were inconsistent with best <human rights> practices. He too relied upon the myth of American exceptionalism in making his case, and he is most clearly connected rhetorically to Reagan's understanding of both that myth and the role <human rights> plays within it. And he is the most fully developed neoliberal of the presidents studied here—for him, the global marketplace is of singular significance, and the connection between democratic forms of government, capitalistic modes of economic organization, and the protection of <human rights> is clear. But Bush has also gone further than any of his predecessors in justifying actions that contravene <human rights> through this language, and in so doing, endangers the rhetorical basis of the practices he defends.

The examples of these presidents reveal the potential power of ideographic criticism: all of the presidents studied here relied on the myth of American exceptionalism and all used the language of <human rights> to advance their aims. But those aims served very different ideological ends and resonated very differently among different constituencies.[44] Over time, then, <human rights> has always meant the protection of human freedom as understood through a capitalist view of democracy associated with the myth of American exceptionalism. At different points in time, however, it has been layered with different nuances that have led presidents to support different set of policy choices.

<Human Rights> in Presidential Rhetoric

John Kane defines the exceptionalist tradition via Seymour Martin Lipset, who argues that it has five key terms: liberty, egalitarianism, individualism, populism, and laissez-faire (it is worth noting that each of these has at least the potential to be treated as an ideograph).[45] For Lipset, "exceptional" connotes "different" rather than "better," but that reading "downplays the mythical significance of America as a special nation with an exemplary world mission, a conception that has played such a large role in America's ideological self-understanding."[46] It is on this mythological self-understanding that presidents rely, and this reliance is key to understanding how <human rights> has attained a lasting place on the American political agenda.

<Human Rights> During the Carter Administration

Jimmy Carter was the first U.S. president to rely heavily on human rights as a foundational value and policy goal. It was his insistence on human rights as reflective of the American ethos that established it as an ideograph. But the specific uses and definitions Carter applied to <human rights> were quite consequential, as they colored and influenced the ideological possibilities of <human rights> as it was used and implemented by later presidents.

As the United States began moving toward both globalizing markets and market values during the 1970s, <human rights> became an increasingly important means of justifying policies based on American values that also furthered American economic interests. American presidents have not seen American values, American economic interests, and <human rights> as anything but compatible, so they were treated—both rhetorically and as a matter of policy—as if they were practically synonymous. The ideological implications of this are clear: international <human rights> became all but dependent upon the extension of American markets and market ideology.

The presidency tends to be a conservative office, reflecting the prevailing alignment of political and institutional forces. Because business interests have always been an entrenched element of those institutional and political forces, it is unsurprising that presidents would support those interests both rhetorically and in terms of policy. This, of course, is what is meant when people argue that there is no "true" Left in American politics. But the degree to which this ideology has permeated every aspect of our self-understanding is perhaps made most clear by its infiltration of terms such as <human rights>.

This infiltration begins with presidential adherence to the myth of American exceptionalism—the argument that the United States is both special and that this specialness can be transferred, at least in some degree, to other nations if they adopt our unique blend of individual rights and democratic practices, both of which are rooted in transcendent values. Carter said, "Ours was the first society openly to define itself in terms of both spirituality and human liberty."[47] That combination, according to Carter, "has given us an exceptional appeal. But," he continued, "it also imposes on us a special obligation to take on those moral duties which, when assumed, seem invariably to be in our own best interests."[48] The ideal and the practical were thus clearly connected from the earliest days of his administration. And practically, expanding the reach of American values also meant expanding the reach of American political and economic forms of organization.

This belief in American exceptionalism implied that <human rights> is linked to democratization. For Carter, "the freedom and vigor of our own national public life is evidence of the rights and the liberties that we have achieved. I believe that public life everywhere, in all nations, should have that same freedom and vigor."[49] He stopped just short of arguing that the United States would press for democratization, saying, "We have no wish to tell other nations what political or social systems they should have, but we want our own world-wide influence to reduce human suffering and not to increase it. This is equally true whether the cause of suffering be hunger on the one hand or tyranny on the other."[50] Given the Cold War context, the meaning here was obvious: through democratization, nations could be free of both tyranny and hunger.

Speaking to the Organization of American States, for instance, he said, "The future of our hemisphere is not to be found in authoritarianism that wears the mask of common consent, nor totalitarianism that wears the mask of justice. Instead, let us find our future in the voice of human liberty, and the human hand of economic development."[51] For Carter, liberty was best understood as a product of economic development—and that development took the specific forms demanded by neoliberal market ideology.

Essentially, the claim that <human rights> was a matter of pragmatic concern to Americans rather than merely a moral one led to the linkage between <human rights>, democracy, and capitalism. His <human rights> policy, according to Carter, was "compatible with our constitutional stance, the framework of our societal structure."[52] That is, <human rights> was a reflection of democracy, American style. He said, "The best way to enhance human rights around the world is not to go to war and to kill people; it's to keep constantly before the leaders and the people of the world the possibility of freedom, of liberty, of democratic processes, of equality of opportunity."[53] Because of the connection between "liberty," "democracy," and "equality of opportunity," it was natural to make the claim that what was good for American democracy was also good for <human rights>. In a major address at the University of Notre Dame, for instance, he said, "The great democracies are not free because we are strong and prosperous. I believe we are strong and prosperous because we are free."[54] Note the implicit connection between a particular system of government, military might, economic success, and

chiasmus

freedom. Having one implied possession of the other three. Even more explicitly, when asked, "What comes in the first place for you: the private enterprise
and the private system or the human rights policy?" He responded with a clear
statement of the connection between the two: "Well, they're both important
to us. And I don't see any incompatibility between a belief in a free enterprise
system, where government does not dominate the banks or the production of
agricultural products on the one hand, and a deep and consistent and permanent and strong belief in enhancing human rights around the world. I might
say that the American business community, the Congress of the United States,
the general populace of the United States supports completely a commitment
of our Nation to human rights. It's a basic element of our national consciousness that has no violation at all—or no conflict between human rights on the
one hand and the free enterprise system on the other."[55] Carter's ideology could
not be clearer. For him, despite the differences between members of Congress,
the business community, the presidency, and the American public, all agreed
on (at least) this one thing: that there was no incompatibility between <human
rights> and private enterprise.

This linkage was also easy to make because <human rights>, as understood
in the American context, is primarily about *individual* rights: "I don't have
any regrets at all," Carter stated, "about our enthusiastic endorsement of the
principle of human rights, basic human freedoms, and the respect for the indi-
viduality of persons."[56] For Carter, human rights were understood as individual
rights. And in a society dominated by capitalistic ideology, it is a short step
from individual rights to property rights, and from there to free markets.
Answering a question on his first hundred days in office, Carter first mentioned
energy policy and arms control and then said, "I have, I think, accurately
mirrored the American people's beliefs on public espousal of human rights.
We have begun to reorganize our own Nation's Government and to com-
mence proposals which will ultimately transform our welfare system and our
income tax structure. I have made some—sometimes controversial—decisions
to prevent the raising of trade barriers and have had an almost unprecedented
stream of distinguished visitors here from other countries."[57] The fluidity with
which he moved from energy and arms control to <human rights> and from
there to welfare, taxes, and trade is revealing—for Carter, <human rights> was
not merely a matter of civil liberties but by association, extended into the economic realm as well.[58] For Carter, the "new yearnings for economic justice and
human rights among people everywhere"[59] was a natural linkage—economic
justice and <human rights> were identified with one another, and with the
economic and political systems favored in the United States.[60]

Summarizing his foreign policy, he said, "Our policy is based on an historical vision of America's role. Our policy is derived from a larger view of global change. Our policy is rooted in our moral values, which never change. Our policy is reinforced by our material wealth and by our military power. Our policy is designed to serve mankind."[61] All of the elements are there: the reliance on the myth of American exceptionalism, the claim that <human rights> is a foundational value of the republic, and the implicit connection between <human rights>, material well-being, and military power.

It is important to remember that for Carter, <human rights> was primarily a *moral* matter. For him poverty and economic inequality were affronts to individual freedom and individual rights. He said, "I think all human beings have the same basic yearnings for freedom, for human self-respect, for a home in which they can live, for a right to raise their family, to have education, health care, food."[62] In other words, they all wanted access to the advantages associated with the affluent West in general, and with the United States in particular. And participation in the global economy was the way to extend those benefits to the world. For Carter, that was (and is) a deeply held, morally grounded belief.

But it is significant that even Carter did not see a contradiction between the extension of American market ideology and the spread of freedom across the globe. He argued, "I want to see our country set a standard of morality. . . . I want our country to be the focal point for deep concern about human beings all over the world,"[63] clearly enunciating the position that America had a unique ability to be a world leader, in keeping with the tenets of American exceptionalism. But note how that leadership is defined: "I see a hopeful world," he told the United Nations in 1977, "a world dominated by increasing demands for basic freedoms, for fundamental rights, for higher standards of human existence."[64] Under his leadership, America would take a leading role in facilitating the fulfillment of these demands through specific actions: arms control, policy aimed at reducing poverty, and advancing <human rights>.[65]

It is interesting that these three things would be included together as implying one another, indicating all of them were necessary for a more peaceful world.[66] For Carter, international peace was furthered by the reduction of arms, international trade, and respect for individual rights. The first of these needs no discussion here; but the connection between the second and the third are vitally important for how <human rights> would come to be understood. He said, "But the search for peace also means the search for justice. One of the greatest challenges before us as a nation, and therefore one of our greatest opportunities, is to participate in molding a global economic system which will bring greater prosperity to all the people of all countries."[67] As a practical matter, this meant foreign aid, and increasing support from the U.N. Development Program and the International Development Association of the World Bank. It also meant "an open international trading system," and multinational trade agreements.[68] In other words, it meant that by encouraging the growth of capitalistic economies around the world, other nations could enjoy the "justice" that was the hallmark of the American system.

That justice now went under the label of <human rights>. Carter promised to work for American ratification of important U.N. covenants on <human rights>, to support the United Nations' Human Rights Division, and to strengthen "international machinery" for the protection of <human rights>.[69] In other words, he was going to support the institutionalization of what was already happening on the world stage in terms of actual <human rights> protections but would also work to ensure "justice" through the extension of global capitalism.

It is important to point out here that this is not necessarily a malign or even manipulative expression of American self-interest cloaked in the language of rights. This is ideology at work. Carter enunciated the entrenched faith in the American system and in the economic processes and preferences that underlie it. So deeply embedded in the American psyche is the connection between democracy and capitalism that they are virtually impossible to disentangle.[70]

The Left is more likely to attempt to disentangle these elements than the Right, however, and Carter was at least able to acknowledge that American morality had limits. "Oppression," he said, "is reprehensible whether its victims are blacks in South Africa or American Indians in the Western Hemisphere or Jews in the Soviet Union or political dissidents in Chile or Czechoslovakia."[71] For Carter, <human rights> meant both the affirmation of American ideals and the respect for the limits of those ideals. He did not hesitate to admit that the United States also had work to do in the matter of <human rights>.[72] But perversely, by acknowledging the fact of American fallibility, he built his case for America as a moral exemplar—the United States was so moral that it could admit to its own moral failings.

As a new ideograph, <human rights> was particularly contested during the Carter years. He and other members of the administration were continually pushed to define <human rights>, to defend their definitions, and to contend with alternative visions of what <human rights> ought to mean.

Carter argued that <human rights> was a moral imperative based on deeply held American values and grounded in the national faith in the importance of individual rights as a foundation for government and, indeed, all collective action. As he argued that <human rights> also had a pragmatic basis, the argument that human rights were individual rights fused with the belief that individual freedom meant freedom to produce and consume—that democratic values were identical to free market values. This was easily accomplished, as in the United States, democracy has long been associated with capitalism, and presidents readily argue that the extension of one has implied the extension of the other.

This is, of course, a slippery ideological slope, as respect for other cultures and other forms of economic organization, implied by some definitions of <human rights>, all too easily becomes diminished by the imperative that the best form of protection for <human rights> is American-style capitalistic democracy. Presidents following Carter illustrate just how slippery that slope can be.

<Human Rights> During the Reagan Administration

While Ronald Reagan and Jimmy Carter had many ideological differences, they shared the argument that <human rights> was integral to the American mission and sense of national self. They also agreed that <human rights> was a matter of deep moral concern. Finally, they both argued that human rights were best protected through the globalization of American market ideology, especially as it was understood to be rooted in Western conceptions of freedom. So in many ways, Reagan continued and built upon Carter's understanding of <human rights>.

There were also important differences, however, namely Reagan's insistence upon American preeminence and virtue where Carter was willing to concede American sin and tended to stress more communalism. Where Carter had understood governmental action as important to the protection of <human rights>, Reagan saw government as an impediment to those rights.

Clearly, Reagan was heavily invested in the myth of American exceptionalism.[73] Speaking at the University of Notre Dame in 1981, for example, he said, "This nation was born when a band of men, the Founding Fathers, a group so unique we've never seen their like since, rose to such selfless heights. Lawyers, tradesmen, merchants, farmers—56 men achieved security and standing in life but valued freedom more. They pledged their lives, their fortunes, and their sacred honor. Sixteen of them gave their lives. Most gave their fortunes. All preserved their sacred honor. They gave us more than a nation. They brought to all mankind for the first time the concept that man was born free, that each of us has inalienable rights, ours by the grace of God, and that government was created by us for our convenience, having only the powers that we choose to give it."[74] This is fairly standard presidential ceremonial prose. But it is also typical of Reagan's speech in general—he often argued for American exceptionalism and for its power to affect the world both at home and abroad.[75] The cause of "human dignity and freedom," he declared, "goes to the heart of our national character and defines our national purpose."[76] At the very end of his presidency, in fact, he stated, "The way I see it, there were two great triumphs" during his time in office: "One is the economic recovery. . . . The other is the recovery of our morale. America is respected again in the world and looked to for leadership."[77] One of Reagan's proudest accomplishments was what he understood as the restoration of America's belief in itself as the beacon light of freedom—and for Reagan, if Americans continued to believe in themselves, the rest of the world followed.

But Reagan considered the United States a particular sort of exemplar. In the same address, he said, "Countries across the globe are turning to free markets and free speech and turning away from the ideologies of the past. For them, the great rediscovery of the 1980's (*sic*) has been that, lo and behold, the moral way of government is the practical way of government. Democracy, the profoundly good, is also the profoundly productive."[78] Reagan here clearly articulated the ideology underpinning <human rights>: rights are best protected under democracy, which is intimately connected to market productivity. That which is moral is also that which is productive. He said, "democratic and free-market revolutions are really the same evolution. They are based on the vital nexus between economic and political freedom and on the Jeffersonian idea that freedom is indivisible, that government's attempts to encroach on that freedom—whether it be through political restrictions on the rights of assembly, speech, or publication, or economic repression through high taxation and excessive bureaucracy—have been the principal institutional barrier to human progress."[79] Governments that behave morally will be rewarded with stable and growing economies—immoral government, whether it be directed by Soviets or Democrats, will lead to weakened economies. What is good for General Motors, then, is not only good for America; it is also good for America's soul.

I do not mean that merely facetiously. For Reagan, the absolute key value in the American pantheon was freedom. It was "the greatest of all ideas of Western thought and civilization: freedom, human dignity under God."[80]

Freedom was foundational, and Reagan argued consistently that people could only thrive in free societies. He would often argue for the connection between freedom and the human soul. He lauded Andrei Sakharov, for instance, as "A Russian patriot in the best sense of the word because he perceived his people's greatness to lie not in militarism and conquest abroad but in building a free and lawful society at home. His principled declarations on behalf of freedom and peace reinforce our belief in these ideals."[81] What Reagan believed about freedom was a true for Soviet citizens as for American ones—freedom was his *sine qua non* for human existence.

For Reagan, freedom meant the protection and nurturing of individual rights. When Reagan used the phrase <human rights>, he tended to preface it with the word "individual," and he argued, "ours is a nation based on the sacredness of the individual."[82] For Reagan, it seemed that all human rights were rights accorded to individuals, and that this element should never be forgotten. Indeed, even when it came to protecting individual <human rights>, individual action was preferable to that of governments: "Whatever the regime," he said, "if progress is to be made, it will require not only support from governments but the active commitment of citizens, individuals unhampered in their humanitarian activities by politics of affairs of state. I've always been an advocate of this kind of personal involvement, knowing that energetic, dedicated individuals inside and outside of government are essential to solving problems."[83] For Reagan, rights attached to individuals, and individuals rather than governments were the preferred form of protecting rights.

The natural product of a society of free individuals was a capitalistic economy. He was, of course, adamantly opposed to communism in all its manifestations. He was particularly intent upon castigating the Soviet Union for its treatment of Solidarity, the Polish worker's movement, and for Soviet and Cuban involvement in Central America. For Reagan, the Polish people "have been betrayed by their own government,"[84] which, in collaboration with their Soviet allies, engaged in a "brutal wave of repression."[85] The repression was necessary because "they fear the infectiousness of even a little freedom."[86] Reagan was, if nothing else, a consistent and dedicated cold warrior.[87]

The Soviets were not just complicit in the Polish situation, but were also guilty of interference much closer to our shores. Reagan's battle over the various wars in Central America during his time in office is too complicated to go into here, but it is worth noting that he consistently contrasted the "freedom fighters" of Nicaragua and the people of El Salvador who "continued to strive toward an orderly and democratic society"[88] to those who opposed freedom and <human rights> in both nations, and who sought a communist-dominated world that would suppress both individual rights and national freedom.[89] To protect <human rights>, we had to fight communism, in all of its forms, all over the world.

Reagan consistently argued for the virtues of democracy over the vices of totalitarian rule. And one of the main reasons advanced for the superiority of democracy was the intersection of "human rights and constitutional democracy."[90] The connection between rights, democracy, and market capitalism were clear. Rights were protected under democracy, and democracy fueled the engines of capitalism—"we know," he said, "that democratic governments are the best guarantors of human rights, and that economic growth will always flourish when men and women are free."[91] Like Carter before him, Reagan argued, "America's foreign policy supports freedom, democracy, and human dignity for all mankind, and we make no apologies for it. The opportunity society that we want for ourselves we also want for others, not because we're imposing our system on others but because those opportunities belong to all peoples as God-given birthrights and because by promoting democracy and economic opportunity, we make peace more secure."[92] Reagan, like Carter, saw advocating <human rights> as both an ideal goal and a practical policy; it was in keeping with the moral values underpinning American national life, it was of practical benefit, and it was clearly consistent with free enterprise and the growth of global markets.

Because America was both free and capitalistic, it was uniquely virtuous. Our nation," he said one Labor Day, "has prospered because we're a nation of workers."[93] But these values and the prosperity that accompanied them was not restricted to the United States. In 1983, for example, he noted that the "fundamental goals of the nations of the Americas" included "justice under law, protection of human rights, and economic and social development."[94] Again, like Carter, Reagan saw no contradiction between advocacy of democracy and capitalism. They combined to justify America's unique virtue; and because America was virtuous, so were the political and economic systems associated with it.

For Reagan, American virtue depended on limited government, which he argued was the "true" democratic government.[95] He said, "there is a threat posed to human freedom by the power of the modern state,"[96] and "Mankind's best defense against tyranny and want is limited government."[97] The connection between the freedom from tyranny and absence of want is not accidental, for he continued, "For above all, human rights are rights of individuals: rights to conscience, rights of choice, rights of association, rights of emigration, rights of self-directed action, and the right to own property."[98] In other words, human rights are not best protected by active governmental intervention, as Carter had argued, but by the active restraint of governmental interference in human affairs. Government's role was restricted to the protection of rights involving free action, chief among them the right to own property. Accepting the Republican nomination in 1984, he said, "Isn't our choice really not one of left or right, but of up or down? Down through the welfare state to statism, to more and more government largesse accompanied always by more government authority, less individual liberty and, ultimately, totalitarianism, always advanced as for our own good. The alternative is the dream conceived by our Founding Fathers, up to the ultimate in individual freedom consistent with an orderly society."[99] Carter had argued that governmental action was crucial to the protection of <human rights>—that as long as he was president, that action would be forthcoming. Reagan argued that the absence of governmental interference in private affairs was practically the definition of <human rights>.

Reagan and Carter agreed that America was defined by its nature as a uniquely free society. The United States had a responsibility to the world to protect <human rights> and spread capitalism. Carter's view of this amounted to something of a globalized community (although he did not talk about globalization in the ways to which we now have become accustomed). His vision was of a world that included the United States as first among equals in the fight for the furtherance and protection of individual dignity. This vision meant that the United States would listen as well as talk and that it would seek accommodations with other nations, respecting the diversity of cultures around the world. Reagan's vision was one of unquestioned and unquestionable American dominance, a world in which the United States led by example and maintained military as well as moral strength. The protection of <human rights> was still an important goal, but for Reagan, that meant the protection of individual rights, especially as they were understood through the lens of capitalism—protection of basic political and civil rights, along with a reverence for private property and the promulgation of global markets.

Both Carter and Reagan argued for <human rights>, and used <human rights> as a powerful warrant for their preferred policies. But it is important to note that those policies were in some cases similar—both favored the expansion of American economic influence, for instance, and both saw the proliferation of market economies in the developing world as crucial to the expansion of

<human rights> around the world. But Carter's communal vision led to differ-
ent places than did Reagan's understanding of American preeminence, and
the presidents who followed them thus had a variety of policy options from
which to choose when justifying their policy preferences in the name of <hu-
man rights>.[100]

<Human Rights> During the Clinton Administration

Clinton also based his <human rights> talk on the myth of American exceptionalism. Like Carter, Clinton was willing to admit America's imperfections,
but also like Carter, argued that improvement on matters of <human rights>
was what mattered—and America led the way. He told the Turkish Grand
National Assembly, for instance, to "Keep in mind that I come from a nation
that was founded on the creed that all are created equal; and yet, when we
were founded, we had slavery; women could not vote; even men could not
vote unless they owned property. I know something about the imperfect realization of a country's ideals. We have had a long journey in America, from
our founding to where we are, but the journey has been worth making."[101]
The path of progress was to admit imperfections and move toward perfec-
tion. By admitting to its imperfections, America was thus a leader on the
journey to a more perfect realization of national ideals—it was thus, despite
its flaws, a good example for the world to follow.[102]

Clinton also shared Carter's and Reagan's views on the connection between
the American version of democracy, <human rights>, and market capitalism:
"Democracies are highly unlikely to go to war with each other. They are
more likely to keep their word to each other. They are more likely to see their
future greatness in terms of developing the human potential of their people
rather than building walls around their country, either economic or military
walls."[103] Trade barriers for Clinton were equated with militarized borders—
both were equally inimical to the development of human potential. The age
of globalization for Clinton meant integration—it meant permeable borders
and economic interdependence. It meant an increased need for international
understanding and tolerance.[104]

Western democracies, in particular, shared "the idea that people can find
strength in diversity of opinions, cultures, and faiths, so long as they are
commonly committed to democracy and human rights; the idea that people
can be united without being uniform, and that if the community we loosely
refer to as the West is an idea, it has no fixed frontiers. It stretches as far as
the frontiers of freedom can go."[105] Again, democracy, freedom, and <human
rights> are intimately connected, and they are of the West, but not confined

to it—in the age of globalization, we can all be Westerners. He said, "We believe all individuals, as a condition of their humanity, have the right to life, liberty, and the pursuit of happiness. We believe liberty includes freedom of religion, freedom of speech, freedom of association. We believe governments must protect those rights. These ideas grew out of the European Enlightenment, but today they are enshrined in the Universal Declaration of Human Rights, not as the birthright of Americans or Westerners, but of people everywhere."[106] America's birthright had become the world's.

Here, Clinton is more like Carter than Reagan—he offers a more communal, less jingoistic version of the myth of American exceptionalism, but the ideological ends being served are not that different—if the world becomes as America is, democracy and global capitalism both expand—and that is in America's self-interest; this belief is shared by all three of these presidents.

Like Carter and Reagan, Clinton argued that the best hope for the developing world lay in the growth of international market economies. Regarding Guatemala, for instance, he said, "I would also hope to discuss other matters critical to peace and to development and reconciliation, including economic liberalization, market-opening measures, increased trade and investment, all of which are critical to the overall well-being of the people of Guatemala."[107] Like Carter and Reagan, he argued that participation in the global economy was the surest route toward increased democratization and the best way to protect <human rights>. In the same speech, he said, "the rule of law is essential to get more investment and more economic opportunity and to protect the investments that exist. It is also essential to establish, in an orderly way, human rights and the institutions of justice."[108] <Human rights> and "the institutions of justice" were important both in their own right and for their connection to enabling global capitalism. So it is not surprising that, like both Carter and Reagan, Clinton would link "peace and prosperity," the protection of <human rights> and economic development.[109] In 1997, for instance, he told the United Nations that "We are off to a promising start. For the first time in history, more than half the people represented in this Assembly freely choose their own governments. Free markets are spreading individual opportunity and national well-being."[110] For American presidents, the connection between free government and free markets was too natural to need explanation or defense.

But Clinton governed in a new context—the first president to have no experience governing during the Cold War, Clinton assumed office as the first president to have no rivals on the world stage. That fact, for Clinton, magnified the importance of America's role as exemplar:

Now it falls to our generation to make good on its promise to put into practice the principle that those who violate universal human rights must be called to account for those actions. This mission demands the abiding commitment of all people. And like many of the other challenges of our time, it requires the power of our nation's example and leadership, first, because America was founded on the proposition that all God's children have the right to life, liberty, and the pursuit of happiness. . . . Second, we have to do it because while fascism and communism are dead or discredited, the forces of hatred and intolerance live on as they will for as long as human beings are permitted to exist on this planet Earth. Today, it is ethnic violence, religious strife, terrorism. . . . And finally, we must do it because, in the aftermath of the cold war, we are the world's only superpower. We have to do it because while we seek to do everything we possibly can in the world in cooperation with other nations they find it difficult to proceed in cooperation if we are not there as a partner and very often as a leader.[111]

Here, Clinton clearly echoed Carter more than Reagan—the need to cooperate with other nations, along with the assumption of a leadership role, were more in line with Carter's view of the United States as first among equals that with Reagan's vision of the United States as unequivocally dominant. But Clinton here also reflects one of the dominant themes of his presidency— that we now live in a different sort of world, and it is imperative that we adapt to it.

For Clinton, this new context provided both challenges and opportunities: "The forces of global integration are a great tide," he said, "inexorably wearing away the established order of things. But we must decide what will be left in its wake. People fear change when they feel its burden but not its benefits. They are susceptible to misguided protectionism, to the poisoned appeals of extreme nationalism, and ethnic, racial, and religious hatred. New global environmental challenges require us to find ways to work together without damaging legitimate aspirations for progress."[112] For Clinton, globalization offered both political and economic dangers and opportunities; it is significant that he saw politics and economics as so closely interwoven. He argued that "these new forces of integration also carry with them the seeds of disintegration and destruction."[113] For him, the task of government had become the management of change such that opportunity was protected, and integration could proceed without falling victim to the forces of disintegration and destruction.[114]

Especially in this new world, Clinton argued, the protection of <human

rights> led to greater prosperity: "Supporting the spread of democracy, with respect for human rights, advances the values that make life worth living. It also helps nations in the information age to achieve their true wealth, for it lies now in people's ability to create, to communicate, to innovate. Fully developing those kinds of human resources requires people who are free to speak, free to associate, free to worship, and feel free to do those things. It requires, therefore, accountable, open, consistent governments that earn people's trust."[115] In this new age, as in the past ages, American presidents argued for democratic processes as a way of ensuring capitalistic development, which would imply and lead to the protection of <human rights>.[116]

He derived some principles from Carter—the importance of international cooperation, and a communalist view of interdependence, for instance. For Clinton, this meant that "engagement" was critical: "Our engagement policy means using the best tools we have, incentives and disincentives alike, to advance core American interests. Engagement does not mean closing our eyes to the policies in China we oppose. We have serious and continuing concerns in areas like human rights, non-proliferation, and trade. When we disagree with China, we will continue to defend our interests and to assert our values. But by engaging China, we have achieved important benefits for our people and the rest of the world."[117] This language, very similar to that used by Jimmy Carter, had earned for Carter the charge of inconsistency on <human rights>. It was, however, so common to connect <human rights> and American interests twenty years later, that by Clinton's time it passed as entirely unremarkable.

From Reagan, though, Clinton took a stress on individualism and a certain mistrust of government—it was Clinton, after all, who declared that the "era of big government is over."[118] Like Carter, Clinton seemed to find a role for government in the protection of <human rights>, at least insofar as the government was the manager of change; but like Reagan, he also argued that extragovernmental activity also had an important place: "Ultimately, support for human rights means preparing to act to stop suffering and violence when our values and our interests demand it. We cannot right every wrong, of course, but we cannot choose inaction either. I have been reminded again and again that much of the best work in promoting human rights and defending freedom is done by people outside Government, students, activists, religious leaders from all walks of life, sharing an unshakeable belief in the simple message of the Universal Declaration of Human Rights, that all humans are free and equal in dignity and rights."[119] These words could have come out of Reagan's mouth—the emphasis on freedom, on the limits of governmental action, and the importance of individual efforts—all were completely consistent with Reagan's view of how human rights were best protected.

Like Reagan, Clinton assumed that process and result were the same. In condemning the sentencing of Cuban dissidents, for instance, Clinton said, "They did nothing more than assert their right to speak freely about their country's future, call on their Government to respect basic human rights, and seek a peaceful transition to democracy for the long-suffering Cuban people. They were tried without a fair process, behind closed doors."[120] It is hard to tell if he objects more to the sentencing or to the way in which it was carried out. He argued that commitment to democratic processes was tantamount to the protection of <human rights>—as if democracies never committed <human rights> abuses. He said, "We continue speaking out for human rights without arrogance or apology, through our annual human rights reports, in meetings with foreign officials, in intensified advocacy for religious freedom around the world. As long as America is determined to stand for human rights, the rest of the world will choose to stand with America. But for all our efforts to prevent abuses, promote accountability, and push for reform, enduring changes must come from within the nations themselves. Democracy, the rule of law, civil society: Those things are the best guarantee of human rights over the long run."[121]

For Clinton, as for Carter, the question was how to promote <human rights> in an international culture that demanded respect for national sovereignty.[122] The problem was made easier by a focus on process, for if arguing for process meant arguing for the protection of <human rights>, all that was required was the establishment of democratic forms of government and capitalist economics.

So, by the 1990s, human rights as connected to Western notions of democratic process and capitalist forms of economic organization were fully entrenched. There was some flexibility about the role of government as a protector of <human rights>, with Carter and Clinton arguing for a strong governmental role, and Reagan less certain that government is not the problem. There was also flexibility about the way in which America serves as a role model of democracy—whether it is an exemplar because of its ability to admit and correct mistakes, or if those mistakes are better ignored. But for all these presidents, the United States, <human rights>, democracy, and market capitalism are all strongly identified, even though the policies pursued by each differed. In the rhetoric of George W. Bush, however, that identification becomes distorted, as he used <human rights> to justify abrogations of the policies and values he claimed to defend.

<Human Rights> During the George W. Bush Administration

From the early days of his administration, George W. Bush offered the promise that "the United States will continue to stand for greater consolidation of pluralism and religious freedom, wider access to information, and respect for human rights and for the rule of law."[123] He also "asked my Administration to examine our programs to support democracy and human rights movements,"[124] so he was willing to support this rhetoric with at least some policy action.

But such facile definitions of <human rights> became problematic after September 11, 2001. Bush quickly decided that the assault was not on the United States or its policies, but on "freedom and democracy,"[125] and on <human rights>, which he tended to treat as synonymous terms. For example, he stated, "The terrible tragedies of September 11 served as a grievous reminder that the enemies of freedom do not respect or value individual human rights. Their brutal attacks were an attack on these very rights."[126] The terrorists, he repeatedly announced, "hate us because we love freedom."[127] <Human rights> were thus connected to freedom and to the United States, which became completely identified.

For Bush, as for other presidents, the American commitment to <human rights> can be traced back to the Founding, and is thus intimately connected to the exceptionalist tradition. Bush said: "The advance of freedom is the story of our time, and new chapters are being written before our eyes. Around the world, freedom is replacing tyranny and giving men and women the opportunity to enjoy lives of purpose and dignity. Because Americans are committed to the God-given value of every life, we cherish the freedom of every person in every nation and strive to promote respect for human rights. By standing with those who desire liberty, we will help extend freedom to many who have not known it and lay the foundations of peace for generations to come."[128] <Human rights> here is clearly connected to the cause of freedom and to the exceptionalist tradition—America stands with those who promulgate <human rights> and freedom, and those America stands with are automatically on the side of <human rights> and freedom.

For Bush, <human rights> are both the reason for and the product of America's unique role in the world: "America believes that all people are entitled to hope and human rights, to the non-negotiable demands of human dignity."[129] That belief has led to a historically driven need to act: "America has always had a special mission," Bush argued, "to defend justice and advance freedom around the world."[130] These "American values" are then embodied within American foreign policy: "Support for human rights," Bush declared, "is the cornerstone of American foreign policy."[131] He connected the mission of "American democracy"—the obligation to spread freedom around the world—to its support of <human rights>. History, destiny, democracy, freedom, and <human rights> were all treated as implying one another—evoking one meant evoking the whole cluster of ideas.

In this rhetoric, democracy is connected to freedom, which is also "the strategic imperative of our age,"[132] and to free markets.[133] In the document introducing our national security strategy, for instance, Bush said, "Freedom is the non-negotiable demand of human dignity; the birthright of every person—in every civilization."[134] Later in that same document, he defined the "non-negotiable demands of human dignity" in terms that clearly indicate he is talking about <human rights>: "the rule of law; limits on the absolute power of the state; free speech; freedom of worship; equal justice; respect for women; religious and ethnic tolerance; and respect for private property."[135] Only the last of these is not traditionally associated with <human rights>, but private property is always associated with free markets via neoliberalism.[136] And certainly, he was here being completely consistent with past presidents.

Importantly, Bush connects these elements of human dignity, including free markets, to the myth of American exceptionalism, citing "America's history as a great multi-ethnic democracy,"[137] claiming that the United States is a country that "opens her doors so that people can realize their dreams."[138] Implicitly relying on FDR's famous "Four Freedoms," Bush argued, "in the war against global terrorism we will never forget that we are ultimately fighting for our democratic values and way of life. Freedom and fear are at war."[139] The United States, exemplar of <freedom> in the world, was on one side, and "fear," represented by the terrorists, on the other. "Every day," according to Bush, "we stand with those who reject tyranny and torture and embrace liberty and life."[140] Again, note how the terms implicate one another through association. To be on America's side is to protect freedom and <human rights>. To oppose the United States is to oppose those things. Bush clearly echoes Reagan's insistence on American dominance here.

For Bush, "Political and economic freedoms go hand in hand,"[141] and restrictions on the latter are intimately connected to restrictions on the former. In Bush's rhetoric, freedom is only possible under democracy, which is also the only system of government that will protect <human rights>. In turn, <human rights> is understood as including the right to private property and all the other elements of the free market system. He attacked Cuban leader Fidel Castro, for instance, on <human rights> grounds. Bush asserted that during Castro's "career of oppression," he was best understood as "a tyrant who uses brutal methods to enforce a bankrupt system,"[142] and who "chooses to jail, to torture, and exile Cuban people for speaking their minds."[143] Among his other crimes was the "stranglehold" he placed on "private economic activity."[144] According to Bush, "America's national ambition is the spread of free markets, free trade, and free societies. These goals are not achieved at the expense of other nations; they are achieved for the benefit of all nations. America seeks to expand not the borders of our country but the realm of liberty,"[145] which is, for Bush, synonymous with neoliberalism as it is articulated through his neoconservative discourse.

This language is consistent with nearly all presidential rhetoric on <human rights>. American presidents continually claim that the national mission is for the benefit of other, less free and less fortunate nations, and that self-interest is not a motivation for American action, despite that fact that self-interest is precisely what drives free market capitalism. It comes as no surprise that Bush used similar language when promoting and defending his decision to go to war in Iraq: "Listen," he said, "we've got people living in Iraq that are tortured and brutalized in order to keep this man in power. I weep for those who suffer."[146] American military power was used only to support its neoconservative mission, which was the defense of neoliberalism, under the guise of international <human rights>: "Yet, the national interest of America involves more than eliminating aggressive threats to our safety. We also stand for the values that defeat violence and the hope that overcomes hatred. We find our greatest security in the advance of human freedom. Free societies look to the possibilities of the future, instead of feeding old resentments and bitterness. Free countries build wealth and prosperity for their people in an atmosphere of stability and order, instead of seeking weapons of mass murder and attacking their neighbors. Because America loves peace, America will always work and sacrifice for the expansion of freedom."[147] Again, the connections between claims that American action was taken in defense of <human rights> and the exceptionalist tradition are evident, but the language Bush used to make his case was not consistent with his actual behavior as a wartime president, a point that is made clear with respect to his decisions regarding detainees and the revelations of torture.

Despite his insistence that the war on terror is a "new kind of war"[148] or a "different kind of war,"[149] Bush also argued that this war would be conducted with full attention to and respect for the best of American traditions: "Consistent with our common values, we will ensure that measures taken to combat terrorism comply fully with our international obligations, including human rights law, refugee law and international humanitarian law."[150] Even in this different war, America would concentrate, whenever possible, on "solving issues in a peaceful way, with respect for the human rights of minorities within countries,"[151] he said, a policy that facilitated the connections between defense of ‹human rights› and American military action.

And yet, once he decided that those captured in Afghanistan (and later in Iraq) would be treated as "illegal combatants" rather than as prisoners of war,[152] the door was opened for mistreatment of these prisoners. Indeed, according to Shirley Warshaw, "One of the most contested decisions that President Bush made following the terrorist attacks was that prisoners of war captured in Afghanistan would be referred to as detainees rather than as prisoners of war," which allowed the use of secret military tribunals rather than the civilian court system.[153]

These prisoners were held in what Amnesty International has called a "new gulag," a characterization the president called "absurd."[154] He continued to insist that these prisoners would be treated in "the spirit of the Geneva Convention,"[155] but also that his administration had sole power to decide their status. Despite his insistence that the procedures taken to deal with these prisoners would conform to all the important legalities, he also characterized the detainees as "killers" and "terrorists" who needed to be "held in a way that was safe."[156] To the extent that due process requires the presumption of innocence, it was doubtful from the start that the civil and political rights of these detainees would be protected.

Having opened the door for the treatment of those captured on battlefields as other than that mandated for prisoners of war, he continued that policy as the American military headed into Iraq, and increasing numbers of people were held at a military facility on Guantanamo Bay in Cuba. He labeled those detainees "enemy combatants," and claimed they could be held as long as necessary, in clear violation of the Geneva Conventions.[157] There is no due process for those labeled "enemy combatants"; and as John Bovard argues, "The power to designate people enemy combatants is the power to nullify all their rights."[158] So to protect ‹human rights›, Bush felt the need to abrogate due process when dealing with those who threatened ‹freedom› as he understood it.

In addition, Bush argued coalition actions were taken in the service of those shared values, which he grounded in the myth of American exceptionalism:

"We're going to continue to lead the cause of freedom, in the world" he said. "The only way to defeat a dark ideology is through the hopeful vision of human liberty."[159] Ironically, the rights of the detainees, who had been rendered rhetorically as less than human, were sacrificed in order to protect America's ability to promote freedom and protect <human rights>. In service of that goal, the Bush Administration was even willing to authorize torture.[160]

In defending military and administration actions regarding the torture of detainees, and to attempt to alleviate some of the burden accrued by his self-contradictory rhetorical style, Bush tended to make distinctions between what others were claiming and the facts as he saw them, modifying important claims in the process. First, for instance, Bush argued that only a few soldiers were involved, claiming that such practices were the exception and not the rule. Bush said of Abu Ghraib, "No question, it's a terrible example. . . . But I also want people to understand, here and around the world, that 99.9 percent of our troops are honorable, decent people who are serving our country under difficult conditions, and I'm proud of them."[161] So it wasn't "the American military," or practices authorized by elements of that military that were at fault, but only a few individual soldiers.

He also lauded the "transparent" nature of the "multiple" investigations into the allegations of torture, and respect for the legal process.[162] Human rights, it was implied, were protected through the court system, and thus were not at risk through the torture of detainees: "And in our system of law, it's essential that those criminal charges go forward without prejudice."[163] The <human rights> of those accused of torture had to be protected, because that is what made America special—its adherence to the rule of law—only the "enemy" deserved punishment and the abrogation of their rights, since, as "evil terrorists," as something less than human, they deserved it.

In addition, he repeatedly stated, "This is not America,"[164] making a clear claim that "America" stood for one thing, and it precluded the possibility of torture. He said, "We've discovered these abuses. They're abhorrent abuses. They do not reflect—the actions of these few people do not reflect the hearts of the American people. The American people are just as appalled by what they have seen on TV as the Iraqi people."[165] By being appalled by torture, it was rendered rhetorically impossible that Americans could also be responsible for it.

Bush was equally appalled, and thus equally free from responsibility: "I'm sorry for the humiliation suffered by those individuals. It makes me sick to my stomach to see that happen. I'll tell you what I'm sorry about. I'm sorry that the truth about our soldiers in Iraq becomes obscured. In other words, we've got fantastic citizens in Iraq, good kids, good soldiers, men and women who are working every day to make Iraqi citizens' lives better. And there are a thousand acts of kindness that take place every day of these great Americans who really do care about the citizens in Iraq."[166] In other words, "good kids" who "care about Iraqi citizens" are the "true" representatives of "America"; they could not be the same, or even identified with, those few soldiers who were (allegedly) guilty of prisoner abuse.

Ideographs help rhetors make these moves by casting events, issues, and people in an ideological light in which "good" and "bad" are a priori moralistic categories. By conflating <human rights>, "America," "freedom," and various elements of neoliberal capitalist thought through the myth of American exceptionalism, Bush crafted powerful apodeictic justifications for his political and military actions in the Middle East. But this rhetoric has also undermined the very values and practices it has claimed to engender and support. As former career U.S. foreign service officer John Brady Kiesling said in his widely discussed letter of resignation, "The policies we are now asked to advance are incompatible not only with American values, but also with American interests. Our fervent pursuit of war with Iraq is driving us to squander the international legitimacy that has been America's most potent weapon of both offense and defense since the days of Woodrow Wilson."[167] Bush's actions and his justifications for those actions threaten both American democracy and the discourse that sustains it. Yet, Bush's neoconservative discourse is entirely consistent and necessary in order to maintain and perpetuate the neoliberal "democratic" ideal of the right to consume.

Conclusion

The point of ideographic criticism is not to label a given term an ideograph, but to make us aware of how specific articulations of ideographic terms can assist in tracing the workings of ideology as it is instantiated into policy through rhetoric. The use of <human rights> by Presidents Carter, Reagan, Clinton, and George W. Bush is one way to understand how they justified their policies by grounding them in specific terms that are foundational to certain forms of American ideology and connected those terms to the myth of American exceptionalism with its heavy reliance on the neoliberal doctrines of economic "rights," free markets, and a consumer citizenship.

David Harvey is only one of several scholars who note that the myth of American exceptionalism has both a bright and dark side. The bright side of

the myth allows Americans to believe that the   ving
God, and that it is a duty imposed upon ther   and
protect freedom—to provide a beacon of light   The
dark side of that myth, however, leads Americ: e of
their status as a chosen people—suspicious of f   l all
manner of "Others."[168] In George W. Bush's use of the ideograph <human
rights> as a justification for military and political action, Harvey justly notes,
there is a fusion of these two strains of exceptionalism enacted in a way that
seems likely to undermine the power of the benign version in favor of its
malignant twin.

It is both easy and common for American presidents to connect <human
rights> to the myth of American exceptionalism, for that myth rests on the
claim that the United States has a special relationship with those rights, and
a special responsibility to protect.[169] The notion of America as an exemplar—

a shining city on a hill, a beacon of freedom's light in a world made dark
by tyranny—is one way of connecting <human rights> to that myth. But
the notion that America must play a more active role, that it must fight for
oppressed people everywhere, that it will "bear any burden" in the cause
of human freedom, also depends on the national commitment to <human
rights>.

Defining <human rights> in these particular ways meant that presidents
since Carter have been able to find a certain utility in <human rights>, thus
contributing to its longevity as a national agenda item. Presidents have unequivocally accepted promotion of <human rights> as connected to the
American national mission and sense of national identity. Protection of <hu-
man rights> is treated by all presidents as entirely consistent with our national responsibilities as dictated by the myth of American exceptionalism.
Presidents have also all agreed that this protection implies the global expansion of democratic forms of government and capitalistic forms of economic
organization.

They differ on the role of governments in the protection of <human
rights>; Carter argued that it was the central job of government, and he
placed <human rights> at the core of his presidency. Reagan claimed that
governments, by definition, tended to abrogate the individual liberties that
lay at the core of <human rights>. Clinton steered a middle course between these two poles, arguing that government and the private sector
both had important roles. Bush deviated from his predecessors in claiming
that whatever the government did was consistent with the protection of
<human rights>.

By so consistently connecting democracy, <human rights>, and capitalism, all of these presidents use language that masks hierarchies implied by capitalism through equality implied by democracy. Ideologically, this contributes to the stabilization of those hierarchies, because it becomes very difficult to separate <human rights> from capitalism, and this renders arguments in favor of other forms of economic organization difficult to make.

Finally, it seems clear that Bush is using <human rights> in ways that undermine his use of the term, and consequently, his rhetoric on <human rights> has lost a great deal of credibility. Ideographs are flexible, but are not infinitely elastic, and as Bush uses <human rights> in ways that fail the test of narrative rationality, his rhetoric loses much of the power an ideograph can afford. All presidents connect America and <human rights>; but Bush so completely identified the two that, in his rhetoric, whatever the United States did was automatically consistent with the protection of <human rights>. Reagan had been unwilling to admit American sin; Bush seemed incapable of doing so. And the difference is profound.

The United States, for instance, went to Iraq at least in part to defend the <human rights> of Iraqi citizens, and we now find ourselves in a moment when the phrase <human rights> conjures up images of free speech zones, Abu Ghraib, prisoner abuses at Guantanamo Bay, torture by members of the American military, and more recently, admissions by Attorney General Alberto Gonzales that the FBI is illegally spying on American citizens under the auspices of the Patriot Act. All of these actions are defended through recourse to some conception of <human rights>. As Bush wields <human rights> in ways that are unacceptable to his audiences, it may lose some of its power to act as a warrant for national action, and he loses the support such terms can provide.

CHAPTER 5

Implementing Human Rights

By talking—in the right ways and often enough—presidents may be able to focus public attention on issues that are important to them. But that alone will not keep an issue on the public agenda—especially not in a media-saturated environment, where there is more and more information available and a seemingly endless array of issues demanding our attention. But if an issue can become bureaucratized—if there are administrative mechanisms and people in the executive branch and on congressional staffs whose careers depend on the advancement of that issue, then public attention may not be so important in the long run—most of the work of government, after all, goes on within the executive bureaucracy and receives little to no public attention.

So it seems possible that a large part of presidential power vis-à-vis national issues is in garnering enough public attention to merit at least some legislation—and some mandate for executive action. After that, if the problem is perceived as "solved," then the issue fades away. But, if there is enough governmental structure dedicated to the issue, then it will continue, albeit at a low level of public attention. Significantly, if there is an office, bureau, or agency dedicated to the promotion of that issue, those who inhabit that office, bureau, or agency can capitalize on events that pertain to their issue and may be able to call public attention to it when the opportunity presents itself.

In terms of the national agenda, the bureaucratization of an issue may well be more important, both in terms of on-going action on an issue and in terms of its episodic attention, than a high degree of public attention over a short period of time. Presidents who want to get their issue to endure after they leave office may do well to ensure that they develop institutional mechanisms that will continue to work on the issue.

Carter was clearly as interested in getting human rights acknowledged as a key component of U.S. foreign policy in general as he was in acting on any particular issue. He saw "human rights" as a large concern, one that transcended any particular event or person. Consequently, by the end of the Carter Administration, "human rights" was synonymous with "Jimmy Carter."[1] Carter himself explained,

> Our country has been the strongest and most effective when morality and a commitment to freedom and democracy have been most clearly emphasized in our foreign policy. Under President Lyndon Johnson, quantum leaps forward were taken within the United States, effectively reducing racial discrimination and providing for the economic and social needs of our own people. But in recent history, President Harry Truman was the strongest and most effective advocate of human rights on an international scale. His encouragement of the formation of the United Nations and his steadfastness in the face of great pressure as he quickly recognized the new nation of Israel were vivid demonstrations of American influence at its finest. . . . However, since Truman's days in the White House, persistent support of such a foreign policy has often been lacking. Much of the time we failed to exhibit as an American characteristic the idealism of Jefferson or Wilson. In the process we forfeited one of our most effective ways to meet threats from totalitarian ideologies and arouse the spirit of our own people.[2]

Because Carter made human rights an umbrella term, interpreting all of recent American history through the lens it provided, he was able to praise the Democratic Party (as supporters of human rights), implicitly castigate the Republicans (as either ignoring or working against human rights), and defend his own administration as acting in line with the best traditions of his party and also of the nation.

Upon entering office, Carter seemed determined to follow through on this understanding of history and famously declared in his inaugural that "our commitment to human rights must be absolute,"[3] but, like all presidents, he implemented policy in ways that allowed him maximum flexibility and diplomatic maneuverability.

This stress on flexibility may have hampered his ability to get major gains in specific nations or on specific events, but it did mean that the executive was able to take control of human rights as an issue from Congress, and it also meant that there would be those members of the executive bureaucracy who would develop a vested interest in promoting human rights, both for its intrinsic value and as part of a career. This in turn increased the chances of human rights staying on the national agenda once Jimmy Carter left office.

The Role of Congress

Much of the impetus for human rights came initially from Congress. In acting on human rights, members of Congress were motivated by several concerns: detente had led to an easing of Cold War tensions, making an emphasis on human rights practically possible; there was concern over the damaged image of the nation in the wake of Vietnam; there was a perception that this image was being continually damaged by American support for repressive regimes; and finally, the civil rights movement gave impetus to similar issues on a global scale.[4] For all of these reasons, members of Congress were motivated to act on human rights. For some members, that motivation was deepened by their perception that the executive did not share their enthusiasm. Because they believed that Nixon, Kissinger, and Ford were all relatively hostile to human rights intrusions into foreign policy, these members were more likely to press for legislative mandates than to trust the president.

Beginning as early as 1968, members of Congress began demanding that the executive take action on human rights, demands that took on added urgency by the early 1970s.[5] One House committee alone held more than forty hearings from 1973 to 1976, intending to educate Congress, the executive branch, and the public on human rights matters.[6] Congress began to attach increasingly restrictive human rights provisions to major aid bills, including security assistance and trade bills. When the Nixon and Ford administrations did not respond as Congress wished (indeed, under both presidents there was only one full-time desk officer dedicated to human rights[7]), they moved from expressing the "sense of the Congress" to imposing these restrictions as a matter of law.[8]

The major focus of such action was the Foreign Assistance Act of 1961. Congress first passed nonbinding amendments,[9] and then dissatisfied with the lack of executive action, amended the Act to prohibit economic aid to nations that engaged in a "consistent pattern" of "gross violations" unless such aid "directly" benefited "needy people."[10] Known as the Harkin Amendment after its chief sponsor Senator Tom Harkin (D-IA), this became the foundation for human rights legislation in the next decade. In 1976, Congress added a similar amendment to section 502B of the Foreign Assistance Act, specifically tying human rights to security assistance.[11] They objected to offering American arms to governments that seemed likely to use them against their own citizens.

In all, between 1973 and 1978, Congress passed several major pieces of legislation affecting human rights policy. They included the two provisions discussed above as well as amendments to the Food for Peace program, the Financial Institutions Act, the Export-Import Bank Act, the Foreign Assistance Appropriations Act, and the Foreign Assistance Act. All of these amendments sought to limit U.S. aid to nations that did not support human rights.[12] This, of course, interfered with the president's ability to provide allies with armaments that were seen as vital to both securing and protecting amiable relationships with those governments[13] and to protect U.S. security interests—an especially difficult problem given the Cold War mentality that became increasingly relevant as the SALT II talks faltered, the Soviets invaded Afghanistan, and Americans were taken hostage in Iran.[14]

Presidents always object to such legislation, especially on matters of foreign policy, because it reduces their flexibility. And, in fact, both Carter and his successors made frequent use of the laws' loopholes to continue to offer assistance—both economic and military—to nations with less than stellar records on human rights.[15] Carter preferred the carrot of rewarding countries with good or "improving" records to the stick of mandated sanctions against countries with poor or deteriorating records on human rights.[16]

So already, there are two sources of tension between Congress and the executive on human rights. Under Nixon and Ford, and even into the Carter Administration, presidents wanted to maintain maximum flexibility in dealing with both allies and presumptive enemies; they strenuously objected to congressional attempts to mandate executive action of any kind in foreign policy. Thus, human rights became one of the battle grounds where the war of interbranch primacy was fought.[17]

And during the Carter presidency, a new element was added in that members of both branches wanted to claim the initiative in human rights policy making. Carter, relatively new on the scene, was better positioned as president to make nationally visible arguments promoting human rights. Members of Congress, some of whom had been advocating human rights for a decade prior to Carter's election, were both pleased at the attention the issue was receiving and annoyed that Carter persisted in dealing with human rights on his terms and claiming credit for getting the issue the national prominence it enjoyed during these years.

But not all aspects of human rights policy making were contentious. In a move considerably less threatening to the executive, Congress required the

State Department to provide annual reports on the human rights records of all nations receiving security assistance—a total of over seventy nations at the time, a number that grew to over 100 by 1977, and to 154 by 1979.[18] These reports serve to remind members of the administrative bureaucracy that human rights is a matter of on-going national concern. They also guarantee at least some executive attention to the area of human rights and provide Congress with a way to monitor executive action. The awareness of such oversight will help to keep an issue on the national agenda, for presidents may act, however unwillingly, to protect presidential prerogatives even when they are relatively uninterested in the issue area. This has proved to be the case with human rights.[19]

Congress has also sought to exercise more overt control over executive actions and in 1976 established the Bureau of Human Rights and Humanitarian Affairs within the State Department, and by the following year had given all regional and some functional bureaus[20] officers specifically dedicated to human rights. Congress, lacking much direct power over foreign policy, was doing what it could to encourage the executive branch to act on human rights.

The problem here is threefold: the amount of support looks greater on paper than it actually was given the enormity of the task; there was tremendous animosity in the State Department to these new policies, which impeded the implementation (more on this below); and finally, the coalition created for these policies was by no means unanimously dedicated to the cause of human rights. Some members of this coalition were motivated by concern for human rights, and others by disapproval of foreign aid in general and saw human rights as a way of reducing such aid.[21] This meant that the congressional oversight was sporadic and uneven, and with so many differing agendas on the table, such oversight was at least potentially divided against itself. There was clearly enough support to get these measures passed, but once passed, the attention given to human rights concerns was often limited, and depended upon outside events and the press of other business occupying the congressional docket. Still, human rights was clearly a matter of concern to at least some of those on Capitol Hill, and it was subjected to the tug of war that is congressional-presidential relations.

Presidents had other troubles with Congress as well. Members of Congress were not reluctant to impose country-specific sanctions when they believed the executive was not acting in accordance with their preferences. Congress limited aid to Chile during the Nixon years, and cut bilateral aid to Chile, Argentina, and Nicaragua under Carter.[22] Congressional action affected other nations as well, including Brazil, Guatemala, Vietnam, Laos, Cambodia, Uganda, Cuba, Mozambique, and Angola.[23] These actions meant that the president had less flexibility regarding incentives and sanctions in dealing with these nations and had to play by rules enforced by others. Presidents object to this both in theory and in practice, and even Carter worked hard to prevent the passage of such legislation.[24]

Given that this opposition runs counter to Carter's consistent support for human rights, it is worth noting just how strong the executive institution can be. The incentives to preserve and increase executive power seem, in cases like this one, to trump even the specific policies presidents favor. The tendency to protect the institution above their own political preferences—and thus to maintain the long-term interests of presidents—is ingrained among denizens of the office.

But even such protection did not get Carter enough power to mandate his preferences. While he formally submitted the U.N. Covenant on Political and Civil Rights and its Covenant on Economic, Social and Cultural Rights, the Convention for the Elimination of All Forms of Racial Discrimination, and the Organization of American States' (OAS) American Convention on Human Rights in 1978, he failed to get any of them ratified due to conservative fears that they would diminish U.S. sovereignty and impinge on the U.S. Constitution.[25] He faced a similar issue with the Panama Canal treaty, which passed, and SALT II, which did not.[26] Senate apathy and intransigence delayed ratification of the Genocide Convention until 1986, and it took another two years to implement legislation making it part of U.S. law.[27]

The inability to get the United States to ratify these treaties, of course, undercut any attempt by the Carter Administration to demand other countries conform to them. Carter was forced to rely on appeals to the moral authority of the United Nations and its charter. When it came to country-specific sanctions, presidents argued that congressional action impeded their ability to encourage foreign governments to respect human rights; in the case of treaty ratification, the president's inability to move Congress was a key barrier to implementing human rights internationally. Both instances were frustrating to everyone concerned.

Human rights policy, like so many other elements of foreign policy, clearly displays the tension between a resurgent Congress and a struggling executive. As Congress diversified and became less hierarchical in the wake of Watergate-inspired reforms, its traditional deference to the executive in matters of foreign policy diminished.[28] Carter was criticized for not acting decisively enough on human rights and for advocating a policy that was rhetorically but not practically different from that of previous administrations.[29] Human rights, however, was one area in which Carter successfully seized the initiative from Congress and moved the impetus and implementation of human rights into the executive branch, where it has remained ever since.

Developing the Administrative Bureaucracy

One of the key arguments of this project is that presidential rhetoric is best understood as an institutional phenomenon, produced by the presidency as much as by a given president. Such rhetoric is most effective when it is supported by institutional mechanisms. That is, a president's agenda may be clear in the choice of which policies he publicly espouses, but it is infinitely more clear in which policies get administrative attention.

In the case of human rights, Carter's policy represented what most scholars consider a major shift in U.S. foreign policy.[30] According to Hauke Hartmann, "when President Jimmy Carter took office, the advancement of individual human rights as a foreign policy goal was hardly institutionalized and only defined in the broadest terms."[31] When he left, however, there were human rights desks in the State Department and in other departments and agencies, there was a deputy secretary of state for Human Rights, and human rights had been routinely discussed, even if on an ad hoc basis, in the planning groups that made recommendations to the president on, among other issues, foreign aid. The human rights report, which was a mere 137 pages in 1977, had grown to nearly a thousand in the next four years.[32] In short, by the end of the Carter Administration, human rights was part of the routine of foreign policy making and implementation.

While the groundwork for the development of an administrative apparatus for human rights had been laid by congressional action, the president moved quickly to add to that apparatus. He assigned a National Security Council aide to serve as liaison between the Oval Office and the State Department on human rights, and State's policy planning staff was directed to formulate a broad plan for integrating human rights into U.S. foreign policy.[33] He made it clear, through both rhetoric and administrative action, that he expected human rights concerns to play a large part in the foreign policy decision making of his administration.

Not all of that action was at his own discretion, of course. The congressionally mandated requirement that the State Department present country-specific annual reports on human rights conditions around the globe, for instance, meant that an on-going mechanism had to be developed in order to produce these reports. Each embassy had to produce the document for their host country. In doing so, embassy personnel relied on official sources, information from various governmental and nongovernmental human rights organizations (NGOs), the media, and other, more informal sources as well.[34] Every year, embassies received guidelines for the preparation of that year's report, and each embassy had at least one official specifically charged with preparing the report, although it had to be cleared by several embassy personnel.[35] Because regional officers are charged with maintaining good relations with host governments, these reports may be carefully constructed to minimize human rights concerns, although this is by no means always the case.[36] As the process became more advanced, it also became more professionalized and routinized and in time became also a major way to educate members of the Foreign Service on human rights matters.[37]

In addition, these reports have provided a routinized way for members of human rights watchdog organizations such as Amnesty International to communicate with—and often to educate—embassy personnel on the human rights situation in a given country. They are sometimes able to develop solid professional and personal relationships, so that members of these groups can have some influence at the embassy level. In addition, these reports can lead to congressional hearings, and members of these groups have an on-going voice and presence there as well.

None of this happened without controversy, however. As A. Glenn Mower Jr., put it, "Jimmy Carter's declared intention to make human rights a central focus of his foreign policy precipitated an intense bureaucratic struggle, which greatly affected both the content and the implementation of his administration's human rights policy. What emerged as the Carter human rights policy, in short, was the product of conflict; what the administration had in the way of a human rights policy was what it was able to get from a bureaucracy that contained hostile elements."[38] That hostility was specifically directed at the requirements to add human rights considerations to aid programs. The bureaucrats fought these provisions by arguing that human rights was only one among many considerations in determining aid, especially important was security assistance; by distorting information and minimizing human rights abuses in some countries; and by exaggerating improvements in human rights in some nations.[39] Resistance was especially strong in the regional bureaus, which had both turf and substantive ends at stake—both of which they perceived as threatened by the incursions of the human rights bureaucrats.[40]

The regional bureaus, after all, are charged with creating and maintaining good relations with the nations in their region. Neither of these goals was likely to be furthered by policies that mandated public excoriation of nations that were guilty of human rights abuses, and neither goal would be enabled by cutting off security or other forms of aid.[41] In addition, because human rights is not so much a policy itself as a consideration that affects all areas of foreign policy, the bureaucracy was right to feel threatened by it, for it had the potential to force reorganization and reconsideration of standardized routines and norms—careers were potentially at stake.[42]

Moreover, there is no natural constituency—either within the bureaucracy or outside of it—for human rights.[43] Human rights matters were taken on by a variety of groups with divergent ideas; together they produced a movement with "considerable resilience and staying power,"[44] but little in common—members of these groups were interested in religious issues, apartheid, colonialism, and other human rights issues. Their coalition was thus both enduring and fragmented, making it difficult to forge a clear and consistent set of policy preferences that had wide acceptance across the board.

In addition, members of the business community became concerned about how to work with the government when "legitimate private efforts to consummate international business arrangements, whether in trade, investment, or finance—often in the country's economic interests—clash with more generalized national interests in advancing human rights worldwide."[45] Business people worried about Carter's "single-issue zealotry,"[46] and about its effect on their ability to conduct international business.[47] They were not shy about expressing such concerns to Congress and the administrative bureaucracy. "Clientism" was not restricted to the State Department.[48]

And it did not help that the directors of the new human rights bureaucracy were outsiders both to government and to the career bureaucracy.[49] Specifically, Patricia Derian, Carter's choice to head the Human Rights bureau, a veteran of the civil rights movement, was single-mindedly dedicated to the cause of human rights—and was not reluctant to take the fight for human rights wherever she thought it should be taken. Supported by Warren Christopher, she fought consistently and well for human rights within the bureaucracy, but she made few friends there in so doing.[50] What she did accomplish, however, was of singular importance, for under Derian, human rights became a legitimate and frequently considered factor in many areas of the State Department's workings.[51] Once routinized, such factors continue, even after a change in administrations. This proved to be the case for human rights.

Another complicating factor in developing the human rights bureaucracy is that human rights and security interests are often seen in conflict,[52] leading one analyst to condemn Carter for his "unsophisticated" and even "utopian" views and actions in foreign policy.[53] But a more sophisticated critique was based on an understanding of the complexities and cross pressures Carter faced: "The Administration attempts to implement its human rights policy in a manner consistent with . . . legislative mandates . . . in the process it copes as best it can with bureaucratic rivalries, private interest groups, and the practical realities of its program options. In practice, this has resulted in a highly selective enforcement of human rights issues, broad policy commitments notwithstanding, that has been geared to specific conditions and situations in individual countries."[54] Deriving a set of bureaucratic rules for a new policy area is difficult; deriving such rules for a policy area as fragmented, contentious, and inherently contradictory as human rights was challenging indeed. But because of such rules, human rights had staying power it would have otherwise lacked, cross pressures notwithstanding.

Some of these cross pressures were evident within the administration and were reflected in the on-going tensions between Secretary of State Cyrus Vance and National Security Advisor Zbigniew Brzezinski,[55] and in tensions between Vance, who argued for a complex, moderate policy that included but was not entirely beholden to human rights, and his deputy, Patricia Derian, who advocated human rights with unrelenting zeal.[56] The middle ground between these various and competing voices became, eventually, a consideration of human rights, but not an exclusive one. Advocates of human rights became somewhat disillusioned as a result.[57]

In sum, during the Carter Administration, Congress had begun to develop institutional mechanisms for the advocacy of human rights, and these efforts were facilitated by a president who was both willing and eager to think in terms of administration when it came to policy formation. But Carter underestimated both the extent and the power of bureaucratic resistance to human rights advocacy.

He was often accused of underestimating the difficulties of the task of developing human rights policy as well. As David Schmitz and Vanessa Walker claim, "the tension between the quest for a more humane foreign policy and the old imperatives of security and stability has led most commentators to criticize Carter's foreign policy as simplistic and naive. A close examination of the Carter administration's development of a foreign policy based on human rights, and the complexities it faced in implementing its policy, demonstrates that this critique is wrong on both counts."[58] It is less a matter of not understanding the complexities and difficulties of establishing new ideas in a bureaucracy and more a matter of lacking the time to do so. Human rights was, after all, only a part of Carter's presidency, and his efforts to establish an administrative bureaucracy were both impeded and facilitated by the actual policies that were being administered.

Implementing Policy

Carter famously stated in his inaugural that his commitment to human rights was "absolute,"[59] but absolutes do not long survive the policy process. He did not, as some have argued, either change course or lessen his commitment to human rights as his administration progressed. Rather the implementation of human rights throughout his entire administration is best understood as an attempt to apply some standard of human rights, when possible, to all foreign policy actions.[60] It is no surprise that the result was imprecise, uneven and, at times, inconsistent. Interestingly, these fissures may have helped human rights remain on the policy agenda.

When Carter decided to place human rights at the center of his administration, that led to an emphasis on flexibility and integration.[61] The president wanted to retain as much freedom of action as possible—meaning he objected to all congressionally mandated sanctions—so that he could wheedle, cajole, denounce, and sanction as the occasion required. He also wanted human rights to be considered across the board in all matters relevant to foreign policy making. But he never intended human rights to be the *only* factor in such decision making—but that for the first time, it would be *a* factor. This combination of flexibility, integration, and proportionality meant that when (the president decided it was) appropriate, he could balance U.S. security interests, or economic interests, or any other interests against human rights interests. Which also meant that no one factor, not even human rights, would control decision making.[62] Human rights had become an "interest" worthy of consideration, but despite the rhetoric of absolutism and centrism, it was always treated as one among many competing concerns for policy makers.

In practice, this often looked like inconsistency, especially to those who looked only at how human rights were being treated, rather than at the whole complicated constellation of factors that is the policy-making process. There were charges that a lack of integration meant that decisions were too often made on an ad hoc rather than principled basis.[63] And it is true that as a matter of pure principle, human rights did not do as well during the Carter administration as his rhetoric would have had us believe.

In principle, Carter did not see self-interest as separate from humanitarian concerns,[64] but in practice, it became difficult to argue that security or economic interests should be damaged in the name of human rights, and compromises—sometimes even with the most notorious abusers—became common practice. This, of course, is what happens when the rubber of principle meets the road of practice, but because Carter tended to speak in ways that privileged the high moral ground and disallowed the middle ground of compromise, it made him look a bit shoddy and unprincipled.

In addition, Carter was careful to base his claims about human rights on international standards, a fact that caused seemingly endless problems when he translated those standards into the U.S. political context. This was especially true when it came to the issue of economic rights. In his Law Day address at the University of Georgia, for instance, as we have seen, Vance defined human rights as a three-fold concern, entailing "the right to be free from governmental violation of the integrity of the person . . . the right to the fulfillment of such vital needs as food, shelter, health care, and education . . . the right to enjoy civil and political liberties. . . ."[65] Vance argued both for a complicated array of rights and administrative flexibility in promoting them.[66] Carter, as we have seen, echoed this definition in his speech at Notre Dame. But, it is important to note, this understanding of human rights was by no means widely accepted—and even had its detractors within the administration.[67] Because his policy was based on international documents, and because those documents tend to place heavy emphasis on the integrity of the person, so too did the Carter Administration. This stance also reflects the American emphasis on political and civil rights. For the Carter Administration, the "cruelest and ugliest of human rights violations" were those that impinged on the right to be free from arbitrary violence.[68] Thus, even though he spoke in terms of human rights as composed of political, civil, economic, and cultural rights, his focus as an administrator was largely on the first two.

He did try, however, to enact these international standards as a matter of U.S. law. Carter announced his advocacy of the U.N. Covenant on Political and Civil Rights and its Covenant on Economic, Social and Cultural Rights in 1977, signing both in October of that year. He sought Senate ratification of the U.N. Genocide Convention and the Convention for the Elimination of All Forms of Racial Discrimination. In 1977, he also signed the OAS-sponsored American Convention on Human Rights. Despite attaching numerous reservations and conditions, he was unable to get these treaties ratified, a failure that went to the heart of his foreign policy.[69]

At least in part because of internal disagreements and disputes about what

Carter took office at a time when human rights was a natural issue of concern—it allowed both politicians and the American public to redeem the promise of America from the actions of those presidents who had seemed to care more about power than ideals, and who had clearly violated the latter in search of the former. So the nation was ready for a human rights policy of some kind, and Congress had begun to implement such policy.

But the president remains the dominant actor in foreign policy, and Congress could only do so much without the support of the executive. Importantly, while Nixon and Ford had resisted these congressional efforts, Carter embraced them. Perhaps more importantly, he saw in human rights an opportunity to put his own stamp on U.S. foreign policy, and thus, simply by talking about human rights, helped to give the issue prominence that congressional action alone could not (especially given that such action tended to take the form of obscure amendments to little known pieces of legislation). From late in his presidential campaign to his inaugural and throughout his administration, Carter talked about human rights, and simply by the act of talking, helped to put the issue on the national agenda.

The evidence is that when presidents strategically deploy their communication, they do have influence over the media agenda and can thus hope to have some impact on public opinion. During the Carter Administration, the media and the mass public responded to the president's continued emphasis on human rights, and it became a significant element on the national agenda. It has remained there, albeit in a lowly position, ever since.

But of course, Carter did not just talk about human rights, he talked about them in a particular way. He tied human rights to both his own ethos and also to that of his party and his nation. He discussed human rights as an extension of American values and connected them to the myth of American exceptionalism, such that the crusade for human rights became a natural result of U.S. history, and a responsibility that could only be ignored at the peril of the national soul. In so doing, Carter established human rights as an ideograph.

As ideologically laden terms we are socialized to valorize, ideographs are among the most useful of language choices for politicians because they are both replete with historical meaning and also adaptable to present exigencies. <Human rights>, which had one set of meanings under Carter, was also amenable to the preferred meanings imbued by other presidents. The utility of <human rights> gave Carter's successors a reason to keep the phrase in play and thus a reason to keep the issue on the national agenda. As long as presidents justify their foreign policy actions with regard to <human rights>, the contested nature of the term will assure it a place in the national conversation.

Ideographs are not infinitely elastic, however, and George Bush's efforts to wield <human rights> in ways that defied the nation's collective sense of narrative rationality have helped to undermine the rhetorical power of his arguments on <human rights>-related issues.[3] Future presidents will still have <human rights> as a rhetorical resource, but they will have to be attentive to its limits as well as its uses.

Equally important, however, are the structural factors that help to keep human rights before Congress and the American people. Congress began the establishment of an administrative bureaucracy dedicated to the promotion of human rights concerns, but under Nixon and Ford, these efforts were largely subverted when they were not entirely ignored. Under Carter, on the other hand, the administrative mechanisms dedicated to human rights burgeoned. He appointed people with credibility and dedication to the human rights team and gave them personal access to the Oval Office; he put top-ranking officials in charge of entities like the Christopher Group; and he supported their decisions. He routinized communication within the State Department on human rights and mandated interaction between human rights advocacy groups and experts and the foreign policy bureaucracy. He made sure that human rights would become a consideration in foreign policy decision making, and he did so in ways that meant that its presence would endure even after he himself left office.

In all of these areas, however, there were serious problems. These problems, which provided obstacles to his promotion of human rights in the short term, all contributed to a certain level of ambiguity that could be exploited by other political actors. All of these problems therefore facilitated the longevity of human rights as an agenda item.

Short-Term Obstacles, Long-Term Advantages) I'll reverse

The nation wanted action on human rights, and Carter seized on the issue and made it his own. But this in itself presented difficulties, not least of which was the ever-present danger of being perceived as self-righteous on the one hand and hypocritical on the other. The American president may be the chief priest of the national civil religion,[4] and in the late 1970s, the American people apparently wanted a return to a more moral foreign policy, but they still had a low tolerance for the brand of morality that Carter seemed to bring into the White House.[5] In addition, his vision of the American community may well have been internally inconsistent.[6] In any case, by the end of his term, Carter was increasingly viewed as sanctimonious and rigidly certain of his own morality while casting doubt on the morality of those who disagreed with him.[7] To the extent that persuasion is connected to the ethos of the speaker, this is not a public character that is likely to persuade and, indeed, this perception has been considered one of the reasons behind his loss to Ronald Reagan in the 1980 presidential election.[8]

In terms of human rights, this sanctimoniousness may have been related to a sense that he had taken a stand he could not possibly maintain in the face of a complex and multilayered world. By claiming that our commitment to human rights was "absolute," Carter set a standard he could not possibly meet. And in fact, despite allegations to the contrary, it is quite clear that he and members of his administration understood exactly how difficult and inherently contradictory human rights policy making was likely to be.[9] But arguing for an absolute commitment in some contexts and for a more realistic implementation in others made him look weak, uncertain, hypocritical, and vacillating by turns.[10] This may well be a problem that attaches to all efforts at argument from moralistic grounds in the political realm. Absolutes in politics are hard to come by, and rhetors that set up such a standard of judgment may be dooming themselves. Arguments steeped in moralism will always falter in a world governed by pragmatism. For Carter, whose entire administration was steeped in moralism, this created a serious image problem.

This image problem was exacerbated by the perception that human rights policy was being applied inconsistently—that we were more likely to impose sanctions on allies than on enemies, that we would let the Soviets off the hook in favor of criticizing authoritarian regimes who were our putative allies, and that we would ignore violations among the strong while exercising moral outrage against the weak. By arguing that his commitment to human rights was unflinching, and then appearing to flinch in the face of criticism, he undermined both his arguments and his ability to make them.

In addition, much of his public rhetoric on human rights made criticisms that he was hopelessly naive quite plausible. When he "confessed" to being surprised at the degree of Soviet resentment of his criticisms of them on human rights grounds, he looked foolish and played directly into the hands of his critics, who offered the idea that he was a good person, even possibly a noble one, but that he may have been too moral to be a good president, given the nastiness of the world we inhabit.[11] His rhetoric on human rights, and his seeming inability to grasp the negative consequences of that rhetoric, facilitated grave doubts about his competence as chief executive.

Carter's problems were further deepened by his tendency to argue that human rights was central but then to act as if it was interest among many. This allowed people to believe that he was backing down on human rights. This alienated those of his supporters who were fully behind human rights. So on the one hand, he was criticized for doing too much and of endangering U.S. security and other interests by his insistence on human rights as a keystone of American policy making. On the other hand, human rights supporters accused him of doing too little and of failing to make good on his promises and commitments in the area of human rights.[12]

Finally, there is the important issue of context. In this, the Iranian hostage crisis must not be forgotten. As Denise Bostdorff has shown, Carter's rhetoric on the crisis tilted too far toward idealism and thus set up pragmatic constraints when he was unable to resolve the crisis quickly. In addition, surrounding the issue with an aura of "crisis" heightened attention to and belief in the existence of a crisis, yet his efforts at resolving that crisis seemed less than adequate.[13] His treatment of the crisis may well have helped fuel the belief that idealism in foreign policy was misguided if not downright dangerous[14]—a belief that Ronald Reagan did not hesitate to exploit in the 1980 presidential campaign.

Within this context, the inability to meet his own standard, the argument that he was naive, the claim that he was inconsistent, and the criticism that he was not as dedicated to human rights as he claimed, impaired his ability to function. Yet, in all cases, his failures made it possible for other presidents and politicians to argue that they could do better. Carter's rhetorical and political failures gave his successors room to maneuver and provided a way for the issue to remain on the national agenda.

In a similar way, the openness of the term itself made <human rights> a valuable rhetorical resource for later presidents. Reagan could use it to help him wage rhetorical war on the "evil empire"; Clinton found in it a way to justify an actual war in Bosnia; and George W. Bush has used it to justify his war on terror. As an ideograph, <human rights> is elastic enough to serve as a warrant for a wide variety of actions. Ideographs are not, however, infinitely elastic, and George Bush's use of <human rights> as a justification for policies that clearly contravene the accepted use of the phrase have faltered on rhetorical as well as ideological grounds. It remains, however, as a rhetorical resource capable of rehabilitation by other, less obviously misleading uses by other political speakers.

Carter left other, less rhetorical resources as well. In implementing human rights policy, Carter may have made many mistakes, and he certainly found himself having to compromise security interests with other concerns. But he also provided a routinized and legitimate voice in the policy making process for human rights advocates, and once involved in the decision-making process, these people were involved to stay. Later presidents may have seen the role of human rights in the bigger scheme of foreign policy decision making differently than did Carter, but they had to find some role for the issue.

The human rights bureaucracy has also been a constant—and one that presidents have had to manage. Under Ronald Reagan, the human rights bureaucracy may have been given less attention than it had received under Carter, but it was still there, and it was still connected to lobbies and NGOs outside of government and to human rights advocates within Congress and the executive branch. And in the years following Carter's term in office, human rights "talk" has expanded, with an ever-increasing number of issues and concerns being placed under the rubric of "human rights," a development that makes it difficult for any president to ignore human rights.[15] In addition, human rights has attained a level of globalized institutionalization that must be addressed within the national bureaucracy. So while little has been done to add to the human rights bureaucracy within the executive branch, those elements of the bureaucracy have survived and continue to influence policy.[16]

Like all elements of foreign policy making, human rights policy making now involves a greater number of constituents and more sustained attention by those constituents. Foreign policy making in general, and human rights policy in particular, may now more closely resemble domestic policy making, involving competition among various interest groups and NGOs, increasingly specialized areas of knowledge and influence, and outcomes determined by compromise.[17] But while that may mean a less clear direction for human rights policy, it also means that human rights are on the national agenda to stay.[18] Even George W. Bush has had to contend with human rights charges, and the war on terror is being conducted in the midst of a debate about how to manage the tension (or even if there is tension) between protection of human rights at home and abroad and U.S. security interests.[19]

Thus, while all of the efforts made to get human rights on the national agenda could be—and often were—deemed inadequate, contradictory, and incomplete, that very character of human rights policy making may be a large part of what has kept the issue alive.

A Theory of Presidential Influence over the National Agenda

This analysis supports the idea that the presidency is at its most rhetorically powerful when the president's ethos and the messages' content mesh and when both are backed by the power of the institution. For presidential rhetoric to make a significant change in the public agenda, it probably needs to be understood as "presidential" in the institutional, rather than the individual meaning of the term. That is, presidential rhetoric is going to be at its most persuasive when it resonates with prevailing public opinion (it is easier to make small changes than large ones), when that message is consistent with the president's existing ethos such that the president's personal interest seems both sincere and ethically motivated, and when the resources of the institution are consistently mobilized on the issue. This was the case with Jimmy Carter and human rights.

Human rights is, at the least, a vague term, which allowed members of various constituencies to pour their own meanings onto it. For some, it meant social and economic rights, for others integrity of the person, for still others, it was restricted to political and civil rights. Some saw it as a weapon in the ideological war the United States waged against the Soviet Union; for others, it was a way to redeem American claims to moral superiority, damaged by years of support for right-wing regimes in Latin America, neglect of emerging nations in Africa, and ignorance of politics in Asia and the Middle East. That vagueness, and the inconsistencies to which it led, created a host of problems for the Carter Administration and for their attempts to develop a coherent, if not a consistent, policy on human rights.

Interestingly, however, precisely those elements that provided obstacles to the formation of policy may have contributed to his influence on the national agenda. There may be two models for presidents seeking to dominate that agenda. The first is well known to the literature: a president should speak clearly and consistently on one issue; he and members of his administration should train their rhetorical, administrative, and political efforts on that issue; and when legislative or policy victory has been gained, they should loudly claim that victory before moving on to the next issue.[20] This model is ideal for a president with a limited agenda or one whose policy preferences lie in areas that can be clearly delineated.

But there is another model, one that relies less on actual accomplishment. A president who wants to get an issue or set of issues on the national agenda, who wants to begin or further a national conversation on those issues, may have to forge a different path. In such a case, he will have to have a issue that has at least some public resonance or that can be tied to strong ideological beliefs or current events such that it can be given that resonance. He will have to communicate about that issue in ways that flag its importance to the administration in a variety of contexts, across a variety of issues, and over a long period of time. Members of his administration will have to similarly communicate. And there must be administrative mechanisms developed to insure the longevity of the issue over time. Issues like space exploration, which can be tied to an ideograph like <progress> and to myths like the frontier; or welfare reform which can be tied to the ideograph <equality> and the American Dream would be ideal candidates for this sort of communication.

Clear, consistent, and focused presidential communication may actually work against a president in this scenario, because to the extent that a president allows an issue to be understood in only one way, its utility to other presidential administrations and other political actors may be limited. Carter had one understanding of human rights. It was not shared by Ronald Reagan, who nevertheless used human rights to his own advantage, thus perpetuating the conversation. The same can be said for presidents who followed Reagan. Certainly, Carter did not agree with George W. Bush's use of human rights as a justification for the war in Iraq, but the fact that human rights was still an issue that could be so manipulated was in no small way a tribute to Carter. But it is also true that it is all but impossible to talk about human rights at all without also talking about Jimmy Carter, and in that sense, his legacy is secure.

If nothing else, this analysis indicates that presidential persuasive influence is a complex set of phenomena, and no one model is going to be able to explain its functioning, much less its evolution across time. There are many ways presidents can hope to influence the public, and we need to start and continue conversations of our own that cross-disciplinary and subfield boundaries in order to better understand them.

theories of...

Notes

Introduction

1. For discussions of Carter as a poor communicator see Denise Bostdorff, "Idealism held Hostage: Jimmy Carter's Rhetoric on the Crisis in Iran," *Communication Studies* 43 (1992): 14–28; Sonja K. Foss, "Abandonment of Genus: The Evolution of Political Rhetoric," *Central States Speech Journal* 33 (1982): 367–378, 371–73; Dan F. Hahn, "The Rhetoric of Jimmy Carter," *Presidential Studies Quarterly* 14 (1985): 256–288; Dan F. Hahn and Justin Gustainis, "Anatomy of an Enigma: Jimmy Carter's 1980 State of the Union," *Communication Quarterly* 33 (1985): 43–49; Miller Center Interview, Hendrick Hertzberg (including Christopher Matthews, Achsah Nesmith, Gordon Stewart), Miller Center Interviews, Box 1, December 3–4, 1981, Jimmy Carter Presidential Library, Atlanta, Georgia; Ronald Lee, "Electoral Politics and Visions of Community: Jimmy Carter, Virtue, and the Small Town Myth," *Western Journal of Communication* 59 (1995): 39–60; Miller Center Interview with Jody Powell, (with Pat Bario, Al Friendly, Rex Granum, Ray Jenkins, Dale Leibach, Claudia Townsend), final edited transcript, Dec 17–18, 1981, 28, Jimmy Carter Presidential Library; Frank A. Ruechel, "The Articulation and Synthesis of Jimmy Carter's Human Rights Policy," PhD diss., Georgia State University, 1990, 24; Ronald Sudol, "The Rhetoric of Strategic Retreat: Carter and the Panama Canal Debate," *Quarterly Journal of Speech* 65 (1979): 379–391, 381; Jack H. Watson Jr., Miller Center Interview, Final Edited Transcript, April 17–18, 1981, University of Virginia.
2. Burton I. Kaufman, *The Presidency of James Earl Carter, Jr.* (Lawrence: University Press of Kansas, 1993), 12.
3. Campaign brochure, First Lady's Staff File, First Lady's Press Office, Speech Notes of Campaign 1976 through Governor's Dinner, March 1, 1977, Box 1, folder: Notes of Campaign 1976, Jimmy Carter Presidential Library.
4. On the rhetorical workings of Carter's outsider candidacy, see Lee, "Electoral Politics and Visions of Community," 39–60. See also Kaufman, *The Presidency of James Earl Carter, Jr.,*15.
5. On Carter's inexperience, see Sam Donaldson, *Hold On, Mr. President* (New York:

Ballantine, 1987), 104; Kaufman, *The Presidency of James Earl Carter, Jr.,* 19, 30–31; Tip O'Neill with William Novak, *Man of the House: The Life and Political Memoirs of Speaker Tip O'Neill* (New York: Random House, 1987), 308–9.

6. Kaufman, *The Presidency of James Earl Carter, Jr.,* 15

7. Interview with Hamilton Jordan (with Landon Butler), Miller Center Interviews, Carter Presidency Project, vol. VI, November 6, 1981, Jimmy Carter Presidential Library, 3, 11–13.

8. See Kaufman, *The Presidency of James Earl Carter, Jr.,* 19–20; O'Neill, *Man of the House,* 302–3.

9. John Dumbrell, *The Carter Presidency: A Reappraisal* (Manchester: Manchester University Press, 1995), 51.

10. Interview with Hamilton Jordan (with Landon Butler, Thomas Donilon), Miller Center, final transcript, November 6, 1981, Jimmy Carter Presidential Library, 21.

11. Andrew Z. Katz, "Public Opinion and the Contradictions of Jimmy Carter's Foreign Policy," *Presidential Studies Quarterly* 30 (2000): 662.

12. Interview with Hamilton Jordan (with Landon Butler, Thomas Donilon), final transcript, November 6, 1981, Jimmy Carter Presidential Library, 7.

13. Jimmy Carter, *Keeping Faith: Memoirs of a President* (New York: Bantam, 1982), 80.

14. Tip O'Neill, *Man of the House,* 297.

15. See Leslie H. Gelb and Justine A. Rosenthal, "The Rise of Ethics in Foreign Policy: Reaching a Values Consensus," *Foreign Affairs* (May/June) 2003: 2–7.

16. Zbigniew Brzezinski, *Power and Principle: Memoirs of the National Security Advisor, 1977–1981* (New York: Farrar, Straus, and Giroux, 1983), 124.

17. David A. Schmitz and Vanessa Walker, "Jimmy Carter and the Foreign Policy of Human Rights: The Development of a Post-Cold War Foreign Policy," *Diplomatic History* 28 (2004): 117.

18. Members of these organizations have worked long and hard to get their issues heard and institutionalized. For discussions of the impact of NGOs, see the encyclopedic work by William Korey, *NGOs and the Universal Declaration of Human Rights* (New York: St. Martin's Press, 1998). See also Tony Evans, *The Politics of Human Rights: A Global Perspective,* 2nd ed., (London: Pluto Press, 2005); David P. Forsythe, *Human Rights and World Politics,* 2nd ed. rev. (Lincoln: University of Nebraska Press, 1989).

19. Friends Committee on National Legislation Washington Newsletter, December 1976, Staff Offices, Domestic Policy Staff, Special Projects, Stern EPA through Israel, Box 3, folder: Human Rights, Jimmy Carter Presidential Library, 1.

20. Dumbrell, *The Carter Presidency,* 117.

21. Hendrick Hertzberg, Miller Center Interview, 1, 11, 27.

22. See Ruechel, "The Articulation and Synthesis of Jimmy Carter's Human Rights Policy," 24–30.

23. Kaufman, *The Presidency of James Earl Carter, Jr.,* 3.

24. Keith V. Erickson, "Jimmy Carter: The Rhetoric of Private and Civic Piety," *Western Journal of Speech Communication* 44 (Summer 1980): 223.

25. On those troubled by Carter's self-righteousness, see Donaldson, *Hold On, Mr. President,* 111; Kaufman, *The Presidency of James Earl Carter, Jr.,* 28.

26. Robert A. Strong, *Working in the World: Jimmy Carter and the Making of American Foreign Policy* (Baton Rouge: Louisiana State University Press, 2000), 274–75.

27. Jack H. Watson Jr., Miller Center Interview, Final Edited Transcript, April 17–18, 1981, University of Virginia, Jimmy Carter Library, 45.

28. Ibid.

29. Ibid., 82–83.

30. Katz, "Public Opinion and the Contradictions of Jimmy Carter's Foreign Policy," 662.

31. Ibid., 666.

32. This argument is supported by much of Edwards work. See especially, *On Deaf Ears* (New Haven, Conn.: Yale University Press, 2003).

33. Dumbrell, *The Carter Presidency,* 3.

34. Carter, *Keeping Faith,* 21.

35. Dumbrell, *The Carter Presidency,* 63–64.

36. Ibid., 64

37. Les Altenberg and Robert Cathcart, "Jimmy Carter on Human Rights: A Thematic Analysis," *Central States Speech Journal* 33 (Fall 1982): 446.

38. Ibid.

39. Ibid., 456–57.

40. Zbiginiew Brzezinski, Memo to the President, March 5, 1977, Zbiginiew Brzezinski Collection, Subject File, [Trips]–Four Power Meetings: [1977–1/80] through Weekly Reports (to the President), 61–71: [6/78–9/78] Box 41, folder: Weekly Reports [to the President], 1–15: 2/77–6/77, 1.

41. More about this in later chapters, but see, John E. Reilly, ed., *American Public Opinion and Foreign Policy* (Chicago: Chicago Council on Foreign Relations, 1975, 1979, 1983, 1987, 1991, 1995).

42. Commentary, ABC Evening News, Tuesday March 22, 1977. First Lady's Staff File, First Lady's Press Office, Speech Notes of Campaign 1976 through Governor's Dinner, March 1, 1977, Box 1, folder: Human Rights, February–March, 1977, Jimmy Carter Presidential Library.

43. See, for instance, International League for Human Rights, "Report on the Conference on Implementing a Human Rights Commitment in United States Foreign Policy," March 4, 1977, Office of the Public Liaison, Costanza, Earthquakes, 4/77[O/A 5771] through [Gay Rights & Vice Mayor Costanza of Rochester, NY] 1/76–8/76 [O/A 5771 Box 4, folder: Foreign Policy and Human Rights 1/77–3/77 [O/A 5772], 3.

44. Carter, *Keeping Faith,* 143.

45. Kaufman, *The Presidency of James Earl Carter, Jr.,* 38.

46. Schmitz and Walker, "Jimmy Carter and the Foreign Policy of Human Rights," 113.

47. See Jerald A. Rosati, *The Carter Administration's Quest for Global Community: Beliefs and Impact on Behavior* (Columbia: University of South Carolina Press, 1987), 5.

48. Schmitz and Walker, "Jimmy Carter and the Foreign Policy of Human Rights," 114.

49. Ibid., 119.

50. See, most prominently, Douglas Brinkley, "The Rising Stock of Jimmy Carter: The 'Hands On' Legacy of Our Thirty-Ninth President," *Diplomatic History* 20 (1996): 505–529; Dumbrell, *The Carter Presidency;* Erwin Hargrove, *Jimmy Carter as President: Leadership and the Politics of the Public Good* (Baton Rouge: Louisiana State University Press, 1988); Kaufman, *The Presidency of James Earl Carter, Jr.;* Strong, *Working in the World.*

51. See, most prominently, Gaddis Smith, *Morality, Reason, and Power: American Diplomacy in the Carter Years* (New York: Hill and Wang, 1986). See also, Chalmers Johnson, *Blowback: The Costs and Consequences of American Empire* (New York: Henry Holt and Company, 2002); Joshua Muravchik, *The Uncertain Crusade: Jimmy Carter and the Dilemmas of Human Rights Policy* (Lanham, Md.: AEI Press, 1986); Herbert D. Rosenbaum and Alexej Ugrinsky, eds., *Jimmy Carter, Foreign Policy, and the Post-Presidential Years* (Westport, Conn.: Greenwood Press, 1994); David Skidmore, *Reversing Course: Foreign Policy, Domestic Politics, and the Failure of Reform* (Nashville, Tenn.: Vanderbilt University Press, 1996); Tony Smith, *America's Mission: The United States and the Worldwide Struggle for Democracy in the 20th Century* (Princeton, N.J.: Princeton University Press, 1994).

52. Schmitz and Walker, "Jimmy Carter and the Foreign Policy of Human Rights," 115.

53. See especially Michael Hunt, *Ideology and U.S. Foreign Policy* (New Haven, Conn.: Yale University Press, 1987), 185–86.

54. Ibid.

55. See Donald S. Spencer, *The Carter Implosion: Jimmy Carter and the Amateur Style of Diplomacy* (New York: Praeger, 1988), 39.

56. See, for instance, Peter Meyer, *James Earl Carter: The Man and the Myth* (Kansas City, Mo.: Sheed Andrews and McMeel, Inc., 1978), 86–89; Sheldon Neuringer, *The Carter Administration, Human Rights, and the Agony of Cambodia* (Queenston, Lampeter: Edwin Mellon Press, 1993), 66.

57. See William Stueck, "Placing Jimmy Carter's Foreign Policy," in Gary M. Fink and Hugh Davis Grahm, eds., *The Carter Presidency: Policy Choices in the Post–New Deal Era* (Lawrence: University Press of Kansas, 1988), 245–266.

58. Dumbrell, *The Carter Presidency,* vii.

59. On the postpresidency, see Rod Troester, *Jimmy Carter as Peacemaker: A Post-Presidential Biography* (New York: Praeger, 1996).

60. Jody Powell's Miller Center Oral History, December 17–18, 1981, 111.

61. See Peter G. Bourne, *Jimmy Carter: A Comprehensive Biography From Plains to Presidency* (New York: Scribner, 1997), 383.

62. As author John Dumbrell points out, human rights cannot "solve America's post-Liberal dilemma." Dumbrell, *The Carter Presidency,* 210.

63. See Gelb and Rosenthal, "The Rise of Ethics in Foreign Policy," 2–7.

64. White House Staff Exit Interviews, Box 1, folder: White House Staff Exit Interview, Aaron, David, December 15, 1980, Jimmy Carter Presidential Library.

65. Brzezinski, *Power and Principle,* 129.

66. Because George H.W. Bush and Ronald Reagan were so similar in their use of <human rights>, for reasons of space, I omitted his presidency from examination here. This allowed me to use only presidents since Carter who had two terms in office, and gave the analysis a partisan balance—two Democrats and two Republicans.

67. For theoretical work on polysemy as it relates to the topic of this book, see Leah Ceccarelli, "Polysemy: Multiple Meanings in Rhetoric Criticism," *Quarterly Journal of Speech* 84 (1998): 395–415. For analyses of how strategic ambiguity may be wielded by presidents and those who oppose them, see W. Lance Bennett, "The Ritualistic and Pragmatic Bases of Political Campaign Discourse," *Quarterly Journal of Speech* 63 (1977): 219–238; Denise Bostdorff, *The Presidency and the Rhetoric of Foreign Crisis* (Columbia: University of South Carolina Press, 1994); J. Michael Hogan, *The Panama Canal in American Politics: Domestic Advocacy and the Evolution of Policy* (Carbondale: Southern Illinois University Press, 1986); Kathryn M. Olsen, "The Controversy Over President Reagan's Visit to Bitburg: Strategies of Definition and Redefinition," *Quarterly Journal of Speech* 75 (1989): 129–151; John H. Patton, "A Government as Good as its People: Jimmy Carter and the Restoration of Transcendence to Politics," *Quarterly Journal of Speech* 63 (1977): 249–257.

Chapter 1

1. For a discussion of the evolution of human rights internationally, see Olwen Hufton, ed., *Historical Change and Human Rights: The Oxford Amnesty Lectures* (New York: Basic Books, 1995).

2. For details on the Code of Hammurabi and other early examples of ethical guidelines, see W. W. Davies, *The Codes of Hammurabi and Moses* (New York: Book Jungle, 2006).

3. Jack Mahoney, *The Challenge of Human Rights: Origins, Development, and Significance* (Malden, Mass: Blackwell Publishing, 2007), 1.

4. Arthur Schlesinger Jr., "Human Rights and the American Tradition," *Foreign Affairs* 57 (1978): 503.

5. Among the early examples of a human rights tradition are the Persian Empire's Cyrus the Great, Ashoka the Great's Maurayan Empire of India, and other extra-governmental examples, such as the Koran, the Bible, and the Talmud, all of which address issues of individual rights and responsibilities.
6. Schlesinger, "Human Rights and the American Tradition," 504.
7. Ibid.
8. Mahoney, *The Challenge of Human Rights*, 1.
9. For more on the Magna Carta, see J. C. Holt, *Magna Carta*, 2nd ed., (New York: Cambridge University Press, 2006).
10. The modern period in philosophy is variously dated to include Kant, Rousseau, Hobbes, and Locke. For brevity's sake, I am limiting the discussion to the latter two.
11. For a fine discussion of human rights as understood by various seventeenth century philosophers, see Knud Haakonssen, *Natural Law and Moral Philosophy: From Grotius to the Scottish Enlightenment* (New York: Cambridge University Press: 1996).
12. Celeste Michelle Condit and John Louis Lucaites, *Crafting Equality: America's Anglo-African Word* (Chicago: University of Chicago Press, 1993), 52.
13. Thomas Hobbes, *The Leviathan* (New York: Dutton, 1950), chap. xiii, 103–4. For more on Hobbes, see Laurence Berns, "Thomas Hobbes," in Leo Strauss and Joseph Cropsey, eds., *History of Political Philosophy* (Chicago: Rand McNally, 1972), 370–394.
14. Haakonssen, *Natural Law and Moral Philosophy*.
15. Michael Zuckert in particular defends this understanding of the American Revolution. See his *Natural Rights and the New Republicanism* (Princeton, N.J.: Princeton University Press, 1994); *The Natural Rights Republic* (Notre Dame, Ind.: University of Notre Dame Press, 1996); *Launching Liberalism: On Lockean Political Philosophy* (Lawrence: University Press of Kansas, 2002).
16. For more on the influence of the Declaration of Independence, see David Armitage, *The Declaration of Independence: A Global History* (Cambridge, Mass: Harvard University Press, 2007).
17. For a further discussion of human rights and the French Revolution, see Lynn Hunt, ed., *The French Revolution and Human Rights: A Brief Documentary History* (Boston: Bedford St. Martin's, 1966); Dale Van Kley, ed., *The French Idea of Freedom: The Old Regime and the Declaration of Rights of 1789* (Stanford, Calif.: Stanford University Press, 1994).
18. For a fascinating discussion of the development of human rights, see Lynn Hunt, *Inventing Human Rights: A History* (New York: W. W. Norton, 2007). See also, Mahoney, *The Challenge of Human Rights*.
19. Henry David Thoreau, *Civil Disobedience* (Bedford, Mass.: Applewood Books, 2000).
20. William Lloyd Garrison, William E. Cain, ed., *William Lloyd Garrison and the Fight Against Slavery: Selections From The Liberator* (New York: Bedford St. Martin's, 1994).

21. See Joseph R. Thysell Jr., "*Ex Parte Milligan:* Lincoln's Use of Military Tribunals," *White House Studies* 5 (2005): 443–456.

22. Hunt, *Inventing Human Rights,* 147.

23. Charles W. Mills, *The Racial Contract,* new ed. (Ithaca, N.Y.: Cornell University Press, 1997).

24. Condit and Lucaites, *Crafting Equality,* 83.

25. Ibid., 101–146.

26. Joshua Muravchik, "Weakening Human Rights to Save Them," *Los Angeles Times,* September 15, 2006, B13.

27. On Woodrow Wilson and these issues, see Forrest McDonald, *The American Presidency: An Intellectual History* (Lawrence: University Press of Kansas, 1994), 396; Mary E. Stuckey, "'The Domain of Public Conscience': Woodrow Wilson and the Establishment of a Transcendent Political Order," *Rhetoric and Public Affairs* 6 (2003): 1–24.

28. Kenneth Cmiel, "The Recent History of Human Rights," *American Historical Review* 109 (2004): 128; Mary Ann Glendon, *A World Made New: Eleanor Roosevelt and the Declaration of Human Rights,* reprint ed. (New York: Random House, 2001); Geoffrey Robertson, *Crimes Against Humanity: The Struggle for Global Justice* (New York: New Press, 2003); A. W. Brian Simpson, *Human Rights and the End of Empire* (New York: Oxford University Press, 2001).

29. Paul Lauren, *Evolution of International Human Rights,* 2nd ed. (Philadelphia: University of Pennsylvania Press, 2003).

30. See Jan Herman Burgers, "The Road to San Francisco: The Revival of the Human Rights Idea in the Twentieth Century," *Human Rights Quarterly* 4 (1992): 448; Burns H. Weston, "Human Rights," *The Encyclopedia Britannica Online.* http://search .eb.com/eb/print?articleId=106289. Web site accessed February 2, 2007.

31. Franklin D. Roosevelt, "Four Freedoms" January 6, 1941, http://www.presidential rhetoric.com/historicspeeches/roosevelt_franklin/fourfreedoms.html. Web site accessed February 18, 2007.

32. Cmiel, "The Recent History of Human Rights," 117.

33. Burns H. Weston, "Human Rights," *The Encyclopedia Britannica Online,* http:// search.eb.com/eb/print?articleId=106289. Web site accessed February 2, 2007.

34. For the best histories of human rights in the twentieth century, see Simpson, *Human Rights and the End of Empire;* Burgers, "The Road to San Francisco," 447–77; Lauren, *Evolution of International Human Rights.*

35. For more on the document, see Burgers, "The Road to San Francisco," 447–77; Johannes Morsink, *The Universal Declaration of Human Rights: Origins, Drafting, and Intent* (Philadelphia: University of Pennsylvania Press, 1999); Barend van der Heijden and Bahiaq Tahziib-Lie, eds. *Reflections on the Universal Declaration of Human Rights: A Fiftieth Anniversary Anthology* (The Hague: Maartin Nijhoff, 1998).

36. See Samantha Powers, *A Problem From Hell: America in the Age of Genocide,* reprint ed. (New York: Harper Perennial, 2003).

37. For a good discussion of the history of women's rights in the context of human rights, see Arvonne S. Fraser, "Becoming Human: The Origins and Development of Women's Human Rights," *Human Rights Quarterly* 21 (1999): 853–906.

38. For more on the process that led to the Universal Declaration of Human Rights, see Mary Ann Glendon, "John P. Humphrey and the Drafting of the Universal Declaration of Human Rights," *Journal of the History of International Law* 2000: 250–60. See also, Hunt, *Inventing Human Rights: A History,* 203–6.

39. Adrian Karatnycky, "Human Rights Depend on American Power," *Wall Street Journal,* December 10, 1998, A22.

40. For more on the conflict between the superpowers and the early days of the United Nations, see Mahoney, *The Challenge of Human Rights,* 48–51.

41. The United Nations has also passed conventions on the prevention and punishment of genocide, prohibiting torture, eliminating racial discrimination, and discrimination based on gender, and protecting the rights of children.

42. These complexities are revealed and exacerbated in the controversies surrounding U.S. governmental actions regarding the global war on terror, especially as those action pertain to issues of the applicability of habeas corpus and governmental treatment of enemy and non-enemy combatants, the use of torture, and the tension between protecting human rights on the one hand and U.S. security on the other.

43. See, for instance, Han Zhen, "On the Historical and Ideal Nature of Human Rights: Reading *Human Rights and Human Diversity* by A. J. M. Milne," *Educational Philosophy and Theory* 34 (2002): 239–46.

44. For a discussion of this point, see Cmiel, "The Recent History of Human Rights," 127–34.

45. Schlesinger, "Human Rights and the American Tradition," 511.

46. Cmiel, "The Recent History of Human Rights," 125.

47. See David Hume, *Enquiry Concerning the Principles of Morals* (Whitefish, Mont. Kessinger Publishing, 2004).

48. John Finnis, *Natural Law and Natural Rights* (New York: Oxford University Press, 2004).

49. John Rawls, *A Theory of Justice* (Cambridge, Mass.: Belknap Press, 1999).

50. Jeremy Bentham, "Anarchical Fallacies," vol. 2, *The Works* (Edinburgh: William Tell, 1843), http://jan.usc.nau.edu/~dss4/bentham1.pdf. Web site accessed February 2, 2007, L-6, line 229.

51. Ibid., L-4, line 151.

52. He is joined in this belief by conservative thinker Edmund Burke. See *Reflections on the Revolution in France,* new ed., edited by L. G. Mitchell (New York: Oxford University Press, 1999).

53. Jeremy Bentham, "Anarchical Fallacies," L-8, line 275–276.

54. See Richard Rorty, *Philosophy and Social Hope* (New York: Penguin, 2000).

55. Alasdair MacIntyre, *After Virtue: A Study in Moral Theory* (Notre Dame, Ind.: University of Notre Dame Press, 1984).

56. For an astute analysis of these criticisms and responses to them, see Mahoney, *The Challenge of Human Rights,* 71–114, 126–27.

57. Burns H. Weston, "Human Rights," *The Encyclopedia Britannica Online,* http://search. eb.com/eb/print?articleId=106289. Web site accessed February 2, 2007. For discussions of various categories of rights, see Maurice Cranston, *What Are Human Rights?* (New York: Taplinger, 1973); Jack Donnelly, *Universal Human Rights in Theory and Practice,* 2nd ed., (Ithaca, N.Y.: Cornell University Press, 2003); Ronald Dworkin, *Taking Rights Seriously* (Cambridge, Mass: Harvard University Press, 1978); Onora O'Neill, *Bounds of Justice* (Cambridge: Cambridge University Press, 2000); Henry Shue, *Basic Rights: Subsistence, Affluence, and U.S. Foreign Policy,* 2nd ed. (Princeton, N.J.: Princeton University Press, 1996).

58. For discussions of these categories, see Lauren, *Evolution of International Human Rights;* Burns H. Weston, "Human Rights."

59. John Kennedy, "Statement of the President Following Ratification of the 23rd Amendment of the Constitution," March 29, 1961. John T. Woolley and Gerhard Peters, *The American Presidency Project* [online]. Santa Barbara, Cal: University of California (hosted), Gerhard Peters (database). Available from World Wide Web: http://www. presidency.ucsb.edu/ws/?pid=8038. Website accessed December 15, 2007.

60. Kennedy, "Address in Honolulu Before the United States Conference of Mayors," June 9, 1963, Woolley and Peters, *The American Presidency Project.* http://www.presidency. ucsb.edu/ws/?pid=9264. Website accessed December 15, 2007.

61. Kennedy, "Joint Statement Following Discussions with the President of Venezuela," December 17, 1961, Woolley and Peters, *The American Presidency Project.* http://www. presidency.ucsb.edu/ws/?pid=8490. Website accessed December 15, 2007.

62. For a discussion of these issues, see Daniel P. Moynihan, "The Politics of Human Rights," *Commentary* (August 1977): 19–27.

63. Certainly the Shah of Iran would fall into this category, and many of our allies in Latin America, notably Manuel Noriega and Augusto Pinochet were accused of gross violations of human rights.

64. The Stonewall Rebellion took place in 1969, for instance, and the 1966 "sip in" that preceded it led to complaints to the New York Human Rights Commission—gay men were, by the mid 1960s, making explicit claims to human rights.

65. Jeffrey E. Cohen, *Presidential Responsiveness and Public Policy-making: The Public and the Policies That Presidents Choose* (Ann Arbor: University of Michigan Press, 1997), 1.

66. See Dumbrell, *The Carter Presidency,* 116; White House Staff Exit Interviews, Box 1, folder: White House Staff Exit Interview, Aaron, David. Dec. 15, 1980, 6, Jimmy Carter Presidential Library.

67. Staff Offices, Domestic Policy Staff, Special Projects, Stern, EPA through Israel, Box 3, folder: Human Rights, Jimmy Carter Presidential Library; Friends Committee on National Legislation Washington Newsletter, dated December 1976, headline: "Congress Focuses on Human Rights," 1.

68. On Helsinki, see Burns H. Weston, "Human Rights."

69. See Korey, *NGOs and the Universal Declaration of Human Rights,* 181–203.

70. Kenneth Cmiel, "The Emergence of Human Rights Politics in the United States," *Journal of American History* 86 (3) (1999): 1231–50.

71. For more on the Jackson-Vanik Amendment, see Schlesinger, "Human Rights and the American Tradition," 503–526, 513.

72. Cmiel, "The Emergence of Human Rights Politics in the United States," 1234.

73. Ibid., 1235, 1246.

74. Ibid., 1237

75. Cmiel, "The Recent History of Human Rights," 129.

76. Office of Public Liaison, Costanza, Human Rights Speeches and Newsletters, 6/74–6/77 [O/A 4460] through [Indian American Task Force: ACTION] 2/77–3/77 [O/A 4475] Box 7, folder: Human Rights Speeches and Newsletters, 6/74–6/77 [O/A 4460], Carter Library.

77. Cmiel, "The Emergence of Human Rights Politics in the United States," 1244. See also, Margaret E. Keck and Kathryn Sikkink, *Activists Beyond Borders: Advocacy Networks in International Politics* (Ithaca, N.Y.: Cornell University Press, 1998).

78. Lynn Hunt, on the other hand, dates the growth of Non-governmental organizations (NGOs) to the 1980s. See Hunt, *Inventing Human Rights,* 207–8.

79. John Kane, "American Values or Human Rights? U.S. Foreign Policy and the Fractured Myth of Virtuous Power," *Presidential Studies Quarterly* 33 (4) (December 2003): 775.

80. Jeanne Kirkpatrick, "Forward," in Muravchik, *The Uncertain Crusade,* ix.

81. Schlesinger, "Human Rights and the American Tradition," 514.

82. Chief of Staff Hamilton Jordan, Note to the President on WH stationary, from Hamilton Jordan, dated December 3, 1977, Camp David, 1979 (Changes, etc.) through Iran, 3/80, Box 34, folder: Human Rights Policy, 1977, Carter Library.

83. Cmiel, "The Emergence of Human Rights Politics in the United States," 1248. See also, Elizabeth Drew, "A Reporter at Large: Human Rights," *New Yorker,* July 18, 1977, 37; Elizabeth Drew, "Human Rights Groups are Riding a Wave of Popularity," *New York Times,* February 28, 1977, B2.

84. Schmitz and Walker, "Jimmy Carter and the Foreign Policy of Human Rights," 114.

85. See Betty Glad, *Jimmy Carter: In Search of the Great White House* (New York: W. W. Norton, 1980); Randy Sanders, "The Sad Duty of Politics": Jimmy Carter and the Issue of Race in his 1970 Gubernatorial Campaign," *The Georgia Historical Quarterly* LXXVI (3) (Fall 1992): 612–638.

86. Griffin Bell, "Interview with Griffin Bell," Miller Center Interviews, Carter Presidency Project, vol. XXIV, March 23, 1988, 34, Jimmy Carter Presidential Library.

87. Glad, *Jimmy Carter: In Search of the Great White House,* 323–330. Although she also notes (pages 292–95) the potential of his remarks on maintaining "ethnic purity" had of derailing his campaign.

88. Dumbrell, *The Carter Presidency,* 1.

89. Muravchik, *The Uncertain Crusade,* 2.

90. Moynihan, "The Politics of Human Rights," 22. On the platform's ability to unite the Democrats, see also, Dumbrell, *The Carter Presidency,* 20.

91. Moynihan, "The Politics of Human Rights," 22.

92. Glad, *Jimmy Carter: In Search of the Great White House,* 380–88.

93. For a discussion of this point, see Glad, *Jimmy Carter: In Search of the Great White House,* 390; Muravchik, *The Uncertain Crusade,* 5–7.

94. Moynihan, "The Politics of Human Rights," 23.

95. Dumbrell, *The Carter Presidency,* 4.

96. Henry M. Jackson, "Human Rights and the Jackson-Vinik Amendment," Congressional Forum, National Conference on Soviet Jewry, June 14, no year, International Inn, Washington D.C. Staff Offices, Domestic Policy Staff, Civil Rights and Justice, Gutierrez, Human Rights through Institutionalized Persons, Box 22, Jimmy Carter Presidential Library.

97. Schlesinger, "Human Rights and the American Tradition," 513.

98. Neuringer, *The Carter Administration, Human Rights, and the Agony of Cambodia,* 1.

99. His assistant attorney general for Civil Rights, for instance, noted the "thousands of letters" received by the White House and the Justice Department in the first year of the administration. See Drew S. Days III, Assistant Attorney General, Civil Rights Division, Department of Justice, Speech Before the Alabama Black Lawyers Association, Birmingham, Ala., November 11, 1977, Staff Offices, Domestic Policy Staff, Civil Rights and Justice, Gutierrez, Human Rights through Institutionalized Persons, Box 22, Jimmy Carter Presidential Library, 3.

100. Drew S. Days III, 3–4.

101. William Raspberry, "The Human Rights of the Wilmington 10," with no citation information, Staff Offices, Domestic Policy Staff, Civil Rights and Justice, Gutierrez, Human Rights through Institutionalized Persons, Box 22, Jimmy Carter Presidential Library.

102. See Dumbrell, *The Carter Presidency,* 20; Schlesinger, "Human Rights and the American Tradition," 515–18.

103. See Gary Gerstle, *American Crucible: Race and Nation in the Twentieth Century* (Princeton, N.J.: Princeton University Press, 2001); Rogers M. Smith, *Civic Ideals: Conflicting Views of Citizenship in U.S. History* (New Haven, Conn.: Yale University Press, 1997).

Chapter 2

1. See, for example, Catherine Cassara, "U.S. Newspaper Coverage of Human Rights in Latin America, 1975–1982: Exploring President Carter's Agenda-Building Influence," *Journalism and Mass Communication Quarterly* 75:3 (Autumn 1998): 478, 481–2; Hahn and Gustainis, "Anatomy of an Enigma"; Ernst B. Haas, "Human Rights: To Act or Not to Act?" in Kenneth A. Oye, Donald Rothchild, and Robert J. Leiber, eds., *Eagle Entangled: U.S. Foreign Policy in a Complex World* (New York: Longman, 1979), 167–98.

2. John E. Reilly, ed., *American Public Opinion and Foreign Policy* (Chicago: Chicago Council on Foreign Relations, 1975, 1979).

3. Kane, "American Values or Human Rights?"

4. Donna Hoffman and Alison D. Howard, "Agendas, Rhetoric, and Social Change: State of the Union Addresses from Eisenhower to Clinton," Paper presented at the 2003 annual meeting of the Midwest Political Science Association, April 3–6, Chicago, Ill.

5. The Gallup Organization, *Attitudes of the American People Related to Foreign Policy,* Submitted to the Chicago Council on Foreign Relations, December 1998, 8.

6. Ibid., 10. See also, Ole R. Holsti, *Public Opinion and American Foreign Policy,* rev. ed. (Ann Arbor: University of Michigan Press, 2004), 92.

7. Holsti, *Public Opinion and American Foreign Policy,* 92, 170.

8. http://www.americans-world.ord/digest/global/_issues/human_rights/PromotingHR .cfm. Web site accessed March 14, 2006.

9. Ibid.

10. Anne E. Geyer and Robert Y. Shapiro, "The Polls—A Report," *Public Opinion Quarterly* 52 (1988): 386.

11. See, for example, Cassara, "U.S. Newspaper Coverage of Human Rights in Latin America," 478.

12. Anthony Lewis, "Raising a Standard," 6-23-77, Box 2: Hendrik Hertzberg Speech Files Jefferson-Jackson ENERGY, Des Moines Iowa, October 21, 1977 through Human Rights, 1977 [2], folder: Human Rights 1977 [1], Jimmy Carter Presidential Library.

13. *Newsweek,* June 22, 1977, "The Push for Human Rights," Box 2: Hendrik Hertzberg Speech Files Jefferson-Jackson ENERGY, Des Moines Iowa, October 21, 1977 through Human Rights, 1977 [2], folder: Human Rights 1977 [1], Jimmy Carter Presidential Library.

14. David Hawk, "Human Rights at Half-Time," *The New Republic,* April 7, 1979, no discernible page numbers, Hendrick Hertzberg Speech Files, Jefferson-Jackson. ENERGY, Des Moines, Iowa, October 21, 1977 through Human Rights, 1977 [2], Box 2, folder: Human Rights [2], Jimmy Carter Presidential Library.

15. Carter Presidential Papers–Staff Offices Ethnic Affairs, Aiello, Housing and Urban Devel-

opment [Research Reports] 10/79 through Human Rights J of Current Social Issues 6/78 [OA 9891], folder: Human Rights 5/78–6/80, Jimmy Carter Presidential Library.

16. ABC News, "Commentary," Tuesday, March 22, 1977, Box: First Lady's Staff Files, First Lady's Press Office, Speech Notes of Campaign 1976 through Governor's Dinner March 1, 1977, Box 1, Folder: Human Rights February–March 1977, Jimmy Carter Presidential Library.

17. Geyer and Shapiro, "The Polls—A Report," 387.

18. Cassara, "U.S. Newspaper Coverage of Human Rights in Latin America," 479.

19. Rowland Evans and Robert Novak, "Human Rights: Carter Blinked First," *Washington Post,* June 25, 1979, Carter Presidential Papers–Staff Offices, Ethnic Affairs, Aiello, Housing and Urban Development [Research Reports] 10/79 through Human Rights J of Current Social Issues 6/78 [OA 989] Box 29, Jimmy Carter Presidential Library.

20. See the media coverage of the Ginzburg and Scharansky trials, Carter Presidential Papers–Staff Offices Ethnic Affairs, Aiello, Housing and Urban Development [Research Reports] 10/79 through Human Rights J of Current Social Issues 6/78 [OA 9891], folder: Human Rights 5/78–6/80, Jimmy Carter Presidential Library.

21. See the News Summary prepared for Rick Hertzberg, H. Hertzberg Speech Files State of the Union January 1978 through Urban Policy March 27, 1978 [2], Box 3, folder: Drop by Meeting Commemorating 30th Anniversary of Declaration of Human Rights, 2/6/78 [1], Jimmy Carter Presidential Library.

22. Such criticism is cited in Edward Walsh, "Carter Asserts Human Rights is 'Soul' of Our Foreign Policy," *Washington Post* December 7, 1978; H. Hertzberg Speech Files. See also, AP, "Carter Softening Rights Posture, Packwood Says," A-16, Friday, July 15, 1977, [name of paper not available] H. Hertzberg Speech Files, Jefferson-Jackson. ENERGY, Des Moines, Iowa, October 21, 1977 through Human Rights, 1977 [2], Box 2, folder: Human Rights 1977 [1], Jimmy Carter Presidential Library.

23. Mark Rozell, *The Press and the Carter Presidency* (Boulder, Colo: Westview Press, 1989), 39.

24. Jeffrey E. Cohen, "Presidential Rhetoric and the Public Agenda," *American Journal of Political Science* 39 (1) (February 1995): 88.

25. This debate is grounded in research on the "rhetorical presidency." See, among numerous others, Roderick P. Hart, *The Sound of Leadership: Presidential Communication in the Modern Age* (Chicago: University of Chicago Press, 1987). Jeffrey Tulis, *The Rhetorical Presidency* (Princeton, N.J.: Princeton University Press, 1987); Samuel Kernell, *Going Public: New Strategies of Presidential Leadership* (Washington, D.C.: Congressional Quarterly Press, 1997).

26. See, for example, Hart, *The Sound of Leadership;* Kathleeen Hall Jamieson, *Eloquence in an Electronic Age: The Transformation of Political Speechmaking* (New York: Oxford University Press, 1988).

27. See, for instance, Martin J. Medhurst, "Introduction," in Martin J. Medhurst, ed., *Beyond the Rhetorical Presidency* (College Station: Texas A&M University Press, 1996).

28. Cohen, "Presidential Rhetoric and the Public Agenda," 87.

29. Ibid., 88

30. Cohen, *Presidential Responsiveness and Public Policy-making,* 21.

31. See Mary E. Stuckey, *Defining Americans: The Presidency and National Identity* (Lawrence: University Press of Kansas, 2004).

32. Kim Quaile Hill, "The Policy Agenda of the President and the Mass Public: A Research Validation and Extension," *American Journal of Political Science* 42 (1998): 1328–34.

33. See Dietram A. Scheufele, "Agenda-Setting, Priming, and Framing Revisited: Another Look at Cognitive Effects of Political Communication," *Mass Communication and Society* 3 (2000): 300.

34. Erving Goffman, *Frame Analysis: An Essay on the Organization of Experience* (New York: Harper and Row, 1974); Shanto Iyengar *Is Anyone Responsible? How Television Frames Political Issues* (Chicago: University of Chicago Press, 1991); Scheufele, "Agenda-Setting, Priming, and Framing Revisited," 300–301.

35. Robert M. Entman, "Framing: Toward Clarification of a Fractured Paradigm," *Journal of Communication* 43 (1993): 51–58.

36. Shanto Iyengar and Donald R. Kinder, *News that Matters* (Chicago: University of Chicago Press, 1987).

37. See Maxwell McCombs and Donald E. Shaw, "The Agenda Setting Function of Mass Media," *Public Opinion Quarterly* 36 (1972): 176–87.

38. James. W. Dearing and Everett. M. Rogers, *Communication Concepts 6: Agenda Setting* (Thousand Oaks, Calif: Sage, 1996).

39. See, for example, Shanto Iyengar and Adam Simon, "News Coverage of the Gulf Crisis and Public Opinion: A Study of Agenda-Setting, Priming, and Framing," *Communication Research* 20 (1993): 365–83.

40. Todd M. Schaefer, "Persuading the Persuaders: Presidential Speeches and the Editorial Opinion," *Political Communication* 14 (1997): 97–111.

41. For work on presidents as reactive to media agendas, see Sheldon Gilberg, Chaim Eyal, Maxwell McCombs, and David Nichols, "The State of the Union and the Press Agenda," *Journalism Quarterly* 57 (1980), 584–88; B. Dan Wood and Jeffrey S. Peake, "The Dynamics of Foreign Policy Agenda Setting" *American Political Science Review* 92 (1998): 173–84.

42. Lawrence R. Jacobs and Robert Y. Shapiro, *Politicians Don't Pander: Political Manipulation and the Loss of Democratic Responsiveness* (Chicago: University of Chicago Press, 2000).

43. See, for example Reed I. Welch, "Presidential Success in Communicating with the Public through Televised Addresses," *Presidential Studies Quarterly* 33 (2003): 347–65.

44. Jeffrey S. Peake, "Presidential Agenda Setting in Foreign Policy," *Political Research Quarterly* 54 (2001): 69–86.

45. Robert M. Entman, "Cascading Activation: Contesting the White House's Frame after 9/11," *Political Communication* 20 (2003): 415–32.

46. Entman, "Framing: Toward Clarification of a Fractured Paradigm," 52.

47. Mary E. Stuckey, *The President as Interpreter-in-Chief* (Chatham, Mass.: Chatham Press, 1999).

48. Donna Hoffman and Alison D. Howard, "Agendas, Rhetoric, and Social Change: State of the Union Addresses from Eisenhower to Clinton."

49. Cohen, *Presidential Responsiveness and Public Policy-making,* 32.

50. Karen Callaghan and Frauke Schnell, "Introduction: Framing Political Issues in American Politics," in Karen Callaghan and Frauke Schnell, eds., *Framing American Politics* (Pittsburgh, Pa.: University of Pittsburgh Press, 2005), 2.

51. See, for instance, Michael X. Delli Carpini, "News From Somewhere: Journalistic Frames and the Debate Over 'Public Journalism,'" in Karen Callaghan and Frauke Schnell, eds., *Framing American Politics* (Pittsburgh, Penn: University of Pittsburgh Press, 2005), 24; T. E. Nelson and Z. M. Oxley, "Framing Effects on Belief Importance and Opinion," *Journal of Politics* 61 (4) (1999): 1040–67; Thomas E. Nelson, Rosalee A. Clawson and Zoe M. Oxley, "Media Framing of a Civil Liberties Conflict and Its Effect on Tolerance," *The American Political Science Review* 91 (1997): 567–83.

52. Callaghan and Schnell, "Introduction," 6.

53. See, for instance, John R. Zaller, *The Nature and Origins of Mass Opinion* (Cambridge: Cambridge University Press, 1992).

54. Paul M. Sniderman and Sean M. Theriault, "The Structure of Political Argument and the Logic of Issue Framing," in William E. Saris and Paul M. Sniderman, eds., *Studies in Public Opinion: Attitudes, Nonattitudes, Measurement Error, and Change* (Princeton, N.J.: Princeton University Press, 2004), 148.

55. See Stuckey, *The President as Interpreter-in-Chief.*

56. James N. Druckman, "On the Limits of Framing Effects: Who Can Frame?" *Journal of Politics* 63 (November 2001): 1043. See also, Callaghan and Schnell, "Introduction," 14; Nelson and Oxley, 1999; Nelson, et al., "Media Framing of a Civil Liberties Conflict and Its Effect on Tolerance."

57. Donald R. Kinder and Thomas E. Nelson, "Democratic Debate and Real Opinions," in Callaghan and Schnell, eds., *Framing American Politics,* 103. See also, Entman, "Framing: Toward Clarification of a Fractured Paradigm," 53.

58. Entman, "Framing: Toward Clarification of a Fractured Paradigm," 54.

59. See Druckman, "On the Limits of Framing Effects: Who Can Frame?" 1045.

60. Teena Gabrielson, "Obstacles and Opportunities: Factors that Constrain Elected Officials' Ability to Frame Political Issues," in Callaghan and Schnell, *Framing American Politics,* 77.

61. Schaefer, "Persuading the Persuaders"; Wood and Peake, "The Dynamics of Foreign Policy Agenda Setting."

62. Hill, "The Policy Agenda of the President and the Mass Public."

63. As Entman notes, because frames rely on individual schemata, "the presence of frames in the text, as detected by researchers, does not guarantee their influence in audience thinking." Entman, "Framing: Toward Clarification of a Fractured Paradigm," 53.

64. Kinder and Nelson, "Democratic Debate and Real Opinions," 111.

65. See David Zarefsky, *President Johnson's War on Poverty: Rhetoric and History* (Tuscaloosa: University of Alabama Press, 2005). For work on metaphor and politics, see Francis A. Beer and Christ'l de Landtsheer, *Metaphorical World Politics* (East Lansing: Michigan State University Press, 2004).

66. See, for example, Robert M. Entman, "Framing U.S. Coverage of International News: Contrasts in Narratives of the KAL and Iran Air Incidents," *Journal of Communication* 41 (1991): 6–26.

67. See, for instance, Doris A. Graber, *Processing the News: How People Tame the Information Tide,* 2nd ed. (New York: Longman, 1988); Marion R. Just, Ann N. Crigler, Dean E. Alger and Timothy E. Cook, *Crosstalk: Citizens, Candidates, and the Media in a Presidential Campaign* (Chicago: University of Chicago Press, 1996); W. Russell Newman, Marion R. Just, and Ann N. Crigler, *Common Knowledge: News and the Construction of Political Meaning* (Chicago: University of Chicago Press, 1992).

68. Donald R. Kinder and Lynn M. Sanders, *Divided by Color: Racial Politics and Democratic Ideals* (Chicago: University of Chicago Press, 1996); William A. Gamson, *Talking Politics* (New York: Cambridge University Press, 1992); William A. Gamson and Andre Modigliani, "The Changing Culture of Affirmative Action," *Research in Political Sociology* 3 (1987): 137–77; William A. Gamson and Andre Modigliani, "Media Discourse and Public Opinion on Nuclear Power: A Constructionist Approach," *American Journal of Sociology* 95 (1989): 1–37; Amos Tversky and Daniel Kahneman, "The Framing of Decisions and the Psychology of Choice," *Science* 211 (1981): 453–58; Iyengar, *Is Anyone Responsible?*

69. Gabrielson, "Obstacles and Opportunities," 83. See also Zaller, *The Nature and Origins of Mass Opinion;* John R. Zaller, "The Myth of Massive Media Impact Revised: New Support for a Discredited Idea," in Diana C. Mutz, Paul Sniderman, and Richard A. Brody, eds., *Political Persuasion and Attitude Change* (Ann Arbor: University of Michigan Press, 1996).

70. Callaghan and Schnell, "Introduction," 14.

71. Paul M. Sniderman and Sean M. Theriault, "The Structure of Political Argument and the Logic of Issue Framing," in Saris and Sniderman, *Studies in Public Opinion,* 142.

72. Joanne M. Miller and Jon A. Krosnick, "News Media Impact on the Ingredients of

Presidential Evaluations: Politically Knowledgeable Citizens Are Guided by a Trusted Source," *American Journal of Political Science* 44 (2000): 301.

73. See Dana Milbank and Claudia Deane, "Poll Finds Dimmer View of Iraq War; 52% Say U.S. Has Not Become Safer," *Washington Post Online,* http://www.washingtonpost.com/wp-dyn/content/article/2005/06/07/AR2005060700296.html. Website accessed December 15, 2007.

74. James N. Druckman and Justin W. Holmes, "Does Presidential Rhetoric Matter? Priming and Presidential Approval," *Presidential Studies Quarterly* 34 (2004): 755–78.

75. See George C. Edwards III and Alec M. Gallup, *Presidential Approval: A Sourcebook* (Baltimore: Johns Hopkins University Press, 1990); J. Michael Hogan, "The Rhetoric of Presidential Approval," in Robert E. Denton and Rachel L. Holloway, eds., *Images, Scandal, and Communication Strategies of the Clinton Presidency* (Westport, Conn: Praeger, 2003), 271–298; Kathleen A. Frankovic, "Public Opinion and Polling," in Doris A. Graber, Denis McQuail, and Pippa Norris, eds., *The Politics of News and the News of Politics* (Washington D.C.: Congressional Quarterly Press, 1998), 150–70.

76. Gabrielson, "Obstacles and Opportunities," 86.

77. On agenda setting, see Iyengar and Kinder, *News that Matters;* Shanto Iyengar, Donald R. Kinder, Mark D. Peters, and Jon A. Krosnick, "The Evening News and Presidential Evaluations," *Journal of Personality and Social Psychology* 46 (1984): 778–87; Michael B. MacKuen, "Social Communication and the Mass Policy Agenda," in Michael B. MacKuen and Steven L. Coombs, eds., *More than News Media Power in Public Affairs* (Thousand Oaks, Calif: Sage, 1981), 19–44; Maxwell McCombs, "The Agenda-Setting Approach," in Dan Nimmo and Keith R. Sanders, eds., *Handbook of Political Communication* (Beverly Hills, Calif: Sage, 1981), 121–40; On priming, see Iyengar and Kinder, *News that Matters;* Jon A. Krosnick and Laura Brannon, "The Impact of the Gulf War on the Ingredients of Presidential Evaluations: Mulitdimensional Effects of Political Involvement," *American Political Science Review* 87 (1993): 963–75; Jon A. Krosnick and Donal E. Kinder, "Altering the Foundations of Support for the President Through Priming," *American Political Science Review* 84 (1990): 497–512.

78. Teena Gabrielson, "Obstacles and Opportunities," 83. See also Zaller, *The Nature and Origins of Mass Opinion;* Zaller, "The Myth of Massive Media Impact Revised."

79. Tulis, *The Rhetorical Presidency.* There is considerable debate on the merits and limitations of the rhetorical presidency as a model. See among others, Matthew A. Bodnick, "'Going Public' Reconsidered: Reagan's 1981 Tax and Budget Cuts, and Revisionist Theories of Presidential Power," *Congress and the Presidency* 17 (1990), 13–29; Matthew Corrigan, "The Transformation of Going Public: President Clinton, the First Lady, and Health Care Reform," *Political Communication* 17 (2000), 149–69; George C. Edwards III, *At the Margins: Presidential Leadership of Congress* (New Haven

Conn.: Yale University Press, 1989); Edwards, *On Deaf Ears;* Hart, *The Sound of Leadership.*

80. Kernell, *Going Public.*

81. There is also good evidence that these attempts at presidential persuasion go back much further in history than Tulis and Kernell consider, although the means of persuasion varied. Rather than addressing the people directly, for instance, presidents used partisan newspapers and other means. See Richard J. Ellis, ed., *Speaking to the People: The Rhetorical Presidency in Historical Perspective* (Amherst: University of Massachusetts Press, 1998); Karen S. Hoffman, "Going Public in the Nineteenth Century: Grover Cleveland's Repeal of the Sherman Silver Purchase Act," *Rhetoric and Public Affairs* 5 (2002), 57–77; Mel Laracey, *Presidents and the People: The Partisan Story of Going Public* (College Station: Texas A&M University Press, 2002).

82. For a thorough and insightful discussion of these issues, see J. Michael Hogan, George C. Edwards III, Wynton C. Hall, Christine L. Harold, Gerard A. Hauser, Susan Herbst, Robert Y. Shapiro, and Ted J. Smith III, "National Task Force Report: The Presidency and Public Opinion," in Martin Medhurst and James A. Aune, eds. (College Station: Texas A&M University Press, 1988), 293–316.

83. Brandon Rottinghaus, "Measure of the Mind of the Public: Patterns of Presidential Rhetoric and Public Opinion from Dwight Eisenhower to Bill Clinton," PhD diss., Northwestern University, 2005, 178.

84. Ibid., 148.

85. See among many others, Joel D. Aberbach and Bert A. Rockman, "Hard Times for Presidential Leadership? (And How Would We Know?)" *Presidential Studies Quarterly* 29 (1999): 757–778; Bruce E. Altschuler, *Keeping a Finger on the Public Pulse: Private Polling and Presidential Elections* (Westport, Conn: Greenwood, 1982); Paul Brace and Barbara Hinckley, *Follow the Leader: Public Opinion Polls and the Modern Presidents* ((New York: Harper Collins, 1992); Richard Brody, *Assessing the President: The Media, Elite Opinion, and Public Support* (Palo Alto, Calif.: Stanford University Press, 1991); Cohen, *Presidential Responsiveness and Public Policy-making;* Michael X. Delli Carpini and Scott Keeter, *What Americans Know About Politics and Why it Matters* (New Haven, Conn.: Yale University Press, 1996); George C. Edwards III, *The Public Presidency: The Pursuit of Popular Support* (New York: St. Martin's Press, 1983); John G. Geer, *From Tea Leaves to Opinion Polls: A Theory of Democratic Leadership* (New York: Columbia University Press, 1996); Diane J. Heith, *Polling to Govern* (Palo Alto, Calif.: Stanford University Press, 2004); Susan Herbst, *Numbered Voices: How Opinion Polling Has Shaped American Politics* (Chicago: University of Chicago Press, 1993); Justin Lewis, *Constructing Public Opinion: How Political Elites Do What They Like and Why We Seem to Go Along With It* (New York: Columbia University Press, 2001); Michael J. Towle, *Out of Touch: The Presidency and Public Opinion* (College Station: Texas A&M University Press, 2004).

86. Edwards has been a prolific author on this subject. See, most prominently, George C. Edwards III, *At the Margins: Presidential Leadership of Congress* (New Haven Conn.: Yale University Press, 1989); Edwards, *On Deaf Ears*.

87. Matthew Eshbaugh-Soha, *The President's Speeches: Beyond "Going Public"* (Boulder, Colo: Lynne Rienner Publishers, 2006).

88. Ibid., 7.

89. For an excellent review of this debate, see Robert Y. Shapiro, "Public Opinion, Elites, and Democracy," *Critical Review* 12 (1998): 501–28.

90. See, for instance, John R. Hibbing and Elizabeth Theiss-Morse, eds., *What is About Government that Americans Dislike?* (Cambridge: Cambridge University Press, 2001).

91. Eshbaugh-Soha, *The President's Speeches: Beyond "Going Public,"* (Boulder, Colo.: Lynne Rienner Publishers, 2006), 15.

92. See, for example. Philip E. Converse, "The Nature of Belief Systems in Mass Publics," in D. E. Apter, ed., *Ideology and Discontent* (New York: Free Press of Glencoe, 1964), 206–61; Philip E. Converse, "Attitudes and Nonattitudes: Continuation of a Dialogue," in Edward R. Tufte, ed., *The Quantitative Analysis of Social Problems* (Reading, Mass: Addison-Wesley, 1975), 168–89; Philip E. Converse, "Public Opinion and Voting Behavior," in Nelson W. Polsby, ed., *Handbook of Political Science,* vol 4 (Reading, Mass: Addison-Wesley, 1975), 75–169; Philip E. Converse, "Nonattitudes and American Public Opinion: Comment: The Status of Nonattitudes," *American Political Science Review* 68 (1974): 650–60.

93. This research began with Angus Campbell, Philip E. Converse, Warren E. Miller and Donald E. Stokes, *The American Voter* (New York: Wiley, 1960). Other important contributions to this stream of research include Norman H. Nie, Sidney Verba, and John R. Petrocik, *The Changing American Voter,* enlarged ed. (Cambridge, Mass: Harvard University Press, 1979); Samuel L. Popkin, *The Reasoning Voter: Communication and Persuasion in Presidential Campaigns* (Chicago: University of Chicago Press, 1992); Benjamin I. Page and Robert Y. Shapiro, *The Rational Public: Fifty Years of Trends in Americans' Policy Preferences* (Chicago: University of Chicago Press, 1992); Warren E. Miller and J. Merrilll Shanks, *The New American Voter* (Cambridge, Mass: Harvard University Press, 1996).

94. See especially Converse, "Nonattitudes and American Public Opinion."

95. "Nonattitudes" are found when the public responds to survey questions on invented issues as if they were real. They are used as evidence of public ignorance regarding politics. See, among many others, George D. Bishop, David L. Hamilton, and John B. McConahay, "Attitudes and Nonattitudes in the Belief Systems of Mass Publics," *The Journal of Social Psychology* 110 (1980): 53–64; Converse, "The Nature of Belief Systems in Mass Publics"; Converse, "Attitudes and Nonattitudes"; Converse, "Public Opinion and Voting Behavior"; Converse, "Nonattitudes and American Public Opinion"; Marcia Franze, "Nonattitudes/Pseudo Opinions: Definitional Problems,

Critical Variables, Cognitive Components, and Solutions," C/D Extended Essay, Department of Human Work Sciences, Division of Engineering Psychology, Lulea University of Technology, 2001; Helmut Norpoth and Milton Lodge, "The Difference Between Attitudes and Nonattitudes in the Mass Public: Just Measurements?" *American Journal of Political Science* 29 (1985): 291–307; John C. Pierce and Douglas D. Rose, "Nonattitudes and American Public Opinion: The Examination of a Thesis," *The American Political Science Review* 68 (1974): 626–49; Douglas D. Rose and John C. Pierce, "Nonattitudes and American Public Opinion: Rejoinder to 'Comment' by Philip E. Converse," *The American Political Science Review* 68 (1974): 661–66; Howard Schuman and Stanley Presser, "Public Opinion and Public Ignorance: The Fine Line Between Attitudes and Nonattitudes," *The American Journal of Sociology* 85 (1980): 1214–25.

96. Zaller, *The Nature and Origins of Mass Opinion.*

97. Ibid.

98. See Shapiro, "Public Opinion, Elites, and Democracy," 512.

99. For a thorough review of the work on framing, see Druckman, "On the Limits of Framing Effects: Who Can Frame?"

100. I am indebted to Denise Bostdorff for highlighting and providing language for this argument.

101. In one example of Carter's importance to international attention to human rights, in the International League for Human Rights, "Report on the Conference on Implementing a Human Rights Commitment in United States Foreign Policy" March 4, 1977, 3, they claimed that "The President's leadership is regarded by the members of the Conference as a vital factor in advancing human rights." Office of the Public Liaison, Costanza, Earthquakes, 4/77 [O/A 5771] through [Gay Rights & Vice Mayor Costanza of Rochester NY] 1/76–8/76 [O/A 5771] Box 4, folder: Foreign Policy & Human Rights 1/77–3/77 [O/A 5772], Jimmy Carter Presidential Library. An example of local attention includes the resolution by a New Jersey township council on the statute of limitations on Nazi war crimes, brought to the president's attention as a human rights issue (see letter from Eva M. Worrick, Township Clerk, Township of Cherry Hill, N.J., dated Jan 15, 1979, Carter Presidential Papers, Staff Offices: Cabinet Secretary and Intergovernmental Affairs, Hispanics through Insurance, Box 35, Human Rights folder, Jimmy Carter Presidential Library). That folder is full of letters asking Carter to intercede on behalf of dissidents in the Ukraine, in Northern Ireland, in Columbia, asking him to prevent the teaching of Mao in Madagascar schools, to protect Jehovah's Witnesses in Argentina, asking him to intervene in favor of specific families trying to emigrate from the Soviet Union, Turkey's action vis-à-vis Cyprus—all under the rubric of his human rights policy.

102. Geyer and Shapiro, "The Polls—A Report," 387.

Chapter 3

1. This may be a controversial claim, as many scholars argue that individual factors are determinative. See, for example, Fred I. Greenstein, *The Presidential Difference: Leadership Style From FDR to George W. Bush* (Princeton, N.J.: Princeton University Press, 2004).

2. Richard M. Weaver, *The Ethics of Rhetoric* (Davis, Calif.: Hermagoras Press, 1985).

3. Jimmy Carter, "Address to the Nation on the State of the Union," January 19, 1978, *Public Papers of the Presidents, Jimmy Carter* (Washington, D.C.: U.S. Government Printing Office), 95.

4. For information on the Church Commission, see L. K. Johnson, "Congressional Supervision of America's Secret Agencies: The Experience and Legacy of the Church Commission," *Public Administration Review* 64 (2004): 3–14.

5. Kaufman, *The Presidency of James Earl Carter, Jr.*, 15; Lincoln Bloomfield, "The Carter Human Rights Policy: A Provisional Appraisal," January 11, 1981, 13, Donated Historical Material—Brzezinski, Box 34, Jimmy Carter Presidential Library, 1.

6. Kaufman, *The Presidency of James Earl Carter, Jr.*, 15.

7. Jon H. Patton, "A Government as Good as its People: Jimmy Carter and the Restoration of Transcendence to Politics," *Quarterly Journal of Speech* 65 (1977): 249–57.

8. Carter, "Address at Commencement Exercises at the University of Notre Dame," May 22, 1977, *Public Papers*, 957.

9. Carter, "Interview with the President: Remarks and a Question-and-Answer Session with a Group of Publishers, Editors, and Broadcasters," May 27, 1977, *Public Papers*, 946. See also, Jimmy Carter, "Question-and-Answer Session with Reporters on Air Force One en Route to the United States," January 6, 1978, *Public Papers*, 41, 42, 47; Jimmy Carter, "Interview with the President: Remarks and a Question-and-Answer Session with Members of the American Society of Magazine Editors," August 11, 1978, *Public Papers*, 1410.

10. See, for instance, Christopher Brady, *United States Foreign Policy Toward Cambodia, 1977–92: A Question of Realities* (New York: MacMillan, 1999), 13.

11. Carter, "Inaugural Address," January 20, 1977, *Public Papers*, 2.

12. Carter, "Remarks at a 'Get Out the Vote,' Rally," Duluth, Minnesota, November 3, 1978, *Public Papers*, 1951.

13. Carter, "Address to the Nation on the State of the Union," January 19, 1978, *Public Papers*, 90.

14. For a detailed analysis of this point, see Stuckey, *Defining Americans*.

15. Carter, "Address Delivered Before a Joint Session of the Congress on The State of the Union," January 19, 1978, *Public Papers*, 95.

16. Carter, "Address at the Commencement Exercises of the United States Naval Academy," June 7, 1978, *Public Papers*, 1056.

17. Carter, "Question-and-Answer Session with European News Journalists," April 25, 1977, *Public Papers,* 782. See also Jimmy Carter, "The President's News Conference," December 15, 1977, *Public Papers,* 2116; Jimmy Carter, "The President's News Conference," Brasilia, Brazil, March 30, 1978, *Public Papers,* 629.

18. Carter, "Remarks at the Hibernian Society Dinner," Savannah, Georgia, March 17, 1978, *Public Papers,* 542. See also, "Remarks at a State Democratic Party Fundraising Dinner," Bedford, New Hampshire, April 25, 1979, *Public Papers,* 720.

19. Carter, *Keeping Faith,* 145.

20. See, for instance, the discussion of foreign policy in Kaufman, *The Presidency of James Earl Carter, Jr.,* 38–40.

21. Carter, "Remarks to the National Association for the Advancement of Colored People," July 4, 1980, *Public Papers,* 1322.

22. Carter, "Address at Commencement Exercises at the University of Notre Dame," May 22, 1977, *Public Papers,* 957.

23. See, for example, Carter, "Remarks at the Annual Convention of the American Legion," Boston, Massachusetts, August 21, 1980, *Public Papers,* 1551.

24. Carter, "Remarks at the 31st Annual Meeting of the Southern Legislative Conference," Charleston, South Carolina, July 21, 1977, *Public Papers,* 1310. He maintained this claim to morality and unselfishness in even his responses to the Iranian hostage crisis. See Carter, "Remarks at the 13th Constitutional Convention of the American Federation of Labor and the Congress of Industrial Organizations," November 13, 1979, *Public Papers,* 2126.

25. Carter, "Inaugural Address," January 20, 1977, *Public Papers,* 3.

26. Carter, "Remarks and a Question-and-Answer Session in a Townhall Meeting," Flint Michigan, October 1, 1980, *Public Papers,* 1995.

27. Carter, "Remarks to Members of the Southern Baptist Brotherhood Commission," Atlanta, Georgia, June 16, 1978, *Public Papers,* 1117.

28. Carter, "Farewell Address to the Nation," January 14, 1981, *Public Papers,* 2890.

29. See, among many others, Druckman, "Limits of Framing Effects," 1061; Nelson, et al., "Media Framing of a Civil Liberties Conflict and Its Effect on Tolerance."

30. On the potential of human rights to unite the Democrats, see John Dumbrell, *American Foreign Policy: Carter to Clinton* (New York: St. Martin's Press, 1997), 17. On the importance of national fragmentation, see Miller Center Interview with Hamilton Jordan (with Landon Butler, Thomas Donilon), final edited transcript, November 6, 1981, Jimmy Carter Presidential Library.

31. See Erickson, "Jimmy Carter: The Rhetoric of Private and Civic Piety"; Kaufman, *The Presidency of James Earl Carter, Jr.,* 12–16; Bruce Mazlish and Edwin Diamond, *Jimmy Carter: A Character Portrait* (New York: Simon & Schuster, 1979), 216.

32. Erickson, "Jimmy Carter: The Rhetoric of Private and Civic Piety."

33. Kaufman, *The Presidency of James Earl Carter, Jr.,* 10.

34. Ibid., 38.

35. Miller Center Interview with Jimmy Carter, Jimmy Carter Presidential Library, November 29, 1982, 70.

36. As two of his top aides (Brzezinski and Rafshoon) wrote to the president, "With the possible exception of peace in the Middle East, no aspect of your foreign policy is more popular or more widely known than human rights." Memo from Brzezinski and Rafshoon to JC; December 4, 1978, Subject: Human Rights Speech, H. Hertzberg Speech Files State of the Union, January 1978 through Urban Policy, March 27, 1978 [2], Box 3, folder: Drop by meeting commemorating 30th anniversary of declaration of human rights, 2/6/78 [1], Jimmy Carter Presidential Library.

37. Carter, "Inaugural Address," *Public Papers,* 2.

38. Ruechel, "The Articulation and Synthesis of Jimmy Carter's Human Rights Policy," 136

39. Zbigniew Brzezinski, *Power and Principle: Memoirs of the National Security Advisor, 1977–1981* (New York: Farrar, Straus, Giroux, 1983), 48.

40. See, for instance, Peter G. Bourne, *Jimmy Carter: A Comprehensive Biography From Plains to the Presidency* (New York: Scribner, 1997), 383.

41. He continues to do so. See Jimmy Carter, *Our Endangered Values: America's Moral Crisis* (New York: Simon and Schuster, 2005), 8.

42. Carter, "Remarks at a Campaign Rally at Spring Park," Tuscumbia, Alabama, September 1, 1980, *Public Papers,* 1602.

43. Here, of course, he followed in the rhetorical footsteps of Lyndon Johnson.

44. Carter, *Keeping Faith,* 142.

45. See Niels C. Neilson Jr., *The Religion of President Carter* (Nashville, Tenn: Thomas Nelson, Inc., 1977), 91.

46. Carter, "The President's Press Conference," Warsaw, Poland, December 30, 1977, *Public Papers,* 2207.

47. Carter, "Remarks and a Question-and-Answer Session with New Hampshire High School Students," Nashua, New Hampshire, February 18, 1978, *Public Papers,* 370.

48. Carter, "Remarks to Members of the Southern Baptist Brotherhood Commission," Atlanta, Georgia, June 16, 1978, *Public Papers,* 1115.

49. Ibid.

50. Carter, "Interview with Correspondents of WPIV-TV," Philadelphia, Pennsylvania, September 3, 1980, *Public Papers,* 1642.

51. Carter, "Interview with European Broadcast Journalists," May 2, 1977, *Public Papers,* 766.

52. Carter, "The President's News Conference," October 27, 1977, *Public Papers,* 1908–16, 1913.

53. Ibid.

54. Carter, "Remarks at the Meeting of the General Council of the World Jewish Congress," November 2, 1977, *Public Papers,* 1954.

55. Carter, "Address at Commencement Exercises at the University of Notre Dame," May 22, 1977, *Public Papers,* 955.

56. Carter, "Remarks at the Meeting of the General Council of the World Jewish Congress," November 2, 1977, *Public Papers,* 1953.

57. Carter, "Remarks to the National Association for the Advancement of Colored People," July 4, 1980, *Public Papers,* 1322.

58. Carter, "Question-and Answer Session with European Journalists," May 2, 1977, *Public Papers,* 765–66. See also, Carter, "Interview with the President: Remarks and a Question-and-Answer Session with American Press Institute Editors," January 27, 1978, *Public Papers,* 237; Carter, "Remarks at a State Democratic Party Reception," Columbus, Ohio, September 23, 1978, *Public Papers,* 1624.

59. For an example of how he used his own history as president to bolster claims to authority on human rights, see Carter, "Remarks at the 10th Regular Session of the General Assembly of the Organization of American States," November 19, 1980, *Public Papers,* 2734.

60. Ibid., 2735.

61. He made a similar argument after leaving office, arguing in his presidential memoirs that, "As President, I hoped and believed that the expansion of human rights might be the wave of the future throughout the world, and I wanted the United States to be at the crest of this movement." See Carter, *Keeping Faith,* 144.

62. Lincoln Bloomfield, "The Carter Human Rights Policy," January 11, 1981, 13, Donated Historical Material—Brzezinski, Box 34, Jimmy Carter Presidential Library, 7.

63. Brzezinski, *Power and Principle,* 124, 49.

64. Carter, "The President's News Conference," December 15, 1977, *Public Papers,* 2115.

65. Carter, "Remarks at the Food and Commercial Workers International Union Founding Convention," June 7, 1979, *Public Papers,* 1009.

66. See, for example, Warren Christopher, "The Diplomacy of Human Rights: The First Year," Speech Before the American Bar Association, February 13, 1978; Patricia M. Derian, "Human Rights: The Role of Law and Lawyers," Speech Before the Lawyer's Committee for Civil Rights Under Law, Division V of the D.C. Bar Assn, March 16, 1978; Mark L. Schneider, "Human Rights Policy Review" Speech Before the House Subcommittee on International Organizations, Oct 25, 1977. Copies of all these speeches are available in Carter Presidential Papers–Staff Offices Ethnic Affairs, Aiello, Housing and Urban Development [Research Reports] 10/79 through Human Rights J of Current Social Issues 6/78 [OA 9891], folder: Human Rights 3/77–6/80, Jimmy Carter Presidential Library.

67. Cyrus R. Vance, "Human Rights Policy" Speech on Law Day at University of Georgia Law School, April 30, 1977, Carter Presidential Papers–Staff Offices Ethnic Affairs, Aiello, Housing and Urban Development [Research Reports] 10/79 through Human

Rights J of Current Social Issues 6/78 [OA 9891], folder: Human Rights 3/77–6/80, Jimmy Carter Presidential Library.

68. For examples of such criticism, see Johnson, *Blowback;* Ruechel, "The Articulation and Synthesis of Jimmy Carter's Human Rights Policy," 24.

69. Carter, "The President's New Conference," July 20, 1978, *Public Papers,* 1325.

70. See Rozell, *The Press and the Carter Presidency,* 39.

71. For discussion of Andrew Young, see Kaufman, *The Presidency of James Earl Carter, Jr.,* 66.

72. The evidence is that they did. See Lincoln Bloomfield, "The Carter Human Rights Policy: A Provisional Appraisal," January 11, 1981, 13, Donated Historical Material—Brzezinski, Box 34, Jimmy Carter Presidential Library, 1; Brzezinski, *Power and Principle,* 49, 124, 129; John H. Patton, "The Concept of Human Rights in the Rhetoric of President Carter and his Administration: A Study of Form, Content, and Significance in Contemporary Political Ideology," in Human Rights Policy, 3/1/77–1/16/78, Staff Offices, Speechwriters Subject File, Human Rights Policy, 3/1/77–1/16/78 through Inflation Statement, 4/15/77, Box 12, Jimmy Carter Presidential Library.

73. Carter, "Remarks at a Democratic National Committee Fundraising Dinner," Los Angeles, California, October 22, 1977, *Public Papers,* 1895–96.

74. Carter, "Remarks at the 1978 Cook County Democratic Dinner," May 25, 1978, *Public Papers,* 986.

75. Carter, "Remarks at a Fundraising Dinner for the Democratic National Committee, September 26, 1979," *Public Papers,* 1769.

76. Carter, "Remarks at a Democratic Party Rally for John Ingram," Wilson, North Carolina, August 5, 1978, *Public Papers,* 1389. See also, Jimmy Carter, "Remarks at a Fundraising Dinner," Democratic National Committee, September 27, 1978, *Public Papers,* 1646.

77. Carter, "Remarks at a Democratic Committee Fundraising Dinner," Hollywood, Florida, July 17, 1980, *Public Papers,* 1364–65.

78. Carter, "Address at the Commencement Exercises at the University of Notre Dame," May 22, 1977, *Public Papers,* 958. For other examples of arguments that human rights were crucial to the American founding, see Carter, "The President's News Conference," December 15, 1977, *Public Papers,* 2115.

79. Carter, "Address at the Commencement Exercises at the University of Notre Dame," *Public Papers,* 961–62.

80. Carter, "Address Before a Joint Session of Congress on the State of the Union," January 23, 1979, *Public Papers,* 108.

81. Carter, "Address at Commencement Exercises at the University of Notre Dame," *Public Papers,* 956.

82. H. Hertzberg Speech Files State of the Union, January 1978 through Urban Policy,

March 27, 1978 [2], Box 3, folder: Drop by meeting commemorating 30th anniversary of declaration of human rights, 2/6/78 [1], Jimmy Carter Presidential Library. In the same folder, see also Edward Walsh, "Carter Asserts Human Rights Is 'Soul of Our Foreign Policy,'" *Washington Post,* December 7, 1978, no page number. The folder contains ample evidence that there was wide coverage of the speech.

83. Carter, "Remarks at a Democratic Party Rally for John Ingram," Wilson, North Carolina, August 5, 1978, *Public Papers,* 1389.

84. "B'nai B'rith speech draft"; draft dated Sept 1–2; speech file dated 9/1/76, Jimmy Carter Papers, Pre-Presidential, 1976 Presidential Campaign Issues Office, Stuart Eizenstat, Arms Control, 2/76–9/76 through Campaign Planning and Strategy, 6/76–11/76 Box 2, folder: B'nai B'rith Speech, 9/1/76, Jimmy Carter Presidential Library.

85. Carter, "B'nai B'rith speech draft"; draft dated Sept 1–2; speech file dated 9/1/76; Jimmy Carter Papers, Pre-Presidential, 1976 Presidential Campaign Issues Office, Stuart Eizenstat, Arms Control, 2/76–9/76 through Campaign Planning and Strategy, 6/76–11/76 Box 2, folder: B'nai B'rith Speech, Jimmy Carter Presidential Library, 9/1/76, 10.

86. Carter, "Remarks at a Democratic Party Rally for John Ingram," Wilson, North Carolina, August 5, 1978, *Public Papers,* 1389. See also, Carter, "Remarks at a State Democratic Party Reception," Columbus, Ohio, September 23, 1978, *Public Papers,* 1623; Carter, "Remarks at a Fundraising Dinner," Democratic National Committee, September 27, 1978, *Public Papers,* 1648; Carter, "Remarks at the Greater Buffalo International Airport," Buffalo, New York, October 28, 1978, *Public Papers,* 1887.

87. Carter, "Inaugural Address," *Public Papers,* 2.

88. Carter, "Remarks at the Food and Commercial Workers International Union Founding Convention," June 7, 1979, *Public Papers,* 1011.

89. Carter, "Remarks at a Democratic Committee Fundraising Dinner," Hollywood, Florida, July 17, 1980, *Public Papers,* 1364.

90. Carter, "Address Before a Joint Session of the Congress on the State of the Union," January 23, 1980, *Public Papers,* 200.

91. Carter, "The President's News Conference," March 19, 1977, *Public Papers,* 346.

92. Carter, "Remarks and a Question-and-Answer Session at the Clinton Town Meeting," Clinton, Massachusetts, March 16, 1977, *Public Papers,* 385.

93. Ibid., 386; see also, Carter, "Remarks at the 31st Annual Meeting of the Southern Legislative Conference," Charleston, South Carolina, July 21, 1977, *Public Papers,* 1310.

94. See, for example, Carter, "Remarks at a Rally for Bill Ray and John Carlin," Wichita, Kansas, October 21, 1978, *Public Papers,* 1817.

95. Carter, "The President's News Conference," March 9, 1977, *Public Papers,* 341.

96. Carter, "Interview with the President: Remarks and a Question-and-Answer Session with a Group of Publishers, Editors, and Broadcasters," May 27, 1977, *Public Papers,* 947.

97. Carter, "Radio Address to the Nation on Foreign Policy," October 19, 1980, *Public Pa-*

pers, 2338–39; Carter, "Remarks Before the Brazilian Congress, Brasilia, Brazil," March 30, 1978, *Public Papers,* 636.

98. Carter, "The President's News Conference," October 27, 1977, *Public Papers,* 1915.

99. Carter, "Address at the Commencement Exercises, United States Naval Academy," June 7, 1978, 1055. See also, Carter, "Address Before a Joint Session of the Congress on the State of the Union," January 23, 1979, *Public Papers,* 106.

100. Carter, "Address Before the General Assembly of the United Nations," March 17, 1977, *Public Papers,* 450.

101. See Carter, "Address at Commencement Exercises at the University of Notre Dame," May 22, 1977, *Public Papers,* 954–62, 959;

102. Carter, "Address Before the General Assembly of the United Nations," March 17, 1977, *Public Papers,* 450.

103. Carter, "Remarks and a Question-and-Answer Session at a Townhall Meeting," Flint, Michigan, October 1, 1980, *Public Papers,* 1995.

104. Carter, "Address at the Commencement Exercises, United States Naval Academy," June 7, 1978, *Public Papers,* 1054.

105. Carter, "The President's Press Conference," June 14, 1978, *Public Papers,* 1099. See also, Carter, "Interview with the President: Question and Answer Session with Heinz Lohfeldt of *Der Spiegel* Magazine," July 11, 1978, *Public Papers,* 1273, 1274; Carter, "The President's New Conference," July 20, 1978, *Public Papers,* 1323.

106. Carter, "Remarks at the 31st Annual Meeting of the Southern Legislative Conference," Charleston, South Carolina, July 21, 1977, *Public Papers,* 1311.

107. Ibid., 1314.

108. Carter, "Remarks at a Campaign Rally at Spring Park," Tuscumbia, Alabama, September 1, 1980, *Public Papers,* 1605.

109. Carter, "Remarks at the Annual Convention of the American Legion," August 21, 1980, *Public Papers,* 1555–56.

110. Carter, "The President's News Conference," June 30, 1977, *Public Papers,* 1200.

111. For a discussion of this point, see Carter, *Keeping Faith,* 149; Kaufman, *The Presidency of James Earl Carter, Jr.,* 94.

112. Carter, "Interview with the President: Remarks and a Question-and-Answer Session with a Group of Publishers, Editors, and Broadcasters," May 27, 1977, *Public Papers,* 946. See also, "Interview with the President: Remarks and a Question-and-Answer Session with Representatives of the Hispanic Media," May 12, 1978, *Public Papers,* 907–8.

113. Carter, "Remarks at the 13th Constitutional Convention of the American Federation of Labor and the Congress of Industrial Organizations," November 13, 1979, *Public Papers,* 2123. See also, Carter, "Remarks at a Democratic Committee Fundraising Dinner," Hollywood, Florida, July 17, 1980, *Public Papers,* 1364.

114. Carter, "Remarks at the 13th Constitutional Convention of the American Federation of Labor and the Congress of Industrial Organizations," November 13, 1979, *Public Papers*, 2123. See also Carter, "Address Before the World Affairs Council of Philadelphia," Philadelphia, Pennsylvania, May 9, 1980, *Public Papers*, 873.

115. Carter, "Remarks on Signing H.R. 4537 Into Law," July 26, 1979, *Public Papers*, 1312.

116. Carter, "Remarks and a Question-and-Answer Session at a Townhall Meeting," Independence, Missouri, September 2, 1980, *Public Papers*, 1616.

117. Carter, "Remarks on Receiving the Final Report of the President's Commission on the Holocaust," September 27, 1979, *Public Papers*, 1773–74.

118. Carter, "Remarks on Signing H.R. 4537 Into Law," July 26, 1979, *Public Papers*, 1312.

119. Carter, "Address Before the World Affairs Council of Philadelphia," Philadelphia, Pennsylvania, May 9, 1980, *Public Papers*, 868.

120. Neilson, *The Religion of President Carter*, 101.

121. Carter, "Remarks at the United Steelworkers of America Convention," Atlantic City, New Jersey, September 20, 1978, *Public Papers*, 1547.

122. Carter, "Remarks at a Fundraising Dinner, Friends of Carter/ Mondale," October 24, 1979, *Public Papers*, 2017.

123. Quoted in Brady, *United States Foreign Policy Toward Cambodia*, 25.

124. Carter, *Keeping Faith*, 146–47.

125. Carter, "Address Before the World Affairs Council of Philadelphia," Philadelphia, Pennsylvania, May 9, 1980, *Public Papers*, 868.

126. Carter, "Address at Commencement Exercises at the University of Notre Dame," May 22, 1977, *Public Papers*, 958.

127. Carter, "Remarks at the 31st Annual Meeting of the Southern Legislative Conference," Charleston, South Carolina, July 21, 1977, *Public Papers*, 1310. See also, Carter, "Address to the Nation on the State of the Union," January 19, 1978, *Public Papers*, 95; Carter, "Remarks at the Opening Ceremonies of the North Atlantic Alliance Summit," May 30, 1978, *Public Papers*, 1013.

128. See also Carter, "Interview with the President: Remarks and a Question-and-Answer Session with American Press Institute Editors," January 27, 1978, *Public Papers*, 237.

129. Carter, "Remarks and a Question-and-Answer Session with New Hampshire High School Students," Nashua, New Hampshire, February 18, 1978, *Public Papers*, 376.

130. For a discussion of how Carter understood the importance of human rights as a domestic as well as international issue, see Miller Center Interview with Alonzo McDonald, final edited transcript, March 13–14, 1981, Carter Library, 81–82.

131. Carter, "Address to the Nation on the State of the Union," January 19, 1978, *Public Papers*, 92.

132. A federal appeals court overturned the convictions in 1981. For more on the Wilmington

10 see Ben Chavis, *Wilmington 10 Editorials and Cartoons* (New York: United Church of Christ Commission for Racial Justice, 1977).

133. Carter, "The President's News Conference," December 15, 1977, *Public Papers,* 2123; Carter, "The President's New Conference," July 20, 1978, *Public Papers,* 1331.

134. Carter, "Interview with the President: Remarks in an Interview for 'Black Perspectives on the News,'" April 3, 1978, *Public Papers,* 695.

135. Carter, "Remarks and a Question-and-Answer Session at the Clinton Town Meeting," Clinton, Massachusetts, March 16, 1977, 392.

136. See, for instance, the exchange between the president and a questioner in Jimmy Carter, "Interview with the President: Remarks and a Question-and-Answer Session with Editors and News Directors," April 6, 1979, *Public Papers,* 626–27.

137. See the question asked by Barbara Walters in which she quotes Henry Kissinger. Carter, "Interview with the President and Mrs. Carter: A Question-and-Answer Session with Barbara Walters of the American Broadcasting Company," December 14, 1978, *Public Papers,* 2256.

138. Carter, "The President's Press Conference," Warsaw, Poland, December 30, 1977, *Public Papers,* 2208.

139. Carter, "Toasts at a White House Dinner Honoring Governors Attending the Governor's Association's Winter Session," February 27, 1979, *Public Papers,* 357.

140. Carter, "Remarks at the 31st Annual Meeting of the Southern Legislative Conference," Charleston, South Carolina, July 21, 1977, *Public Papers,* 1314.

141. Carter, "Remarks at the Meeting of the General Council of the World Jewish Congress," November 2, 1977, *Public Papers,* 1953.

142. Carter, "Remarks at the 10th Regular Session of the General Assembly of the Organization of American States," November 19, 1980, *Public Papers,* 2735.

143. See, for example, Ruechel, "The Articulation and Synthesis of Jimmy Carter's Human Rights Policy," 23.

144. Carter, "The President's New Conference," July 20, 1978, *Public Papers,* 1328.

145. Carter, "Question-and-Answer Session with European News Journalists," April 25, 1977, *Public Papers,* 782.

146. Carter, "The President's News Conference," October 27, 1977, *Public Papers,* 1916.

147. Carter, "Text of Remarks at the First Session of the NATO Ministerial Meeting," May 10, 1977, *Public Papers,* 850; emphasis in original.

148. Carter, "Radio Address to the Nation on Foreign Policy," October 19, 1980, *Public Papers,* 2336.

149. Carter, "Question-and-Answer Session with European Broadcast Journalists," May 2, 1977, *Public Papers,* 766. See also Carter, "Interview with the President: Remarks and a Question-and-Answer Session with American Press Institute Editors," January 27, 1978, *Public Papers,* 237; Carter, "Interview with the President: Remarks and a

Question-and-Answer Session with German Reporters," July 11, 1978, *Public Papers*, 1259; Carter, "Remarks at a Democratic-Farmer-Labor Party Victory Rally," Minneapolis, Minnesota, October 21, 1978, *Public Papers*, 1832.

150. Carter, "Interview with the President: Remarks and a Question-and-Answer Session with a Group of Publishers, Editors, and Broadcasters," May 27, 1977, *Public Papers*, 947. See also, Carter, "Remarks and a Question-and-Answer Session with New Hampshire High School Students," Nashua, New Hampshire, February 18, 1978, *Public Papers*, 376.

151. Carter, "Interview with the President: Remarks and a Question-and-Answer Session with a Group of Publishers, Editors, and Broadcasters," May 27, 1977, *Public Papers*, 947.

152. Carter, "Interview with the President: Remarks and a Question-and-Answer Session with German Reporters," July 11, 1978, *Public Papers*, 1259.

153. Carter, "The President's News Conference," October 27, 1977, *Public Papers*, 1910. See also Carter, "Interview with Correspondents of WPIV-TV," Philadelphia, Pennsylvania, September 3, 1980, *Public Papers*, 1642.

154. Carter, "Address to the Nation on the State of the Union," January 19, 1978, *Public Papers*, 95.

155. Carter, "Remarks at a Cuyahoga County Democratic Party Reception," Cleveland, Ohio, September 16, 1980, *Public Papers*, 1765.

156. Carter, "Remarks at a Fundraising Dinner, Friends of Carter/ Mondale," October 24, 1979, *Public Papers*, 2018. See also, Carter, "Remarks at a State Democratic Party Reception," Columbus, Ohio, September 23, 1978, *Public Papers*, 1623;

157. Carter, "Address Before a Joint Session of the Congress on the State of the Union," January 23, 1979, *Public Papers*, 106.

158. Carter, "Address Before a Joint Session of the Congress on the State of the Union," January 23, 1980, *Public Papers*, 197.

159. Lincoln Bloomfield, "The Carter Human Rights Policy," January 11, 1981, 13, Donated Historical Material—Brzezinski, Box 34, Jimmy Carter Presidential Library, 27; Peter G. Bourne, *Jimmy Carter: A Comprehensive Biography From Plains to the Presidency*, 390.

Chapter 4

1. Ideographs are distinguished as a form of speech by the use of brackets. Thus, "human rights" when used without brackets indicates a simple phrase while <human rights> indicates its use as an ideograph or term whose ideological use and functions are being mapped.

2. In fact, as this is being written, Carter is embroiled in a feud with George W. Bush's

White House involving charges made by Carter about the nature of Bush's foreign policy as among the worst in history, and Bush's administration replying with counter charges about Carter's increasing irrelevance. The argument centers on issues of American values, including human rights, and prestige abroad.

3. Much of the material in this section and in the section concerning Bush comes from Mary E. Stuckey and Joshua Ritter, "George W. Bush, <Human Rights>, and American Democracy," *Presidential Studies Quarterly* 37 (2007): 646–66. I am indebted to the journal, and especially to Josh, for their permission to use this material here.

4. Michael Calvin McGee, "In Search of 'the People': A Rhetorical Alternative," *Quarterly Journal of Speech* 61 (1975): 235–49; Michael Calvin McGee, "Not Men, But Measures: The Origins and Import of an Ideological Principle," *Quarterly Journal of Speech* 64 (1978): 141–55; Michael Calvin McGee, "The 'Ideograph': A Link Between Rhetoric and Ideology," *Quarterly Journal of Speech* 66 (1980): 1–17; Michael Calvin McGee, "Ideograph," in Thomas O. Sloane, ed., *Encyclopedia of Rhetoric.* (New York: Oxford University Press, 2001).

5. Celeste M. Condit, and John L. Lucaites, *Crafting Equality: America's Anglo-African Word* (Chicago: University of Chicago Press, 1993), xiv–xv.

6. See, for example, Condit, and Lucaites, *Crafting Equality;* Eric E. Foner, *The Story of American Freedom* (New York: Norton, 1998).

7. Dana L. Cloud, "To Veil the Threat of Terror: Afghan Women and the <Clash of Civilizations> in the Imagery of the U.S. War on Terrorism," *Quarterly Journal of Speech* 90 (2004): 285–306; Janis Edwards and Carol K.Winkler, "Representative Form and the Visual Ideograph in the Iwo Jima Image in Editorial Cartoons," *Quarterly Journal of Speech* 83 (1997): 289–310; Catherine H. Palczewski, "The Male Madonna and the Feminine Uncle Sam: Visual Argument, Icons and Ideographs in 1909 Anti-Woman's Suffrage Postcards," *Quarterly Journal of Speech* 91 (2005): 365–94.

8. McGee, "Ideograph," 378.

9. Ibid., 380.

10. Walter R. Fisher, "The Narrative Paradigm: An Elaboration," *Communication Monographs* 52 (1985): 347–68; Walter R. Fisher, "The Narrative Paradigm: In the Beginning." *Journal of Communication* 35 (1985): 74–89.

11. Condit and Lucaites, *Crafting Equality.*

12. M. H. Wright, "Gestalt Psychological Theory's Value in Rhetorical Criticism," *Quarterly Journal of Speech* 87 (2001): 208–15.

13. James Jasinski, "Ideograph," in *Sourcebook on Rhetoric* (Thousand Oaks, Calif: Sage, 2001), 309.

14. Maurice Charland, "Constitutive Rhetoric: The Case of the Peuple Quebecois." *Quarterly Journal of Speech* 73 (1987): 133–51.

15. Condit and Lucaites, *Crafting Equality,* xiii.

16. McGee, "Ideograph," 378.

17. Condit and Lucaites, *Crafting Equality,* xiv.

18. Ibid., 20.

19. Michael P. Zuckert, *Natural Rights and the New Republicanism.* (Princeton, N.J.: Princeton University Press, 1994); Michael P. Zuckert, *The Natural Rights Republic* (Notre Dame, Ind.: University of Notre Dame Press, 1996); Michael P. Zuckert, *Launching Liberalism: On Lockean Political Philosophy.* (Lawrence: University Press of Kansas, 2002).

20. Lynn Hunt, *Inventing Human Rights: A History* (New York: W. W. Norton, 2007), 147.

21. Cmiel, "The Recent History of Human Rights"; Schlesinger, "Human Rights and the American Tradition."

22. David Harvey, *A Brief History of Neoliberalism* (New York: Oxford University Press, 2005); John Gray, *False Down: The Delusions of Global Capitalism* (New York: The New Press, 1998). Bretton Woods, New Hampshire, July 1944: After the war, both political and economic interdependence increased as the West coalesced around one set of ideas and the Soviet bloc around another. Both sides created institutional forms to manage the cooperation necessitated by that interdependence, and these institutions, in the West, relied upon the language of political rights, which became increasingly associated with specific forms of economic organization; the rhetoric of "rights" spread to economics as well.

23. Manfred B. Steger, *Globalism: The New Market Ideology* (Lanham, Md.: Rowman & Littlefield Publishers, Inc., 2002), 9.

24. Ibid., 11–12.

25. Albert O. Hirschman, *The Passions and the Interests: Political Arguments for Capitalism Before Its Triumph* (Princeton, N.J.: Princeton University Press, 1977).

26. Steger, *Globalism;* David Held and Anthony McGrew, *Globalization/Anti-Globalization* (Cambridge: Polity Press, 2002).

27. Harvey, *A Brief History of Neoliberalism.*

28. Bradford Vivian, "Neoliberal Epideictic: Rhetorical Form and Commemorative Politics on September 11, 2002." *Quarterly Journal of Speech* 92 (2006): 1–26.

29. Gray, *False Down: The Delusions of Global Capitalism,* 109.

30. Harvey, *A Brief History of Neoliberalism,* 176.

31. Ibid., 178–79.

32. Ibid., 180.

33. Ibid., 82.

34. Ibid., 195.

35. Ibid., 83–84.

36. Ibid., quoting Mary Kaldor, 84.

37. Altenberg and Cathcart, "Jimmy Carter on Human Rights," 446–57.

38. Kane, "American Values or Human Rights?"

39. Ibid., 784.

40. Ibid., 774.

41. Ibid., 785, 787.

42. John Orman, *Comparing Presidential Behavior: Carter, Reagan, and the Macho Presidential Style* (New York: Greenwood, 1987).

43. For more on Clinton and the "Third Way," see Democratic Leadership Committee, "About the Third Way," June 1, 1998, http://www.ndol.org/ndol_ci.cfm?kaid=1288&s ubid=187&contentid=895. Web site accessed June 20, 2007.

44. Kenneeth Cmiel, "The Recent History of Human Rights," *American Historical Review* 109 (2004): 117–35.

45. Seymour Martin Lipset, *American Exceptionalism: A Double-Edged Sword* (New York: Norton, 1996), 19.

46. Kane, "American Values or Human Rights?" 778.

47. Carter, "Inaugural Address of Jimmy Carter," *Public Papers,* 1.

48. Ibid., 1–2; See also, Carter, "Address at the Commencement Exercises, United States Naval Academy," June, 7, 1978, *Public Papers,* 1055.

49. Carter, "The President's News Conference," December 15, 1977, *Public Papers,* 2115. See also, Carter, "Remarks and a Question-and-Answer Session at a Townhall Meeting," Independence, Missouri, September 2, 1980, *Public Papers,* 1616.

50. Carter, "The President's News Conference," December 15, 1977, *Public Papers,* 2115.

51. Carter, "Remarks at the 10th Regular Session of the General Assembly of the Organization of American States," November 19, 1980, *Public Papers,* 2736.

52. Carter, "Remarks and a Question-and-Answer Session with a Group of Publishers, Editors, and Broadcasters," May 20, 1977, *Public Papers,* 947.

53. Carter, "Interview With Correspondents of WPIV-TV," Philadelphia, Penn., September 3, 1980, *Public Papers,* 1642.

54. Carter, "Address at Commencement Exercises at the University of Notre Dame," May 22, 1977, *Public Papers,* 958.

55. Carter, "The President's News Conference," March 30, 1978, *Public Papers,* 629.

56. Carter, "The President's Press Conference," June 30, 1977, *Public,* 1205; see also, Carter, "Remarks to the NAACP," Miami, Florida, July 4, 1980, *Public Papers,* 1322.

57. Carter, "Question-and-Answer Session with European Journalists," April 25, 1977, *Public Papers,* 775.

58. For instance, he made explicit connections between "economic justice" and "minority-owned businesses." See Carter, "Remarks to the NAACP," Miami, Florida, July 4, 1980, *Public Papers,* 1324; and between <human rights> and employment. See Carter, "Remarks at a Democratic National Committee Fundraising Dinner," Hollywood, Florida, July 17, 1980, *Public Papers,* 1365.

59. Carter, "Address to the Nation on the State of the Union," January 23, 1979, *Public Papers,* 106.

60. See also, Carter, "Remarks on Signing the Trade Agreements Act of 1979," July 26, 1979, *Public Papers,* 1312.

61. Carter, "Address at Commencement Exercises at the University of Notre Dame," May 22, 1977, *Public Papers,* 961–62.

62. Carter, "The President's Press Conference," October 27, 1977, *Public Papers,* 1915.

63. Carter, "Remarks and a Question-and-Answer Session at the Clinton Town Meeting," Clinton, Mass., March 16, 1977, *Public Papers,* 385.

64. Carter, "Address Before the General Assembly of the United Nations," New York City, March 17, 1977, *Public Papers,* 445.

65. See also, See Carter, "Address to the Nation on the State of the Union," January 19, 1978, *Public Papers,* 97.

66. Carter, "Address Before the General Assembly of the United Nations," New York City, March 17, 1977, *Public Papers,* 446.

67. Ibid., 448.

68. Ibid., 449.

69. Ibid., 449–50.

70. See H. W. Brands, *The Money Men* (New York: W. W. Norton, 2006); David W. Noble, *The End of American History: Democracy, Capitalism, and the Metaphor of Two Worlds in Anglo-Historical Writing, 1880–1980* (Minneapolis: University of Minnesota Press, 1985).

71. Carter, "Remarks at the Meeting of the General Council of the World Jewish Congress," November 2, 1977, *Public Papers,* 1953.

72. See Carter, "Address to the Nation on the State of the Union," January 19, 1978, *Public Papers,* 92; Jimmy Carter, "Remarks in an Interview for 'Black Perspective on the News,'" April 5, 1978, *Public Papers,* 695.

73. See, among many others, Robert Dallek, *Ronald Reagan: The Politics of Symbolism* (Cambridge, Mass.: Harvard University Press, 1984); Paul D. Erickson, *Reagan Speaks: The Making of an American Myth* (New York: New York University Press, 1985); Gary Wills, *Reagan's America: Innocents at Home* (Garden City, N.Y.: Doubleday, 1985).

74. Ronald Reagan, "Address at the Commencement Exercises at the University of Notre Dame," May 17, 1981. John Woolley and Gerhard Peters, *The American Presidency Project* [online]. Santa Barbara, Calif: University of California (hosted), Gerhard Peters (database), www.presidency.ucsb.edu/ws/?pid=43825.

75. See, for instance, Reagan, "Remarks at the Bicentennial Observance of the Battle of Yorktown in Virginia," October 19, 1981, Woolley and Peters, *American Presidency Project,* www.presidency.ucsb.edu/ws/?pid=43151; Reagan, "Address at Commencement Exercises at Eureka College in Illinois," May 9, 1982, Woolley and Peters, *American Presidency*

Project, www.presidency.ucsb.edu/ws/?pid=42501; Reagan, "Remarks at the Swearing-In Ceremony for New United States Citizens in White House Station, New Jersey," September 17, 1982, Woolley and Peters, *American Presidency Project,* www.presidency.ucsb.edu/ws/?pid=43007.

76. Reagan, "Remarks on Signing the International Human Rights Day Proclamation," December 10, 1984, Woolley and Peters, *American Presidency Project,* www.presidency.ucsb.edu/ws/?pid=39473.

77. Reagan, "Farewell Address to the Nation," January 11, 1989, Woolley and Peters, *American Presidency Project,* www.presidency.ucsb.edu/ws/?pid=29650.

78. Ibid.

79. Reagan, "Remarks and a Question-and-Answer Session at the University of Virginia in Charlottesville," December 16, 1988, Woolley and Peters, *American Presidency Project,* www.presidency.ucsb.edu/ws/?pid=35272.

80. Reagan, "Remarks and a Question-and-Answer Session at a World Affairs Council Luncheon in Los Angeles, California," October 28, 1988, Woolley and Peters, *American Presidency Project,* www.presidency.ucsb.edu/ws/?pid=35084

81. Reagan, "Message on the 60th Birthday of Andrei Sakharov," May 2, 1981, Woolley and Peters, *American Presidency Project,* www.presidency.ucsb.edu/ws/?pid=43772.

82. Reagan, "Remarks at the International Convention of B'nai B'rith," September 6, 1984, Woolley and Peters, *American Presidency Project,* www.presidency.ucsb.edu/ws/?pid=40332.

83. Reagan, "Remarks on Signing the Human Rights Day, Bill of Rights Day, and Human Rights Week Proclamation," December 10, 1986, Woolley and Peters, *American Presidency Project,* www.presidency.ucsb.edu/ws/?pid=36797.

84. Reagan, "Address to the Nation About Christmas and the Situation in Poland," December 23, 1981, Woolley and Peters, *American Presidency Project,* www.presidency.ucsb.edu/ws/?pid=43384.

85. Reagan, "Proclamation," December 4, 1981, and "4891–Solidarity Day," January 20, 1982, Woolley and Peters, *American Presidency Project,* www.presidency.ucsb.edu/ws/?pid=42487.

86. Reagan, "Address at Commencement Exercises at Eureka College in Illinois," May 9, 1982, Woolley and Peters, *American Presidency Project,* www.presidency.ucsb.edu/ws/?pid=42501.

87. See, for instance, Paul Kenger, *The Crusader: Ronald Reagan and the Fall of Communism* (New York: Regan Books, 2006); John Patrick Diggins, *Ronald Reagan: Fate, Freedom, and the Making of History* (New York: W. W. Norton, 2007).

88. Reagan, "Address Before a Joint Session of Congress on Central America," April 27, 1983, Woolley and Peters, *American Presidency Project,* www.presidency.ucsb.edu/ws/?pid=41245.

89. See, for instance, Reagan, "Radio Address to the Nation on Central America," March 24, 1984, Woolley and Peters, *American Presidency Project,* www.presidency.ucsb.edu/ws/?pid=39686; Reagan, "Address to the Nation on United States Policy in Central America," May 9, 1984, Woolley and Peters, *American Presidency Project,* www.presidency.ucsb.edu/ws/?pid=39901.

90. Reagan, "Proclamation 5003–Bill of Rights Day, Human Rights Day and Week 1982," December 10, 1982, Woolley and Peters, *American Presidency Project,* www.presidency.ucsb.edu/ws/?pid=42101.

91. Reagan, "Remarks at the National Leadership Forum of the Center for International and Strategic Studies of Georgetown University," April 6, 1984, Woolley and Peters, *American Presidency Project,* www.presidency.ucsb.edu/ws/?pid=39731; see also, Reagan, "Address Before a Joint Session of Congress on the State of the Union," January 25, 1988, Woolley and Peters, *American Presidency Project,* www.presidency.ucsb.edu/ws/?pid=36035.

92. Reagan, "Remarks at the Annual Conservative Political Action Conference Dinner," March 2, 1984, Woolley and Peters, *American Presidency Project,* www.presidency.ucsb.edu/ws/?pid=39591; see also, Reagan, "Remarks to Soviet Dissidents at Spaso House in Moscow," May 30, 1988, Woolley and Peters, *American Presidency Project,* www.presidency.ucsb.edu/ws/?pid=35894.

93. Reagan, "Address to the Nation on the Observance of Labor Day," September 4, 1982, Woolley and Peters, *American Presidency Project,* www.presidency.ucsb.edu/ws/?pid=42916.

94. Reagan, "Remarks to Organization of American States Ambassadors on Pan American Day," April 14, 1983, Woolley and Peters, *American Presidency Project,* www.presidency.ucsb.edu/ws/?pid=41189; see also, Reagan, Address to the 39th Session of the United Nations General Assembly in New York, New York," September 24, 1984, Woolley and Peters, *American Presidency Project,* www.presidency.ucsb.edu/ws/?pid=40430.

95. See for instance, Reagan, "Statement on the 239th Anniversary of the Birth of Thomas Jefferson," April 13, 1982, Woolley and Peters, *American Presidency Project,* www.presidency.ucsb.edu/ws/?pid=42388; Reagan, "Remarks at the Annual Meeting of the American Bar Association in Atlanta, Georgia," August 1, 1983, Woolley and Peters, *American Presidency Project,* www.presidency.ucsb.edu/ws/?pid=41664.

96. Ronald Reagan, "Address to Members of the British Parliament," June 8, 1982, Woolley and Peters, *American Presidency Project,* www.presidency.ucsb.edu/ws/?pid=42614.

97. Reagan, "Proclamation 4885—Bill of Rights Day, Human Rights Day and Week," December 4, 1981, Woolley and Peters, *American Presidency Project,* www.presidency.ucsb.edu/ws/?pid=43332.

98. Ibid.

99. Ronald Reagan, "Remarks Accepting the Presidential Nomination at the Republican National Convention in Dallas, Texas," August 23, 1984, Woolley and Peters, *American Presidency Project,* www.presidency.ucsb.edu/ws/?pid=40390.

100. It is worth reiterating that in this George H. W. Bush clearly and consistently followed Reagan's path rather than Carter's.

101. William J. Clinton, "Remarks to the Turkish Grand National Assembly in Ankara," November 15, 1999, Woolley and Peters, *American Presidency Project,* www.presidency .ucsb.edu/ws/?pid=56935.

102. Clinton, "Remarks Celebrating the 50th Anniversary of the Universal Declaration of Human Rights in New York City," December 9, 1997, Woolley and Peters, *American Presidency Project,* www.presidency.ucsb.edu/ws/?pid=53684.

103. Clinton, "The President's News Conference with President Fidel Ramos of the Philippines in Manila," November 13, 1994, Woolley and Peters, *American Presidency Project,* www.presidency.ucsb.edu/ws/?pid=49486; see also, Clinton, "Remarks to the Pacific Basin Economic Council" May 20, 1996, Woolley and Peters, *American Presidency Project,* www.presidency.ucsb.edu/ws/?pid=52835.

104. See, for example, Clinton, "Remarks at the American University Centennial Celebration," February 26, 1993, Woolley and Peters, *American Presidency Project,* www .presidency.ucsb.edu/ws/?pid=46220; Clinton, "Remarks to the 48th Session of the United Nations General Assembly in New York City," September 27, 1993, Woolley and Peters, *American Presidency Project,* www.presidency.ucsb.edu/ws/?pid=47119.

105. Clinton, "Remarks to the Turkish Grand National Assembly in Ankara" November 15, 1999, Woolley and Peters, *American Presidency Project,* www.presidency.ucsb.edu/ ws/?pid=56935; see also, Clinton, "Remarks on Presenting the Eleanor Roosevelt Award for Human Rights," December 6, 1999, Woolley and Peters, *American Presidency Project,* www.presidency.ucsb.edu/ws/?pid=57029; Clinton, "Remarks on Signing the Proclamation on Human Rights," December 10, 1996, Woolley and Peters, *American Presidency Project,* www.presidency.ucsb.edu/ws/?pid=52325.

106. Clinton, "The President's News Conference with President Jiang Zemin of China" October 29, 1997, Woolley and Peters, *American Presidency Project,* www.presidency .ucsb.edu/ws/?pid=53468.

107. Clinton, "Remarks in a Roundtable on Peace Efforts in Guatemala City" March 10, 1999, Woolley and Peters, *The American Presidency Project,* www.presidency.ucsb .edu/ws/?pid=57227; Clinton, "Remarks to the 52nd Session of the United Nations General Assembly in New York City," September 22, 1997, www.presidency.ucsb.edu/ ws/?pid=54652.

108. Clinton, "Remarks in a Roundtable on Peace Efforts in Guatemala City" March 10, 1999, Woolley and Peters, *American Presidency Project,* www.presidency.ucsb.edu/ ws/?pid=57227.

109. Clinton, "Remarks on Signing the Proclamation on Human Rights," December 10, 1996, Woolley and Peters, *American Presidency Project*, www.presidency.ucsb.edu/ws/?pid=52325.

110. Clinton, "Remarks to the 52nd Session of the United Nations General Assembly in New York City," September 22, 1997, Woolley and Peters, *American Presidency Project*, www.presidency.ucsb.edu/ws/?pid=54652.

111. Clinton, "Remarks at the University of Connecticut in Storrs," October 15, 1995, Woolley and Peters, *American Presidency Project*, www.presidency.ucsb.edu/ws/?pid=50655.

112. Clinton, "Remarks to the 52nd Session of the United Nations General Assembly in New York City," September 22, 1997, Woolley and Peters, *American Presidency Project*, www.presidency.ucsb.edu/ws/?pid=54652.

113. Clinton, "Remarks on the 50th Anniversary of the United Nations Charter in San Francisco, California," June 26, 1995, Woolley and Peters, *American Presidency Project*, www.presidency.ucsb.edu/ws/?pid=51540.

114. See also, Clinton, "Remarks to the United States Institute of Peace," April 7, 1999, Woolley and Peters, *American Presidency Project*, www.presidency.ucsb.edu/ws/?pid=57368.

115. Clinton, "Remarks Celebrating the 50th Anniversary of the Universal Declaration of Human Rights in New York City," December 9, 1997, Woolley and Peters, *American Presidency Project*, www.presidency.ucsb.edu/ws/?pid=53684.

116. See, for instance, Clinton, "Remarks at the University of Connecticut in Storrs," October 15, 1995, Woolley and Peters, *American Presidency Project*, www.presidency.ucsb.edu/ws/?pid=50655.

117. Clinton, "Remarks to the Pacific Basin Economic Council" May 20, 1996, Woolley and Peters, *The American Presidency Project*, www.presidency.ucsb.edu/ws/?pid=52835.

118. Clinton, "Address to the Nation on the State of the Union" January 23, 1996, Woolley and Peters, *American Presidency Project*, www.presidency.ucsb.edu/ws/?pid=53091.

119. Clinton, "Remarks on Presenting the Eleanor Roosevelt Award for Human Rights and the Presidential Medal of Freedom," December 6, 2000, Woolley and Peters, *American Presidency Project*, www.presidency.ucsb.edu/ws/?pid=956.

120. Clinton, "Statement on the Cuban Government's Sentencing of Human Rights Activists" March 15, 1999, Woolley and Peters, *American Presidency Project*, www.presidency.ucsb.edu/ws/?pid=57261.

121. Clinton, "Remarks Celebrating the 50th Anniversary of the Universal Declaration of Human Rights in New York City," December 9, 1997, Woolley and Peters, *American Presidency Project*, www.presidency.ucsb.edu/ws/?pid=53684.

122. The extent of this problem was perhaps indicated by Hillary Clinton's speech, "Women's Rights are Human Rights," given at the U.N.'s Fourth World Conference on

Women in Beijing, China, September 5, 1995. For a text of the speech, see www
.americanrhetoric.com/speeches/hillaryclintonbeijingspeech.htm. Web site accessed
December 17, 2007.

123. George W. Bush, "Proclamation 7455—Captive Nations Week, 2001." July 12,
2001, Woolley and Peters, *American Presidency Project*, www.presidency.ucsb.edu/
ws/?pid=61752.

124. Ibid.

125. John Bovard, *The Bush Betrayal* (New York: Palgrave MacMillan, 2004), 11.

126. Bush, "Proclamation 7153—Human Rights Day, Bill of Rights Day, and Human
Rights Week," December 9, 2001, Woolley and Peters, *American Presidency Project*,
www.presidency.ucsb.edu/ws/?pid=61810.

127. Bush, "Interview with Radio Free Europe/Radio Liberty," November 18, 2002,
Woolley and Peters, *American Presidency Project*, www.presidency.ucsb.edu/
ws/?pid=64108.

128. Bush, "Proclamation 8090—Human Rights Day, Bill of Rights Day, and Human
Rights Week, 2006," December 8, 2006, Woolley and Peters, *American Presidency Proj-
ect*, www.presidency.ucsb.edu/ws/?pid=24379. See also, Bush, "Address Before a Joint
Session of Congress on the State of the Union," January 28, 2003, Woolley and Peters,
American Presidency Project, www.presidency.ucsb.edu/ws/?pid=29645.)

129. Bush, "Address to the Nation on Iraq from Cincinnati," October 7, 2002, Woolley and
Peters, *American Presidency Project*, www.presidency.ucsb.edu/ws/?pid=73139. See also
Bush, "Proclamation 7802—Captive Nations Week, 2004," July 16, 2004, Woolley
and Peters, *American Presidency Project*, www.presidency.ucsb.edu/ws/?pid=62087.

130. Bush, "Remarks on Compassionate Conservatism in San Jose, California," April 30,
2002, Woolley and Peters, *American Presidency Project*, www.presidency.ucsb.edu/
ws/?pid=62868; Bush, "Remarks at a Dinner for Senator Christopher S. 'Kit' Bond
of Missouri in St. Louis," August 26, 2003, Woolley and Peters, *American Presidency
Project*, www.presidency.ucsb.edu/ws/?pid=63936.

131. Bush, "Remarks on Efforts to Globally Promote Women's Human Rights," March
12, 2004, Woolley and Peters, *American Presidency Project*, www.presidency.ucsb.edu/
ws/?pid=64747.

132. Bush, "The President's News Conference in Savannah, Georgia," June 10, 2004,
Woolley and Peters, *American Presidency Project*, www.presidency.ucsb.edu/
ws/?pid=64460.

133. Ivo H. Daalder, James M. Lindsay, and James B. Steinberg, *The Bush National Security
Strategy: An Evaluation*, Policy Brief #109-2002, Brookings Institution, www.brook
ings.edu/comm/policybriefs/pb109.htm. Web site accessed May 25, 2007.

134. George W. Bush, *The National Security Strategy of the United States of America*, September 17, 2002, www.whitehouse.gov/nsc/nss.html. Web site accessed May 25, 2007.

135. Ibid., 3.

136. Harvey, *A Brief History of Neoliberalism;* Gray, *False Down: The Delusions of Global Capitalism.*

137. Bush, *The National Security Strategy of the United States of America,* 3.

138. Bush, "Remarks on the 100th Anniversary of Cuban Independence in Miami, Florida," May 20, 2002, Woolley and Peters, *American Presidency Project,* www.presidency.ucsb.edu/ws/?pid=63117

139. Bush, *The National Security Strategy of the United States of America,* 7.

140. Bush, "Remarks on the 100th Anniversary of Cuban Independence in Miami, Florida," May 20, 2002, Woolley and Peters, *American Presidency Project,* www.presidency.ucsb.edu/ws/?pid=63117.

141. Bush, "Remarks Announcing the Initiative for a New Cuba," May 20, 2002, Woolley and Peters, *American Presidency Project,* www.presidency.ucsb.edu/ws/?pid=64006.

142. Ibid.

143. George W. Bush, "Remarks on the 100th Anniversary of Cuban Independence in Miami, Florida," May 20, 2002, Woolley and Peters, *American Presidency Project,* www.presidency.ucsb.edu/ws/?pid=63117).

144. Ibid.

145. Bush, "Commencement Address at the United States Coast Guard Academy in New London, Connecticut," May 21, 2003, Woolley and Peters, *American Presidency Project,* www.presidency.ucsb.edu/ws/?pid=915.

146. Bush, "Interview with Radio Free Europe/ Radio Liberty" November 18, 2002, Woolley and Peters, *American Presidency Project,* www.presidency.ucsb.edu/ws/?pid=64108; see also Bush, "Address Before a Joint Session of Congress on the State of the Union," January 28, 2003, Woolley and Peters, *American Presidency Project,* www.presidency.ucsb.edu/ws/?pid=29645; Bush, "Remarks at a Dinner for Senator Christopher S. 'Kit' Bond of Missouri in St. Louis," August 26, 2003, Woolley and Peters, *American Presidency Project,* www.presidency.ucsb.edu/ws/?pid=63936.

147. Bush, "Commencement Address at the United States Coast Guard Academy in New London, Connecticut," May 21, 2003, Woolley and Peters, *American Presidency Project,* www.presidency.ucsb.edu/ws/?pid=915.

148. Bush, "Remarks at Pease Air National Guard Base in Portsmouth, New Hampshire," October 9, 2003, Woolley and Peters, *American Presidency Project,* www.presidency.ucsb.edu/ws/?pid=64247.)

149. Bush, "Interview with Radio Free Europe/Radio Liberty," November 18, 2002, Woolley and Peters, *American Presidency Project,* www.presidency.ucsb.edu/ws/?pid=64108; Bush, "The President's News Conference in Savannah, Georgia," June 10, 2004, Woolley and Peters, *American Presidency Project,* www.presidency.ucsb.edu/ws/?pid=64460.

150. Bush, "Joint Statement: United States-European Union Summit Declaration," June 21, 2006, Woolley and Peters, *American Presidency Project,* www.presidency.ucsb.edu/ ws/?pid=178.

151. Bush, "Interview with Radio Free Europe/Radio Liberty," November 18, 2002, Woolley and Peters, *American Presidency Project,* www.presidency.ucsb.edu/ ws/?pid=64108.

152. Bush, "Remarks Prior to Discussions with Chairman Hamid Karzai of the Afghan Interim Authority and an Exchange with Reporters," January 28, 2002, Woolley and Peters, *American Presidency Project,* www.presidency.ucsb.edu/ws/?pid=62986.

153. Shirley Anne Warshaw, "Mastering Presidential Government: Executive Power and the Bush Administration," in J. Kraus, K. J. Mcmahon, and D. M. Rankin, eds., *Transformed by Crisis: The Presidency of George W. Bush and American Politics* (New York: Palgrave MacMillan, 2004), 114.

154. Bush, "The President's News Conference," May 31, 2005, Woolley and Peters, *American Presidency Project,* www.presidency.ucsb.edu/ws/?pid=73921.

155. Bush, "Interview with David Frost of BBC Television," November 12, 2003, Woolley and Peters, *American Presidency Project,* www.presidency.ucsb.edu/ws/?pid=822.

156. Bush, "Remarks Prior to Discussions with Chairman Hamid Karzai of the Afghan Interim Authority and an Exchange with Reporters," January 28, 2002, Woolley and Peters, *American Presidency Project,* www.presidency.ucsb.edu/ws/?pid=62986.

157. Bovard, *The Bush Betrayal,* 206–213.

158. Ibid., 213.

159. Bush, "The President's News Conference," January 26, 2006, Woolley and Peters, *American Presidency Project,* www.presidency.ucsb.edu/ws/?pid=65146.

160. Amnesty International, "Human Rights Not Hollow Words: An Appeal to President George W. Bush on the Occasion of his Re-Inauguration, 2005," http://web.amnesty. org/library/index/engamr510122005. Website accessed February 27, 2007.

161. Bush, "The President's News Conference," June 14, 1006, Woolley and Peters, *American Presidency Project,* www.presidency.ucsb.edu/ws/?pid=130.

162. Bush, "Interview with Alhurra Television," May 5, 2004, Woolley and Peters, *American Presidency Project,* www.presidency.ucsb.edu/ws/?pid=64600.

163. Ibid.

164. Ibid; George W. Bush, "Interview with Al-Ahram International," May 6, 2004, Woolley and Peters, *American Presidency Project,* www.presidency.ucsb.edu/ ws/?pid=63380.

165. Bush, "Interview with Alhurra Television."

166. Bush, "Interview with Al-Ahram International."

167. John Brady Kiesling, "Resignation Letter," February 24, 2003, www.bradykiesling .com/resignation_letter.htm.

168. Harvey, *A Brief History of Neoliberalism,* 195–96.

169. Eran N. Ben-Porath, "Rhetoric of Atrocities: The Place of Horrific Human Rights Abuses in Presidential Persuasion Efforts," *Presidential Studies Quarterly* 37 (2007): 181–202.

Chapter 5

1. Peter C. Bourne, *Jimmy Carter: A Comprehensive Biography From Plains to Presidency,* 383; Nicolai N. Petro, *The Predicament of Human Rights: The Carter and Reagan Policies,* vol. 5 (Lanham, Md.: University Press of America, 1983), 5.

2. Carter, *Keeping Faith,* 142.

3. Carter, "Inaugural Address of Jimmy Carter," January 22, 1977, *Public Papers,* 2.

4. Petro, *The Predicament of Human Rights,* 10.

5. See, for instance, Lars Schoultz, *Human Rights and United States Policy Toward Latin America* (Princeton, N.J.: Princeton University Press, 1981), 251; Sandy Vogelgesang, *American Dream: Global Nightmare* (New York: W. W. Norton, 1980), 121–25.

6. Ruechel, "The Articulation and Synthesis of Jimmy Carter's Human Rights Policy," 201.

7. Edwin S. Maynard, "The Bureaucracy and Implementation of Human Rights Policy," *Human Rights Quarterly,* 11 (1989): 178.

8. See the fine discussion of this history in Stephen B. Cohen, "Conditioning U.S. Security Assistance on Human Rights Practices," *American Journal of International Law,* 76 (January–April 1982): 246–79.

9. See U.S. Congress, House of Representatives, Committee on Foreign Affairs, *Human Rights Documents: Compilation of Documents Pertaining to Human Rights* (Washington, D.C.: U.S. Government Printing Office, 1983), 28.

10. See Section 113 of the Foreign Assistance Act of 1961, U.S. House of Representatives Committee on International Relations, U.S. Senate Committee on Foreign Relations, *Legislation on Foreign Relations Through 2002, Current Legislation and Related Executive Orders* (Washington, D.C.: U.S. Government Printing Office, 2003).

11. See Maynard, "The Bureaucracy and Implementation of Human Rights Policy," 179; Petro, *The Predicament of Human Rights,* 12.

12. A. Glenn Mower Jr., *Human Rights and American Foreign Policy: The Carter and Reagan Experiences* (Westport, Conn.: Greenwood, 1987), 61–62.

13. Ibid., 67–68.

14. See Cyrus Vance, *Hard Choices: Critical Years in American Foreign Policy* (New York: Simon and Schuster, 1983).

15. See, Mower, *Human Rights and American Foreign Policy,* 63; see also, Stephen B. Cohen, "Conditioning U.S. Security Assistance on Human Rights Practices," 246.

16. Ruechel, "The Articulation and Synthesis of Jimmy Carter's Human Rights Policy," 204.

17. That battle, of course, got quite intense during these years, as Congress passed the War Powers Act and the Impoundment Control Act, both attempts to restrict presidential freedom of action.

18. See Peter C. Brown and Douglas MacLean, eds., *Human Rights and U.S. Foreign Policy* (Lexington,, Mass., Lexington Books, 1979), 9; Ruechel, "The Articulation and Synthesis of Jimmy Carter's Human Rights Policy," 207–8.

19. See Mower, *Human Rights and American Foreign Policy;* Hauke Hartmann, "US Human Rights Policy Under Carter and Reagan, 1977–1981," *Human Rights Quarterly* 23 (2001): 402–30; Petro, *The Predicament of Human Rights.*

20. Within the State Department, there are both regional and functional bureaus. There are five regional bureaus, each dedicated to a continent; they are the traditional loci of power with the department. There are also functional bureaus, whose portfolios cut across geographical lines. Human Rights and Humanitarian Affairs is a functional bureau; and is thus potentially threatening to the regional bureaus. See Maynard, "The Bureaucracy and Implementation of Human Rights Policy," 175, 187.

21. Hartmann, "US Human Rights Policy Under Carter and Reagan, 1977–1981," 405; International Economic Policy Association, *Human Rights and American Foreign Policy: An Analytical Commentary* White House Central Files, Box HU-3, Jimmy Carter Presidential Library, 16–17; Petro, *The Predicament of Human Rights,* 11.

22. See Gaddis Smith, *Morality, Reason, and Power,* 54.

23. Ruechel, "The Articulation and Synthesis of Jimmy Carter's Human Rights Policy," 209.

24. Ibid., 212; Petro, *The Predicament of Human Rights,* 13–14.

25. See U. S. Congress, Senate Foreign Relations Committee, *International Human Rights Treaties: Hearings before the Committee on Foreign Relations, United States Senate, Ninety-Sixth Congress, First Session* (Washington, D.C.: U.S. Government Printing Office, 1980), especially 104–30.

26. On Panama, see Vance, *Hard Choices,* 140–59; on SALT, see the same source, 99–120.

27. Ruechel, "The Articulation and Synthesis of Jimmy Carter's Human Rights Policy," 190.

28. See Robert J. Spitzer, *President and Congress: Executive Hegemony at the Crossroads of American Government* (Philadelphia: Temple University Press, 1993), 84–85.

29. Hartmann, "US Human Rights Policy Under Carter and Reagan, 1977–1981," 413. See also, Neuringer, *The Carter Administration, Human Rights, and the Agony of Cambodia,* 49, 66.

30. See, for example, *Commentary,* ABC Evening News, Tuesday March 22, 1977, Rosalyn Carter Files, Box: First Lady's Staff File, First Lady's Press Office, folder: Human

Rights, February-March, 1977, Carter Library; Rosati, *The Carter Administration's Quest for Global Community*, 5, 44; David E. Schmitz and Vanessa Walker, "Jimmy Carter and the Foreign Policy of Human Rights: The Development of a Post-Cold War Foreign Policy," *Diplomatic History* v 28, n1 (January 2004): 113–43.

31. Hartmann, "US Human Rights Policy Under Carter and Reagan, 1977–1981," 404.

32. Spencer, *The Carter Implosion*, 58.

33. Petro, *The Predicament of Human Rights*, 27.

34. Mower, *Human Rights and American Foreign Policy*, 113.

35. Maynard, "The Bureaucracy and Implementation of Human Rights Policy," 220–21.

36. Ibid., 222

37. Ibid., 229, 232.

38. Mower, *Human Rights and American Foreign Policy*, 68. See also, Bourne, *Jimmy Carter: A Comprehensive Biography From Plains to Presidency*, 390; Stephen B. Cohen, "Conditioning U.S. Security Assistance on Human Rights Practices," 249; Dumbrell, *The Carter Presidency*, 181; Hartmann, "US Human Rights Policy Under Carter and Reagan, 1977–1981," 406.

39. Mower, *Human Rights and American Foreign Policy*, 69.

40. Ibid.

41. Hartmann, "US Human Rights Policy Under Carter and Reagan, 1977–1981," 407.

42. Petro, *The Predicament of Human Rights*, 34–42.

43. Ibid., 61.

44. International Economic Policy Association, *Human Rights and American Foreign Policy: An Analytical Commentary*, White House Central Files, Box HU-3, Jimmy Carter Presidential Library, 21.

45. Timothy W. Stanley, "Foreword," i; International Economic Policy Association, *Human Rights and American Foreign Policy: An Analytical Commentary*, White House Central Files, Box HU-3, Jimmy Carter Presidential Library.

46. International Economic Policy Association, *Human Rights and American Foreign Policy*, ii.

47. Ibid., 20.

48. For a good discussion of the problem of clientism as it relates to human rights, see Stephen B. Cohen, "Conditioning U.S. Security Assistance on Human Rights Practices," 258–61.

49. Maynard, "The Bureaucracy and Implementation of Human Rights Policy," 185.

50. Ibid., 188; Mower, *Human Rights and American Foreign Policy*, 70–71.

51. Petro, *The Predicament of Human Rights*, 28.

52. Ibid., 34.

53. Spencer, *The Carter Implosion*, ix, 59.

54. International Economic Policy Association, *Human Rights and American Foreign Policy*, 24.

55. Vance, *Hard Choices*, 35–38.

56. Petro, *The Predicament of Human Rights,* 43.

57. Ibid., 44.

58. Schmitz and Walker, "Jimmy Carter and the Foreign Policy of Human Rights," 113. See also, Carter, *Keeping Faith,* 145–47.

59. Jimmy Carter, "Inaugural Address of Jimmy Carter," January 22, 1977, *Public Papers,* 2.

60. Mower, *Human Rights and American Foreign Policy,* 31.

61. Vance, *Hard Choices,* 46.

62. Mower, *Human Rights and American Foreign Policy,* 29. See also, David Heaps, *Human Rights and U.S. Foreign Policy: The First Decade, 1973–1983* (New York: American Association for the International Commission of Jurists, 1984), 16–17.

63. Hartmann, "US Human Rights Policy Under Carter and Reagan, 1977–1981," 416.

64. Mower, *Human Rights and American Foreign Policy,* 41.

65. Cyrus R. Vance, "Human Rights Policy Speech on Law Day at University of Georgia Law School," April 30, 1977, 1. Carter Presidential Papers–Staff Offices Ethnic Affairs, Aiello, Housing and Urban Development [Research Reports] 10/79 through Human Rights [J of Current Social Issues 6/78 [OA 9891], folder: Human Rights 3/77–6/80. Jimmy Carter Presidential Library.

66. Hartmann, "US Human Rights Policy Under Carter and Reagan, 1977–1981," 406

67. Ibid., 407–8.

68. Jimmy Carter, "Remarks at a White House Meeting Commemorating the 30th Anniversary of the Signing of the Universal Declaration of Human Rights," December 6, 1978, *Public Papers,* 2162.

69. Mower, *Human Rights and American Foreign Policy,* 59; see also Zbigniew Brzezinski, *Power and Principle,* rev. ed. (New York: Farrar, Strauss, and Giroux, 1985), 55.

70. Hartmann, "US Human Rights Policy Under Carter and Reagan, 1977–1981," 410.

71. See Memorandum, Cyrus Vance and Warren Christopher to the President, March 27, 1978, White House Central Files, Human Rights, Box HU-1, Jimmy Carter Presidential Library.

72. Ruechel, "The Articulation and Synthesis of Jimmy Carter's Human Rights Policy," 176.

73. See Presidential Directive, Human Rights, Staff Office, Counsel Lipshutz, Haitian Drug Trafficking Matter through Human Rights, Box 18, folder: Human Rights, 12/77 [CF, O/A, 710], Jimmy Carter Presidential Library.

74. Maynard, "The Bureaucracy and Implementation of Human Rights Policy," 205; Petro, *The Predicament of Human Rights,* 29–30.

75. Maynard, "The Bureaucracy and Implementation of Human Rights Policy," 205.

76. Ibid., 215.

77. Ibid., 216.

78. Mower, *Human Rights and American Foreign Policy,* 72–73.

79. Maynard, "The Bureaucracy and Implementation of Human Rights Policy," 210.

80. See Stephen B. Cohen, "Conditioning U.S. Security Assistance on Human Rights Practices," 263.

81. Mower, *Human Rights and American Foreign Policy,* 83.

82. Ibid., 91.

83. Ibid., 103.

84. Vance, *Hard Choices,* 46.

85. Mower, *Human Rights and American Foreign Policy,* 93.

86. For specifics, see, ibid., 93–94.

87. These media norms are well known, but see Doris A. Graber, *Mass Media and American Politics,* 6th ed. (Washington, D.C.: Congressional Quarterly Press, 2002), 92–137; Kathleen Hall Jamieson and Paul Waldman, *The Press Effect: Politicians, Journalists and the Stories that Shape the Political World* (New York: Oxford University Press, 2003).

88. Jessica Tuchman, Memo to Zbigniew Brzezinski, February 21, 1977, Staff Offices, Press, Jody Powell [Hostages in US Embassy in Iran, 1979–81] through [Interview]— Des Moines *Register and Tribune,* 12/30/79 [CF, O/A 746] Box 63, folder: Human Rights, 2/77–12/78[CF, O/A 588}, Jimmy Carter Presidential Library, 1.

89. See Interview with Zbigniew Brzezinski, Madeline Albright, Leslie Denend, and William Odom, Miller Center Interviews, Carter Presidency Project, vol. XV, February 18, 1982, 49, Jimmy Carter Presidential Library; Vance, *Hard Choices,* 27.

90. Ruechel, "The Articulation and Synthesis of Jimmy Carter's Human Rights Policy," 219.

91. Vance, *Hard Choices,* 103.

92. Bourne, *Jimmy Carter: A Comprehensive Biography From Plains to Presidency,* 390.

93. Neuringer, *The Carter Administration, Human Rights, and the Agony of Cambodia,* 18.

94. Ruechel, "The Articulation and Synthesis of Jimmy Carter's Human Rights Policy," 228.

95. Petro, *The Predicament of Human Rights,* 20.

96. International Economic Policy Association, *Human Rights and American Foreign Policy,* 34.

97. Ruechel, "The Articulation and Synthesis of Jimmy Carter's Human Rights Policy," 242.

98. Mower, *Human Rights and American Foreign Policy,* 46.

99. Maynard, "The Bureaucracy and Implementation of Human Rights Policy," 191.

100. Ibid., 192.

101. Hartmann, "US Human Rights Policy Under Carter and Reagan, 1977–1981," 428.

102. Mower, *Human Rights and American Foreign Policy;* Hartmann, "US Human Rights Policy Under Carter and Reagan, 1977–1981"; Petro, *The Predicament of Human Rights.*

103. Hartmann, "US Human Rights Policy Under Carter and Reagan, 1977–1981," 424; Mower, *Human Rights and American Foreign Policy,* 34.

104. Maynard, "The Bureaucracy and Implementation of Human Rights Policy," 182, n 37.

105. Mower, *Human Rights and American Foreign Policy.*

106. Ibid., 39; Petro, *The Predicament of Human Rights,* 49.

107. Mower, *Human Rights and American Foreign Policy,* 155–56; Petro, *The Predicament of Human Rights,* 43.

108. Schlesinger, "Human Rights and the American Tradition," 522

109. Ibid., 523.

110. Mower, *Human Rights and American Foreign Policy,* 25.

Conclusion

1. Mower, *Human Rights and American Foreign Policy,* 1.

2. On the postpresidency, see Ronald Lee, "Humility and the Political Servant: Jimmy Carter's Post-Presidential Rhetoric of Virtue and Power," *The Southern Communication Journal* 60 (Summer 1995): 120–30.

3. This worked in much the same way as the use of <equality> and <justice> by those opposing civil rights helped to undermine their argumentative stance.

4. On Carter and American civil religion, see Erickson, "Jimmy Carter: The Rhetoric of Private and Civic Piety."

5. On Carter as preacher, see Peter G. Bourne, *Jimmy Carter: A Comprehensive Biography From Plains to Presidency* (New York: Scribner, 1997), 179; Jody Powell, Miller Center Oral history, December 17–18, 1981, Jimmy Carter Presidential Library, 81.

6. Lee, "Electoral Politics and Visions of Community." See also, Dumbrell, *The Carter Presidency,* 4.

7. See Spencer, *The Carter Implosion,* 49.

8. See Dan Hahn, "The Rhetoric of Jimmy Carter, 1976–1980," *Presidential Studies Quarterly* 14 (1985): 282; Richard A. Melanson, *American Foreign Policy Since the Vietnam War: The Search for Consensus from Nixon to Clinton,* 3rd ed., (Armonk, N.Y.: M. E. Sharpe, 2000), 107.

9. See Warren Christopher, "Draft of PRM on Human Rights," July 8, 1977, Staff Offices Counsel Lipshutz, Human Rights through [Indian Land Claims] Maine: Notes Doug Huron, Box 19, folder: Human Rights PRM 7?77 [CF, O/A 716], Jimmy Carter Presidential Library.

10. See Dumbrell, *The Carter Presidency,* 64; Meyer, *James Earl Carter;* Sheldon Nueringer, *The Carter Administration, Human Rights, and the Agony of Cambodia* (Lewiston, Queenston, Lampeter: Edwin Mellon Press, 1993), 66; Rosati, *The Carter Administration's Quest for Global Community,* 8–12.

11. See Altenberg and Cathcart, "Jimmy Carter on Human Rights," 446.

12. Carter himself recognized this dilemma. See Carter, *Keeping Faith,* 145.

13. See Bostdorff, *The Presidency and the Rhetoric of Foreign Crisis.*

14. See Robert Alexander Kraig, "The Tragic Science: The Uses of Jimmy Carter in Foreign Policy Realism," Rhetoric and Public Affairs 5 (2002): 1–30.

15. See Cmiel, "The Recent History of Human Rights."

16. See Julie Mertius, *Bait and Switch: Human Rights and U.S. Foreign Policy* (New York: Routledge, 2004), 30–40.

17. Mertius, *Bait and Switch,* 38–39.

18. Paulette Chu Miniter, "Why George Bush's 'Freedom Agenda' is Here to Stay," *Foreign Policy,* http:www.foreignpolicy.com/story/cms.php?story_id=3959.

19. See, for instance, Joshua Muravchik, "Weakening Rights to Save Them," *Los Angeles Times,* September 15, 2006, B13.

20. Scholars generally assume that focused communication is always more effective communication. See most recently, D. Domke, E. S. Graham, K. Coe, S. L. John, T. Coopman, "Going Public as a Political Strategy: The Bush Administration, an Echoing Press, and the Passage of the Patriot Act," *Political Communication* 23 (2006): 291–312.

Selected Bibliography

Aberbach, Joel D., and Bert A. Rockman. "Hard Times for Presidential Leadership? (And How Would We Know?)." *Presidential Studies Quarterly* 29 (1999): 757–78.

Altenberg, Les, and Robert Cathcart. "Jimmy Carter on Human Rights: A Thematic Analysis." *Central States Speech Journal* 33 (1982): 446–57.

Altschuler, Bruce E. *Keeping a Finger on the Public Pulse: Private Polling and Presidential Elections.* Westport, Conn: Greenwood, 1982.

Bennett, W. Lance. "The Ritualistic and Pragmatic Bases of Political Campaign Discourse." *Quarterly Journal of Speech* 63 (1977): 219–38.

Bishop, George D., David L. Hamilton, and John B. McConahay. "Attitudes and Nonattitudes in the Belief Systems of Mass Publics." *The Journal of Social Psychology* 110 (1980): 53–64.

Bodnick, Matthew A. "'Going Public' Reconsidered: Reagan's 1981 Tax and Budget Cuts, and Revisionist Theories of Presidential Power." *Congress and the Presidency* 17 (1990): 13–29.

Bostdorff, Denise. "Idealism held Hostage: Jimmy Carter's Rhetoric on the Crisis in Iran." *Communication Studies* 43 (1992): 14–28.

———. *The Presidency and the Rhetoric of Foreign Crisis.* Columbia: University of South Carolina Press, 1994.

Bourne, Peter C. *Jimmy Carter: A Comprehensive Biography From Plains to Presidency.* New York: Scribner, 1997.

Bovard, John. *The Bush Betrayal.* New York: Palgrave MacMillan, 2004.

Brace, Paul, and Barbara Hinckley. *Follow the Leader: Public Opinion Polls and the Modern Presidents.* New York: Harper Collins, 1992

Brady, Christopher. *United States Foreign Policy Toward Cambodia, 1977–92: A Question of Realities.* New York: MacMillan, 1999.

Brands, H. W. *The Money Men.* New York: W. W. Norton, 2006.

Brinkley, Douglas. "The Rising Stock of Jimmy Carter: The 'Hands On' Legacy of Our Thirty-Ninth President." *Diplomatic History* 20 (1996): 505–29.

Brody, Richard. *Assessing the President: The Media, Elite Opinion, and Public Support.* Palo Alto, Calif.: Stanford University Press, 1991.

Brown, Peter C., and Douglas MacLean, eds. *Human Rights and U.S. Foreign Policy.* Lexington, Mass.: Lexington Books, 1979.

Brzezinski, Zbigniew. *Power and Principle: Memoirs of the National Security Advisor, 1977–1981.* New York: Farrar, Straus, Giroux, 1983.

Callaghan, Karen, and Frauke Schnell, eds. *Framing American Politics.* Pittsburgh, Pa.: University of Pittsburgh Press, 2005.

Campbell, Angus, Philip E. Converse, Warren E. Miller, and Donald E. Stokes. *The American Voter.* New York: Wiley, 1960.

Carter, Jimmy. *Keeping Faith: The Memoirs of a President.* New York: Bantam, 1982.

Cassara, Catherine. "U.S. Newspaper Coverage of Human Rights in Latin America, 1975–1982: Exploring President Carter's Agenda-Building Influence." *Journalism and Mass Communication Quarterly* 75:3 (Autumn 1998): 478–86.

Ceccarelli, Leah. "Polysemy: Multiple Meanings in Rhetoric Criticism." *Quarterly Journal of Speech* 84 (1998): 395–415.

Charland, Maurice. "Constitutive Rhetoric: The Case of the Peuple Quebecois." *Quarterly Journal of Speech* 73 (1987): 133–51.

Cloud, Dana L. "'To Veil the Threat of Terror': Afghan Women and the <Clash of Civilizations> in the Imagery of the U.S. War on Terrorism." *Quarterly Journal of Speech* 90 (2004): 285–306.

Cmiel, Kenneth. "The Emergence of Human Rights Politics in the United States." *Journal of American History* 86 (3) (1999): 1231–50.

———. "The Recent History of Human Rights." *American Historical Review* 109 (2004): 117–35.

Cohen, Jeffrey E. "Presidential Rhetoric and the Public Agenda." *American Journal of Political Science* 39 (1) (February 1995): 87–107.

———. *Presidential Responsiveness and Public Policy-making: The Public and the Policies that Presidents Choose.* Ann Arbor: University of Michigan Press, 1997.

Cohen, Stephen B. "Conditioning U.S. Security Assistance on Human Rights Practices." *American Journal of International Law,* 76 (January–April 1982): 246–79.

Condit, Celeste Michelle, and John Louis Lucaites. *Crafting Equality: America's Anglo-African Word.* Chicago: University of Chicago Press, 1993.

Converse, Philip E. "The Nature of Belief Systems in Mass Publics." In *Ideology and Discontent,* edited by D. E. Apter. New York: Free Press of Glencoe, 1964, 206–61.

———. "Attitudes and Nonattitudes: Continuation of a Dialogue." In *The Quantitative Analysis of Social Problems,* edited by Edward R. Tufte. Reading, Mass: Addison-Wesley, 1975, 68–189.

———. "Public Opinion and Voting Behavior." In *Handbook of Political Science,* 01 vol. 4, edited by Nelson W. Polsby. Reading, Mass: Addison-Wesley, 1975, 75–169.

———. "Nonattitudes and American Public Opinion: Comment: The Status of Nonattitudes." *American Political Science Review* 68 (1974): 650–60.

Corrigan, Mathew. "The Transformation of Going Public: President Clinton, the First Lady, and Health Care Reform." *Political Communication* 17 (2000), 149–69.

Cranston, Maurice. *What Are Human Rights?* New York: Taplinger, 1973.

Dallek, Robert. *Ronald Reagan: The Politics of Symbolism.* Cambridge, Mass.: Harvard University Press, 1984.

Delli Carpini, Michael X., and Scott Keeter. *What Americans Know About Politics and Why it Matters.* New Haven, Conn: Yale University Press, 1996.

Diggins, John Patrick. *Ronald Reagan: Fate, Freedom, and the Making of History.* New York: W. W. Norton, 2007.

Donnelly, Jack. *Universal Human Rights in Theory and Practice,* 2nd ed. Ithaca, N.Y.: Cornell University Press, 2003.

Druckman, James N. "On the Limits of Framing Effects: Who Can Frame?" *Journal of Politics* 63 (November 2001): 1041–66.

Druckman, James N., and Justin W. Holmes. "Does Presidential Rhetoric Matter? Priming and Presidential Approval." *Presidential Studies Quarterly* 34 (2004): 755–78.

Dumbrell, John. *The Carter Presidency: A Reevaluation.* Manchester: Manchester University Press, 1993.

Dworkin, Ronald. *Taking Rights Seriously.* Cambridge, Mass: Harvard University Press, 1978.

Edwards, George C. III. *The Public Presidency: The Pursuit of Popular Support.* New York: St. Martin's Press, 1983.

———. *At the Margins: Presidential Leadership of Congress.* New Haven, Conn.: Yale University Press, 1989.

———. *On Deaf Ears.* New Haven, Conn.: Yale University Press, 2003.

Edwards, George C. III, and Alec M. Gallup. *Presidential Approval: A Sourcebook.* Baltimore: Johns Hopkins University Press, 1990.

Edwards, Janis, and Carol K.Winkler. "Representative Form and the Visual Ideograph in the Iwo Jima Image in Editorial Cartoons." *Quarterly Journal of Speech* 83 (1997): 289–310.

Ellis, Richard J., ed. *Speaking to the People: The Rhetorical Presidency in Historical Perspective.* Amherst: University of Massachusetts Press, 1998.

Entman, Robert M. "Framing U.S. Coverage of International News: Contrasts in Narratives of the KAL and Iran Air Incidents." *Journal of Communication* 41 (1991): 6–26.

———. "Framing: Toward Clarification of a Fractured Paradigm." *Journal of Communication* 43 (1993): 51–58.

———. "Cascading Activation: Contesting the White House's Frame After 9/11." *Political Communication* 20 (2003): 415–32.

Erickson, Keith V. "Jimmy Carter: The Rhetoric of Private and Civic Piety." *Western Journal of Speech Communication* 44 (Summer 1980): 221–35.

Erickson, Paul D. *Reagan Speaks: The Making of an American Myth.* New York: New York University Press, 1985.

Eshbaugh-Soha, Mathew. *The President's Speeches: Beyond "Going Public."* Boulder, Colo: Lynne Rienner Publishers, 2006.

Evans, Tony. *The Politics of Human Rights: A Global Perspective,* 2nd ed. London: Pluto Press, 2005.

Fink, Gary M., and Hugh Davis Grahm, eds. *The Carter Presidency: Policy Choices in the Post-New Deal Era.* Lawrence: University Press of Kansas, 1988.

Finnis, John. *Natural Law and Natural Rights.* New York: Oxford University Press, 2004.

Fisher, Walter R. "The Narrative Paradigm: An Elaboration." *Communication Monographs* 52 (1985): 347–68.

———. "The Narrative Paradigm: In the Beginning." *Journal of Communication* 35 (1985): 74–89.

Foner, Eric E. *The Story of American Freedom.* New York: Norton, 1998.

Forsythe, David P. *Human Rights and World Politics,* 2nd ed. rev. Lincoln: University of Nebraska Press, 1989.

Foss, Sonja K. "Abandonment of Genus: The Evolution of Political Rhetoric." *Central States Speech Journal* 33 (1982): 367–78.

Franze, Marcia. "Nonattitudes/ Pseudo Opinions: Definitional Problems, Critical Variables, Cognitive Components, and Solutions." C/D Extended Essay, Lulea University of Technology, 2001.

Gamson, William A. *Talking Politics.* New York: Cambridge University Press, 1992.

Gamson, William A., and Andre Modigliani. "The Changing Culture of Affirmative Action." *Research in Political Sociology* 3 (1987): 137–77.

———. "Media Discourse and Public Opinion on Nuclear Power: A Constructionist Approach." *American Journal of Sociology* 95 (1989): 1–37.

Geer, John G. *From Tea Leaves to Opinion Polls: A Theory of Democratic Leadership.* New York: Columbia University Press, 1996.

Gelb, Leslie H., and Justine A. Rosenthal. "The Rise of Ethics in Foreign Policy: Reaching a Values Consensus." *Foreign Affairs* (May/June) 2003: 2–7.

Gerstle, Gary. *American Crucible: Race and Nation in the Twentieth Century.* Princeton, N.J.: Princeton University Press, 2001.

Geyer, Anne E., and Robert Y. Shapiro. "The Polls—A Report." *Public Opinion Quarterly* 52 (1988): 386–98.

Gilberg, Sheldon, Chaim Eyal, Maxwell McCombs, and David Nichols. "The State of the Union and the Press Agenda." *Journalism Quarterly* 57 (1980): 584–88.

Glad, Betty. *Jimmy Carter: In Search of the Great White House.* New York: W. W. Norton, 1980.

Goffman, Erving. *Frame Analysis: An Essay on the Organization of Experience.* New York: Harper and Row, 1974.

Graber, Doris A. *Processing the News: How People Tame the Information Tide,* 2nd ed. New York: Longman, 1988.

Graber, Doris A., Denis McQuail, and Pippa Norris, eds. *The Politics of News and the News of Politics.* Washington D.C.: Congressional Quarterly Press, 1998.

Gray, John. *False Down: The Delusions of Global Capitalism.* New York: The New Press, 1998.

Greenstein, Fred I. *The Presidential Difference: Leadership Style From FDR to George W. Bush.* Princeton, N.J.: Princeton University Press, 2004.

Hahn, Dan F. "The Rhetoric of Jimmy Carter," *Presidential Studies Quarterly* 14 (1985): 256–88.

Hahn, Dan F., and Justin Gustainis, "Anatomy of an Enigma: Jimmy Carter's 1980 State of the Union." *Communication Quarterly* 33 (1985): 43–49.

Hargrove, Erwin. *Jimmy Carter as President: Leadership and the Politics of the Public Good.* Baton Rouge: Louisiana State University Press, 1988.

Hart, Roderick P. *The Sound of Leadership: Presidential Communication in the Modern Age.* Chicago: University of Chicago Press, 1987.

Hartmann, Hauke. "US Human Rights Policy Under Carter and Reagan, 1977–1981." *Human Rights Quarterly* 23 (2001): 402–30.

Harvey, David. *A Brief History of Neoliberalism.* New York: Oxford University Press. 2005.

Heith, Diane J. *Polling to Govern.* Palo Alto, Calif.: Stanford University Press, 2004.

Herbst, Susan. *Numbered Voices: How Opinion Polling Has Shaped American Politics.* Chicago: University of Chicago Press, 1993.

Hill, Kim Quaile. "The Policy Agenda of the President and the Mass Public: A Research Validation and Extension." *American Journal of Political Science* 42 (1998): 1328–34.

Hirschman, Albert O. *The Passions and the Interests: Political Arguments for Capitalism before Its Triumph.* Princeton, N.J.: Princeton University Press, 1977.

Hoffman, Karen S. "Going Public in the Nineteenth Century: Grover Cleveland's Repeal of the Sherman Silver Purchase Act." *Rhetoric and Public Affairs* 5 (2002), 57–77.

Hogan, J. Michael. *The Panama Canal in American Politics: Domestic Advocacy and the Evolution of Policy.* Carbondale: Southern Illinois University Press, 1986.

Holsti, Ole R. *Public Opinion and American Foreign Policy,* rev. ed. Ann Arbor: University of Michigan Press, 2004.

Hufton, Olwen, ed. *Historical Change and Human Rights: The Oxford Amnesty Lectures.* New York: Basic Books, 1995.

Hunt, Lynn. *Inventing Human Rights: A History.* New York: W. W. Norton, 2007.

Hunt, Michael. *Ideology and U.S. Foreign Policy.* New Haven, Conn.: Yale University Press, 1987.

Iyengar, Shanto. *Is Anyone Responsible? How Television Frames Political Issues.* Chicago: University of Chicago Press, 1991.

Iyengar, Shanto, and Donald R. Kinder. *News that Matters.* Chicago: University of Chicago Press, 1987.

Iyengar, Shanto, Donald R. Kinder, Mark D. Peters, and Jon A. Krosnick, "The Evening News and Presidential Evaluations." *Journal of Personality and Social Psychology* 46 (1984): 778–87.

Iyengar, Shanto, and Adam Simon. "News Coverage of the Gulf Crisis and Public Opinion: A Study of Agenda-Setting, Priming, and Framing." *Communication Research* 20 (1993): 365–83.

Jacobs, Lawrence R., and Robert Y. Shapiro. *Politicians Don't Pander: Political Manipulation and the Loss of Democratic Responsiveness.* Chicago: University of Chicago Press, 2000.

Jamieson, Kathleeen Hall. *Eloquence in an Electronic Age: The Transformation of Political Speechmaking.* New York: Oxford University Press, 1988.

Jasinski, James. *Sourcebook on Rhetoric.* Thousand Oaks, Calif: Sage, 2001.

Johnson, Chalmers. *Blowback: The Costs and Consequences of American Empire.* New York: Henry Holt and Company, 2000.

Just, Marion R., Ann N. Crigler, Dean E. Alger, and Timothy E. Cook. *Crosstalk: Citizens, Candidates, and the Media in a Presidential Campaign.* Chicago: University of Chicago Press, 1996.

Kane, John. "American Values or Human Rights? U.S. Foreign Policy and the Fractured Myth of Virtuous Power." *Presidential Studies Quarterly* 33 (2003): 772–800.

Katz, Andrew Z. "Public Opinion and the Contradictions of Jimmy Carter's Foreign Policy." *Presidential Studies Quarterly* 30 (2000): 662–87.

Kaufman, Burton I. *The Presidency of James Earl Carter, Jr.* Lawrence: University Press of Kansas, 1993.

Kenger, Paul. *The Crusader: Ronald Reagan and the Fall of Communism.* New York: Regan Books, 2006.

Kernell, Samuel. *Going Public: New Strategies of Presidential Leadership.* Washington, D.C.: Congressional Quarterly Press, 1997.

Kinder, Donald R., and Lynn M. Sanders. *Divided by Color: Racial Politics and Democratic Ideals.* Chicago: University of Chicago Press, 1996.

Korey, William. *NGOs and the Universal Declaration of Human Rights.* NewYork: St. Martin's Press, 1998.

Kraig, Robert Alexander. "The Tragic Science: The Uses of Jimmy Carter in Foreign Policy Realism." *Rhetoric and Public Affairs* 5 (2002): 1–30.

Kraus, J., K. J. McMahon, and D. M. Rankin, eds. *Transformed by Crisis: The Presidency of George W. Bush and American Politics.* New York: Palgrave, 2004.

Krosnick, Jon A., and Laura Brannon. "The Impact of the Gulf War on the Ingredients of Presidential Evaluations: Multidimensional Effects of Political Involvement." *American Political Science Review* 87 (1993): 963–75.

Krosnick, Jon A., and Donal E. Kinder. "Altering the Foundations of Support for the President Through Priming." *American Political Science Review* 84 (1990): 497–512.

Laracey, Mel. *Presidents and the People: The Partisan Story of Going Public.* College Station: Texas A&M Press, 2002.

Lauren, Paul. *Evolution of International Human Rights,* 2nd ed. Philadelphia: University of Pennsylvania Press, 2003.

Lee, Ronald. "Electoral Politics and Visions of Community: Jimmy Carter and the Small Town Myth." *Western Journal of Communication* 59 (Winter 1995): 39–60.

———. "Humility and the Political Servant: Jimmy Carter's Post-Presidential Rhetoric of Virtue and Power." *The Southern Communication Journal* 60 (Summer 1995): 120–30.

Lewis, Justin. *Constructing Public Opinion: How Political Elites Do What They Like and Why We Seem to Go Along With It.* New York: Columbia University Press, 2001.

Lipset, Seymour Martin. *American Exceptionalism: A Double-Edged Sword.* New York: Norton, 1996.

MacIntyre, Alasdair. *After Virtue: A Study in Moral Theory.* Notre Dame, Ind.: University of Notre Dame Press, 1984.

MacKuen, Michael B. "Social Communication and the Mass Policy Agenda." In *More than News Media Power in Public Affairs,* edited by Michael B. MacKuen and Steven L. Coombs. Thousand Oaks, Calif: Sage, 1981, 19–44.

Mahoney, Jack. *The Challenge of Human Rights: Origins, Development, and Significance.* Malden, Mass: Blackwell Publishing, 2007.

Mazlish, Bruce, and Edwin Diamond. *Jimmy Carter: A Character Portrait.* New York: Simon & Schuster, 1979.

McCombs, Maxwell. "The Agenda-Setting Approach." In *Handbook of Political Communication,* edited by Dan Nimmo and Keith R. Sanders. Beverly Hills, Calif: Sage, 1981, 121–40.

McCombs, Maxwell, and Donald E. Shaw. "The Agenda Setting Function of Mass Media." *Public Opinion Quarterly* 36 (1972): 176–87.

McGee, Michael Calvin. "In Search of 'the People': A Rhetorical Alternative." *Quarterly Journal of Speech* 61 (1975): 235–49.

———. "Not Men, But Measures: The Origins and Import of an Ideological Principle." *Quarterly Journal of Speech* 64 (1978): 141–55.

———. The "Ideograph: A Link Between Rhetoric and Ideology." *Quarterly Journal of Speech* 66 (1980): 1–17.

———. "Ideograph." In *Encyclopedia of Rhetoric,* edited by Thomas O. Sloane. New York: Oxford University Press, 2001, 378–81.

Maynard, Edwin S. "The Bureaucracy and Implementation of Human Rights Policy." *Human Rights Quarterly,* 11 (1989): 175–248.

Melanson, Richard A. *American Foreign Policy Since the Vietnam War: The Search for Consensus from Nixon to Clinton,* 3rd ed. Armonk, N.Y.: M. E. Sharpe, 2000.

Mertius, Julie. *Bait and Switch: Human Rights and U.S. Foreign Policy.* New York: Rutledge, 2004.

Meyer, Peter. *James Earl Carter: The Man and the Myth.* Kansas City, Mo.: Sheed Andrews and McMeel, Inc, 1978.

Miller, Joanne M., and Jon A. Krosnick. "News Media Impact on the Ingredients of Presidential Evaluations: Politically Knowledgeable Citizens Are Guided By a Trusted Source." *American Journal of Political Science* 44 (2000): 301–15.

Miller, Warren E., and J. Merrill Shanks, *The New American Voter.* Cambridge, Mass: Harvard University Press, 1996.

Mower, A. Glenn Jr. *Human Rights and American Foreign Policy: The Carter and Reagan Experiences.* Westport, Conn.: Greenwood, 1987.

Moynihan, Daniel P. "The Politics of Human Rights." *Commentary* (August 1977): 19–27.

Muravchik, Joshua. *The Uncertain Crusade: Jimmy Carter and the Dilemmas of Human Rights Policy.* Lanham, Md.: AEI Press, 1986.

Neilson, Niels C. Jr. *The Religion of President Carter.* Nashville, Tenn: Thomas Nelson, Inc., 1977.

Nelson, Thomas E., Rosalee A. Clawson, and Zoe M. Oxley. "Media Framing of a Civil Liberties Conflict and Its Effect on Tolerance." *The American Political Science Review* 91 (1997): 567–83.

Newman, W. Russell, Marion R. Just, and Ann N. Crigler. *Common Knowledge: News and the Construction of Political Meaning.* Chicago: University of Chicago Press, 1992.

Nie, Norman E., Sidney Verba, and John R. Petrocik. *The Changing American Voter,* enlarged ed. Cambridge, Mass: Harvard University Press, 1979.

Noble, David W. *The End of American History: Democracy, Capitalism, and the Metaphor of Two Worlds in Anglo-Historical Writing, 1880–1980.* Minneapolis: University of Minnesota Press, 1985.

Norpoth, Helmut, and Milton Lodge. "The Difference Between Attitudes and Nonattitudes in the Mass Public: Just Measurements?" *American Journal of Political Science* 29 (1985): 291–307.

Nueringer, Sheldon. *The Carter Administration, Human Rights, and the Agony of Cambodia.* Lewiston, Queenston, Lampeter: Edwin Mellon Press, 1993.

O'Neill, Onora. *Bounds of Justice.* Cambridge: Cambridge University Press, 2000.

O'Neill, Tip, with William Novak. *Man of the House: The Life and Political Memoirs of Speaker Tip O'Neill.* New York: Random House, 1987.

Olsen, Kathryn M. "The Controversy Over President Reagan's Visit to Bitburg: Strategies of Definition and Redefinition." *Quarterly Journal of Speech* 75 (1989): 129–51.

Orman, John. *Comparing Presidential Behavior: Carter, Reagan, and the Macho Presidential Style.* New York: Greenwood, 1987.

Oye, Kenneth A., Donald Rothchild, and Robert J. Leiber, eds. *Eagle Entangled: U.S. Foreign Policy in a Complex World.* New York: Longman, 1979.

Page, Benjamin I., and Robert Y. Shapiro. *The Rational Public: Fifty Years of Trends in Americans' Policy Preferences.* Chicago: University of Chicago Press, 1992.

Palczewski, Catherine H. "The Male Madonna and the Feminine Uncle Sam: Visual Argument, Icons and Ideographs in 1909 Anti-Woman's Suffrage Postcards." *Quarterly Journal of Speech* 91 (2005): 365–94.

Patton, John H. "A Government as Good as its People: Jimmy Carter and the Restoration of Transcendence to Politics." *Quarterly Journal of Speech* 63 (1977): 249–57.

Petro, Nicolai N. *The Predicament of Human Rights: The Carter and Reagan Policies,* vol. 5. Lanham, Md.: University Press of America, 1983.

Pierce, John C., and Douglas D. Rose, "Nonattitudes and American Public Opinion: The Examination of a Thesis." *The American Political Science Review* 68 (1974): 626–49.

Popkin, Samuel L. *The Reasoning Voter: Communication and Persuasion in Presidential Campaigns.* Chicago: University of Chicago Press, 1992.

Powers, Samantha. *A Problem From Hell: America in the Age of Genocide,* reprint ed. New York: Harper Perennial, 2003.

Rawls, John. *A Theory of Justice.* Cambridge, Mass.: Belknap Press, 1999.

Robertson, Geoffrey. *Crimes Against Humanity: The Struggle for Global Justice.* New York: New Press, 2003.

Rorty, Richard. *Philosophy and Social Hope.* New York: Penguin, 2000.

Rosati, Jerald A. *The Carter Administration's Quest for Global Community: Beliefs and Impact on Behavior.* Columbia: University of South Carolina Press, 1987.

Rose, Douglas D., and John C. Pierce. "Nonattitudes and American Public Opinion: Rejoinder to 'Comment' by Philip E. Converse." *The American Political Science Review* 68 (1974): 661–66.

Rosenbaum, Herbert D., and Alexej Ugrinsky, eds. *Jimmy Carter, Foreign Policy, and the Post-Presidential Years.* Westport, Conn: Greenwood Press, 1994.

Rottinghaus, Brandon. "Measure of the Mind of the Public: Patterns of Presidential Rhetoric and Public Opinion from Dwight Eisenhower to Bill Clinton." PhD diss., Northwestern University, 2005.

Rozell, Mark. *The Press and the Carter Presidency.* Boulder, Colo: Westview Press, 1989.

Ruechel, Frank A. "The Articulation and Synthesis of Jimmy Carter's Human Rights Policy." PhD diss., Georgia State University, 1990.

Sanders, Randy. "The Sad Duty of Politics: Jimmy Carter and the Issue of Race in his 1970 Gubernatorial Campaign." *The Georgia Historical Quarterly* LXXVI (3) (Fall 1992): 612–38.

Saris, William E., and Paul M. Sniderman, eds. *Studies in Public Opinion: Attitudes, Nonattitudes, Measurement Error, and Change.* Princeton, N.J.: Princeton University Press, 2004.

Schaefer, Todd M. "Persuading the Persuaders: Presidential Speeches and the Editorial Opinion." *Political Communication* 14 (1997): 97–111.

Scheufele, Dietram A. "Agenda-Setting, Priming, and Framing Revisited: Another Look at Cognitive Effects of Political Communication." *Mass Communication and Society* 3 (2000): 297–316.

Schlesinger, Arthur Jr. "Human Rights and the American Tradition." *Foreign Affairs* 57 (1978): 503–26.

Schmitz, David A., and Vanessa Walker. "Jimmy Carter and the Foreign Policy of Human Rights: The Development of a Post-Cold War Foreign Policy." *Diplomatic History* 28 (2004): 113–43.

Schuman, Howard, and Stanley Presser. "Public Opinion and Public Ignorance: The Fine Line Between Attitudes and Nonattitudes." *The American Journal of Sociology* 85 (1980): 1214–25.

Shapiro, Robert Y. "Public Opinion, Elites, and Democracy." *Critical Review* 12 (1998): 501–28.

Shue, Henry. *Basic Rights: Subsistence, Affluence, and U.S. Foreign Policy,* 2nd ed. Princeton, N.J.: Princeton University Press, 1996.

Simpson, A. W. Brian. *Human Rights and the End of Empire.* New York: Oxford University Press, 2001.

Skidmore, David. *Reversing Course: Foreign Policy, Domestic Politics, and the Failure of Reform.* Nashville, Tenn.: Vanderbilt University Press, 1996.

Smith, Gaddis. *Morality, Reason, and Power.* New York: Hill and Wang, 1986.

Smith, Rogers M. *Civic Ideals: Conflicting Views of Citizenship in U.S. History.* New Haven, Conn.: Yale University Press, 1997.

Smith, Tony. *America's Mission: The United States and the Worldwide Struggle for Democracy in the 20th Century.* Princeton, N.J.: Princeton University Press, 1994.

Spencer, Donald S. *The Carter Implosion: Jimmy Carter and the Amateur Style of Diplomacy.* New York: Praeger, 1988.

Steger, Manfred B. *Globalism: The New Market Ideology.* Lanham, Md.: Rowman & Littlefield Publishers, Inc., 2002.

Strong, Robert A. *Working in the World: Jimmy Carter and the Making of American Foreign Policy.* Baton Rouge: Louisiana State University Press, 2000.

Stuckey, Mary E. *The President as Interpreter-in-Chief.* Chatham, Mass: Chatham Press, 1990.
———. *Defining Americans: The Presidency and National Identity.* Lawrence: University of Kansas Press, 2004.

Sudol, Ronald. "The Rhetoric of Strategic Retreat: Carter and the Panama Canal Debate." *Quarterly Journal of Speech* 65 (1979): 379–91.

Towle, Michael J. *Out of Touch: The Presidency and Public Opinion.* College Station: Texas A&M University Press, 2004.

Tulis, Jeffrey. *The Rhetorical Presidency.* Princeton, N.J.: Princeton University Press, 1987.

Tversky, Amos, and Daniel Kahneman. "The Framing of Decisions and the Psychology of Choice." *Science* 211 (1981): 453–58.

Vance, Cyrus. *Hard Choices: Critical Years in American Foreign Policy.* New York: Simon and Schuster, 1983.

Vivian, Bradford. "Neoliberal Epideictic: Rhetorical Form and Commemorative Politics on September 11, 2002." *Quarterly Journal of Speech* 92 (2006): 1–26.

Vogelgesang, Sandy. *American Dream: Global Nightmare.* New York: W. W. Norton, 1980.

Weaver, Richard M. *The Ethics of Rhetoric.* Davis, Calif.: Hermagoras Press, 1985.

Wills, Gary. *Reagan's America: Innocents at Home.* Garden City, N.Y.: Doubleday, 1985.

Wood, B. Dan, and Jeffrey S. Peake. "The Dynamics of Foreign Policy Agenda Setting." *American Political Science Review* 92 (1998): 173–84.

Zaller, John R. *The Nature and Origins of Mass Opinion.* Cambridge: Cambridge University Press, 1992.
———. "The Myth of Massive Media Impact Revised: New Support for a Discredited Idea." In *Political Persuasion and Attitude Change,* edited by Diana C. Mutz, Paul Sniderman, and Richard A. Brody. Ann Arbor: University of Michigan Press, 1996, 17–78.

Zarefsky, David. *President Johnson's War on Poverty: Rhetoric and History.* Tuscaloosa: University of Alabama Press, 2005.

Zuckert, Michael P. *Natural Rights and the New Republicanism.* Princeton, N.J.: Princeton University Press, 1994.

———. *The Natural Rights Republic.* Notre Dame, Ind.: University of Notre Dame Press, 1996.

———. *Launching Liberalism: On Lockean Political Philosophy.* Lawrence: University Press of Kansas, 2002.

Index